ALEX McFARLAND

the **21** toughest
questions
your kids *will ask about*
Christianity

& how to
answer them
confidently

TYNDALE HOUSE PUBLISHERS, INC.
CAROL STREAM, ILLINOIS

The 21 Toughest Questions Your Kids Will Ask about Christianity
© 2013 by Alex McFarland
ISBN: 978-1-58997-678-8

A Focus on the Family book published by
Tyndale House Publishers, Inc., Carol Stream, Illinois 60188

Focus on the Family and the accompanying logo and design are federally registered trademarks
of Focus on the Family, Colorado Springs, CO 80995.

TYNDALE and Tyndale's quill logo are registered trademarks of Tyndale House Publishers, Inc.

Editor: Marianne Hering
Cover design by Dan Farrell

Library of Congress Cataloging-in-Publication Data is available at www.loc.gov/help
/contact-general.html.

Printed in the United States of America   ·
2   3   4   5   6   7   8   9 / 19   18   17   16   15   14

*This book is dedicated to all godly adults
who take time away from their busy grown-up world
to invest themselves in the life of a child.*

CONTENTS

Part 5: Questions about the Church

Part 6: Questions Parents Ask and My Question to You

Theology Lessons on the Front Steps

[Children] are like wet cement. Any word that falls on them makes an impact.

—Dr. Haim Ginott, *Between Parent and Child*

When my niece Allie was five, she was *always* asking me imaginative questions about God. One day she arranged a pastoral Q-and-A session for me. I waited on the front steps of her house while she gathered several of her friends. An impromptu study group gathered around, and Allie announced, "My uncle is a preacher, and he can tell you what kinds of ice cream there will be in heaven."

I forced back laughter as the tribunal of little faces turned toward me. Their expressions seemed to say, "Tell us, grown-up, and we *will* receive your words! What kinds of ice cream will we have in heaven?"

My heart just about melted, and my brain fumbled for an answer. I thought about what a privilege it was that, at least for a season, I was the go-to person whenever my niece had a question about God or theology.

Theological Emergencies

The questions children ask may often make us smile or even laugh, but consider this thought: Becoming the Christian Wikipedia for your kids is both a God-ordained privilege and a relationship building block. Remember that when you're presented with questions like these:

"Are Santa's elves angels or humans?"

"Did the baby Jesus have to wear diapers?"

"In Sunday school we read from Hebrews, 'I will remember their sins no more.'[1] How can this be if God knows everything?"

But having an inquisitive child is no cause for alarm. Quite the opposite, in fact. As long as your child is seeking guidance from you, everything is okay. That's not an emergency; that's a gift. The true emergency is when your child *stops* coming to you for answers.

Me, a Theologian? Actually, Yes!

You, as a Christian parent, can be an effective responder to the tough theological questions your children ask. The main purpose of this book is to equip you to do just that. You can become an expert even if you've never read the Bible much before, and you don't know whether the book of Ezekiel is in the Old or New Testament. More than that, you can develop a relationship with your child in which biblical principles are lived out, not merely talked about.

I compiled these twenty-one questions after years of interacting with families, children, teens, and college students, and from dozens of personal interviews conducted during the creation of this book. I'm confident that virtually all the tough questions you'll face about God and Christianity are addressed within the pages of this book in one form or another.

As you use this book to prepare yourself for the questions your kids may ask, your understanding of God and biblical truth will also deepen. Rather than squirming when the tough questions arise, you'll begin to cherish the opportunity to have meaningful conversations about the Bible. *The 21 Toughest Questions Your Kids Will Ask about Christianity* is designed to be your primer and guide for giving answers that are not only scriptural but are also easy for kids to relate to and absorb spiritually.

Proverbs 1:8–9 promises certain benefits to the children who receive their parents' godly teaching: "Listen, my son, to your father's instruction and do not forsake your mother's teaching. They will be a garland to grace your head and a chain to adorn your neck."

What does this mean? Solomon was comparing the adornment of godly wisdom to the clothes and jewels of royalty. Parents are to impart to their children something comparable to, and even preferable to, a type of victor's medal: God's truth. And preparing yourself to answer questions and model truth can be rewarding in and of itself.

Christian parenting involves much more than sending our children off to Sunday school and Wednesday-night youth group. I was a youth pastor for many years, and I poured my heart out to the students under my care. But nothing can compare to the devotion, time, and love parents give to their own precious children. Sure, kids need a Christian community, and even mentors, but they need you more.

First, the Good News! But Then . . .

The good news is *"You can do this!"* You can learn how to better grasp the deep realities of Scripture, and you can also learn to effectively handle the challenging questions related to God's Word. Because God wants everyone to know about Him, each person is promised the Holy Spirit's help and guidance. First John 2:27 says, "His anointing teaches you about all things, and is true and is not a lie" (NASB). Begin the journey, and God will come alongside you in a tangible way.

That's not to say it's easy. After more than a decade of hosting live radio call-in shows, I thought I had heard every possible question and variation thereof. But new, creative, and even odd questions about spiritual topics continue to be brought to my attention. A young lady recently called in to my radio program and asked about two passages from the book of Acts. She noted that the Holy Spirit was so present in the lives of Peter and Paul that people would be healed by simply coming into contact with objects that the apostles had touched. (An apostle was someone who walked with Jesus during Christ's earthly ministry.) In Acts 5:15–16, even Peter's *shadow* passing over someone's afflicted body resulted in a healing. The caller asked, "Could God work through Christians in this way today?"

How do you answer such a question with only sixty seconds left in the broadcast? As succinctly as possible!

In about one minute, and by the time the radio program's ending theme music was starting, I had explained that God works in any way necessary that . . .

1. is in conformity with His sinless and perfect nature;
2. is in harmony with the rest of His written Word; and
3. is reasonable and logically meaningful.

I explained to the caller that Acts is about the early church's beginning. The Lord did whatever was necessary to bring and authenticate the gospel to the world, and part of that initiative included many miracles. Peter, Paul, and the other apostles had been in the presence of the risen Jesus, so it's fair to assume they had a level of anointing, power, and spiritual authority that they needed to do the job.

Could the Holy Spirit do such things again today? Of course. But we'll leave that to Him to decide if and when it's necessary.

My point in sharing this is to show that tough questions don't have to frighten you. With some basic tools and a growing understanding of God's Word, you can be ready for any spiritual questions your children present to you. Through your example, the message you want to pass on to your children is this: "Your word is a lamp to my feet / And a light to my path" (Psalm 119:105, NKJV). This book will help you and your family find God's path to biblical wisdom.

How to Answer a Question

If any of you lacks wisdom, let him ask of God, who gives to all liberally and without reproach, and it will be given to him.

—James 1:5, NKJV

Dr. Lester Morton served as an Old Testament professor at a small Methodist college in the South for many years. He was known for his liberal views on the Bible, which he openly and frequently expressed in the classroom. Many of his former students have told me that on the first day of his Old Testament survey classes, Dr. Morton informed them, "We are going to begin studying the Old Testament in Genesis chapter 12, because the first eleven chapters are a myth." He spent most of the semester refuting the Old Testament miracles—creation, Noah's ark and the flood, the parting of the Red Sea—and casting doubt on the authenticity of the books themselves.

One day Dr. Morton told his students about an incident that happened during his teenage years. Without a doubt, I believe this experience corroded his view of the Bible's authority. The teenage Morton went to his pastor with a question about an Old Testament passage that seemed to contradict another passage. But when Morton approached his pastor, explaining his confusion and expressing doubt, the pastor responded, "You shouldn't ask questions like that. You're just supposed to take the Scriptures as truth."

I believe this woefully inadequate response shaped Morton's

theological views. Instead of receiving satisfying answers to his legitimate questions, he began to believe there were no good answers. Ultimately, this led to Morton sowing similar doubts into the hearts of a generation of young college students.

The answer Morton received is a rendition of another reply commonly used to deflect inquisitive young minds: "Because the Bible says so." This is never a sufficient answer for the theological questions that arise from children and teens. When we give them such off-the-cuff answers with no real biblical basis or thought on our part, we are telling them that Christianity is not worthy of our time, effort, and intellect. Or worse yet, that Christianity and the Bible are not strong enough to bear the scrutiny of a serious study. Out of all the answers that could have been given in response to Morton's question, "You shouldn't ask" was one of the worst.

We shouldn't be surprised or caught off guard when our children ask us tough questions about Christianity and the Bible. After all, they are immersed in a culture that aggressively questions and attacks the Christian worldview. And as much as we would like to think that we have the most influence on our kids, we are just one of many voices vying for their attention. By the time our children reach college, they will have been bombarded with so many conflicting intellectual messages that it may be difficult for them to distinguish God's truth from what the world is telling them. If the answers we give to their questions about faith aren't satisfactory or are laced with contempt toward atheists or other non-Christian groups, our children will begin to search elsewhere. And we may not like where they find their answers.

How to Use This Book

The 21 Toughest Questions Your Kids Will Ask about Christianity was not written as an encyclopedia of theological answers for you to look up on a specific topic and have a pat answer ready to read verbatim. Instead, I wanted to point you in the right direction and give you the tools, skills, and basic information to start your search for the answers to your child's questions.

Regarding the content, my prayer is that this book will provide the foundation for answering virtually any question that comes along. You may be surprised at some of the topics in the book that are *not* addressed. Social issues, such as racism and sex trafficking, are not included. Neither did I tackle the teachings of the Church of Jesus Christ of Latter-Day Saints (Mormonism) or the Jehovah's Witnesses. But we will spend sufficient time establishing the trustworthiness and authority of the Bible and the nature of God, which resolve ambiguity about countless issues.

For example, if your kids thoroughly understand the significance of Jesus' deity and work on the cross, then questions about cults will be much easier to explain. If your children are convinced the Bible's teachings on morality are trustworthy, then the dozens of questions regarding sex, marriage, and homosexuality will be more easily dealt with.

But you can't wait until your children ask a question to flip to this book's table of contents. You need to be prepared with some basic knowledge of the Bible before questions are asked, and then be ready to go deeper as the need arises. Read through this entire book. Develop the Bible-study skills taught in its pages. Build a library of study helps that will assist you in understanding and researching the Word of God. As your understanding of God's Word increases, you will be prepared for almost any question your children ask, or you'll know where to go to find the answers.

I refer to "your child" or "your children" throughout this book, but I realize that some of you may be reading this as youth leaders, teachers, pastors, friends, or relatives. In this light, we are all part of the family of God and as such have a responsibility to teach and train the children of the family, whether or not they are our own offspring.

The Question behind the Question

When children and teens ask questions about God, the Bible, Christianity, or something that touches on a spiritual matter, our first reaction may be to blurt out an answer. There are times when that approach is called for, but it's better to pause and think, *Why is my child asking this question? What information (or misinformation) is in her mind that may be influencing her? Has a recent event or circumstance in his life prompted this line of thinking?*

Often, children are trying to come to terms with a complex issue and will find one point of that issue to ask a question about. It's like a jigsaw puzzle—they are trying to understand the entire picture while only looking at one piece. Our job is to listen to the question and try to figure out the entire puzzle by using their question and our knowledge of their lives. There is very often a question behind the question: a deeper, more personal issue they are wrestling with and may not know how to express yet. You, as the parent, must dig a little deeper to find the real heart of the matter.

Let's say your child comes to you and asks, "Why does God allow bad things to happen?" This seems like a straightforward theological question, right? But what if Grandma had been ill and has just passed away? The real question your child is asking may be, "Why did God allow Grandma to die? I prayed for her. Why didn't He answer my prayer?" This is a much more personal issue.

Or what if your child comes to you and asks, "Does God really send people to hell?" Again, this is another straightforward question. But what if the real question is, "Will God send *me* to hell?" Then your approach to the question will certainly be much different, because the question might indicate that God is working in the heart of your child to draw him or her to Christ.

One of the most effective ways to find the question behind the question is to begin by saying, "That's a great question. What do you think?" When you ask that question, you should remain quiet and allow your child to articulate what he or she is thinking while you listen closely. Listening is not just a good skill for children; adults benefit from it too!

Be sure to observe your child's body language while listening. Does your child look confused, fearful, under conviction, angry, or disappointed? Body language communicates the urgency of the question. Is this just mere curiosity, or is there a vital matter involved? These nonverbal cues are more pieces of the puzzle that can help you understand your child's real questions.

Once you get a better grasp on your child's question, it's a good idea to say, "Let me make sure I understand: You are asking . . . ?" Restating the question helps make sure that you aren't reading your own question into your child's question. It also can help children see their true underlying question, especially if they haven't even understood for themselves what they were really asking. Once you understand what the real question is, you are in a better position to give a satisfying answer.

You may also want to ask further diagnostic questions, such as "What led you to ask about this?" Was it something your child heard in school that prompted the question? Was it something your child heard on television? Did one of his or her friends say something that called into question your child's beliefs? This will give you additional clues to the origins of your child's doubt and will aid you in formulating an answer. As a doctor tries to diagnose an illness by asking diagnostic questions, we should ask questions of a spiritually diagnostic nature to get to the core of the issue.

Additionally, the approach you take when answering a child's tough questions about Christianity is just as important as the actual answers you give. Your tone, body language, and reaction to questions communicate just as much as actual words. Children are looking to see if adults really believe what the Bible teaches. For questioning children, our answers and interactions with them could mean the difference between faith and skepticism, conviction and doubt, or heaven and hell.

Guiding the Conversation

When giving an answer to a spiritual question, it's much more constructive to dialogue with your children rather than to give a monologue—which they may see as a lecture. In other words, talk *with* your children, not *at* them. Children often process what they learn much more efficiently when they are allowed to ask questions and add input into the conversation. One of the best ways to do this is to use the Socratic method of teaching.

Socrates was a well-known philosopher who had a unique method of answering his students' questions. He would answer a question with a question. With this approach, Socrates would steer the conversation along by asking probing questions in an effort to help students arrive at answers on their own.

Consider how Jesus at times answered a question with a question:

> A certain lawyer stood up and tested [Jesus], saying, "Teacher, what shall I do to inherit eternal life?"
>
> He said to him, "What is written in the law? What is your reading of it?" (Luke 10:25–26, NKJV)

In this particular incident, Jesus challenged the lawyer to consider what he already knew about God when seeking the answer to his question. When you apply this method to answering the spiritual questions your children pose, you encourage them to draw on the knowledge they already have about God and apply it to their questions.

While you are talking with your children, consider peppering your conversations with questions like these:

- How do you know that to be true?
- Where did you find your information?
- Can you give me an example to help me understand your question?
- How did you come to that conclusion?
- What do you already know about this?
- Is this situation similar to any Bible stories you know?
- How could you look at this another way?
- What does God say about . . . ?
- What do you think might happen if . . . ?

If your children come up with answers on their own, it may lead to the formation of a firm conviction rather than just an accumulation of facts and knowledge. And when it comes to matters of your children's faith, convictions are better than knowledge because convictions aren't easily abandoned in the heat of the moment.

Don't Give Too Much Information

Eight-year-old Lewis came to his mother and asked, "Mom, what is sex?" After Mom went through a speech about the differences between men and women, dating, love, marriage, and what comes after, Lewis looked utterly confused.

She finally asked, "Do you have any more questions?"

He answered, "Yeah, we had to fill out this form at school, and it asked what our sex was. Am I an M or an F?"

Be careful that you don't give your children too much information. A question about Jesus coming back may not call for a detailed discussion of eschatology, pre- or post-tribulation rapture, and the prophecies of Ezekiel and Daniel as compared to Revelation and Thessalonians. A simple "We don't know exactly when, but here's how we can make sure we are ready when Jesus does come back" may be all your children need at the moment.

How much your children will understand will depend on their age. As they ask their questions, give them just enough information to be accurate and to satisfy their curiosity. Be sure to use language that is appropriate for their understanding and maturity level.

I believe that kids truly appreciate it when adults talk with them about God and life in plain language. Don't be surprised if you get the reputation around the neighborhood as the go-to grown-up for straight answers. God may entrust you with ministry opportunities that reach beyond the bounds of your immediate family.

If your children continue to ask questions, go deeper with them until they are satisfied with your answers.

It's Okay to Say "I Don't Know"

Believe it or not, "I don't know" is an acceptable answer as long as you follow it up with "Let's find out the answer together." Too many Christians never talk about their faith because they're afraid that people, especially their children, are going to ask them a question they can't answer. If your child asks you such a question, you could pass it off to a pastor or a Sunday school teacher, but that has three drawbacks: (1) It needlessly delays the answer; (2) it sends a clear message that "normal" or lay Christians don't have to know the Scriptures well or be able to defend the faith; and (3) you lose an opportunity to build a spiritual relationship with your child.

Unless you are a Bible scholar who spends hours upon hours in study, chances are that your little ones will eventually stump you with a question. That's okay! You can't be expected to know the answer to every question your children, or other people, throw at you about Christianity. But you can and should show a willingness to dig deep and find the answer.

No matter your background or current Bible knowledge, your willingness to invest the time in helping your children find the answers speaks volumes about your personal relationship with Jesus Christ. A favorite verse that is often used to emphasize the importance of Bible study is 2 Timothy 2:15. The King James Version renders the passage this way: "Study to shew thyself approved unto God, a workman that needeth not to be ashamed, rightly dividing the word of truth." The word *study* doesn't necessarily mean "hit the books" or "memorize information." Reading this verse in more modern translations reveals that the meaning points toward being diligent, focused, or committed. But the important principle is there: We are to strive for effectiveness and accurate knowledge of God's Word in our walk and witness. Nourish your own heart and mind with Scripture daily, and you'll also be prepping yourself for your kids' spiritual questions, which *will* come!

While this may seem like a daunting task, don't be afraid! God promises to provide wisdom to those who ask for it (James 1:5). You can pray for understanding (Psalm 119:73) and dig into the Word daily. When it comes to being ready to give effective answers to challenging questions, I truly believe that our Lord's invitation from Matthew 7:7 is applicable: "Ask, and it will be given to you; seek, and you will find; knock, and it will be opened to you" (NKJV).

Part 1

Questions about God, the Father

Why Does God Allow Evil?

Why God no kill the devil,
so make him no more do wicked?

—Friday, in *The Life and Surprising Adventures*
of Robinson Crusoe by Daniel Defoe

This question takes as many forms as there are people to ask it. One common variation is "Why does God allow evil people to live?" Another is "If God knew Adam and Eve would sin, why did He put the tree in the garden of Eden?" Adult skeptics will preface the question with presuppositions, such as "*If God is all-loving,* why does He allow bad things to happen to good people? *If God is all-powerful,* why doesn't He do something about the suffering in the world?"

Almost every person with an active mind has wrestled with the question of evil. Some of the best and brightest thinkers in history have invested much of their lives and intellect in this subject. For the sake of clarity, I've divided evil into two chapters. Chapter 1 covers moral evil (sin), and chapter 2 covers natural evil and suffering (disasters).

Believe it or not, the problem of evil isn't as difficult as most people make it out to be. While it can appear complicated, it's certainly not a theological showstopper. Using a few cups of Scripture mixed with a healthy dose of logic, you can adequately address your children's concerns. As your children mature, however, their questions will change, and you may need to revisit the related Bible passages and reexamine the problem of evil several times.

Key Concepts

QUESTION RECAP: The reality of evil in a world that was supposedly created "good" presents Christianity with one of its most common objections. The apparent dilemma is this: If God is good, wise, and all-powerful, then why doesn't He remove (or at least restrain) the evil in this world?

1. All evil present in this world is traceable to Adam and Eve's fall into sin. That means every human is part of the world's evil. Sin and evil are virtually the same thing.
2. God is patient and loving, however, and He has a plan that will rid the world of evil and evil people. Part of that plan involves Jesus' death on the cross.

HOPE-FILLED ANSWER: Throughout Scripture, especially in the New Testament, we are promised God's victory over sin and evil. Christ's empty tomb is proof that sin and death have been fully conquered, and one day evil will be eternally removed.

Moral Evil—the Answer Begins in Genesis

The word *evil* appears in the Bible as early as Genesis 2. In verse 17, God gave Adam a single command, which Adam later passed on to Eve: "You must not eat from the tree of the knowledge of good and evil, for when you eat of it you will surely die."

Did Adam and Eve eat the fruit from the Tree of Knowledge of Good and Evil? Yes. So by the third chapter of Genesis, we arrive at the answer to the question about why there is evil in the world. The answer is that Adam and Eve chose evil, or sin, by disobeying God.

An ancillary question immediately follows: Why did God allow Adam and Eve to live when He said in Genesis 2:17 that they would surely die if they ate from the tree in the center of the garden?

The answer is this: Starting with Adam and Eve, throughout history everyone has sinned, and sinning is "evil." If God had destroyed Adam and Eve on the spot, there would have been no one left—there would have been no human race. However, there was still a penalty or punishment that was imposed on Adam and Eve and all subsequent human beings— physical degradation and death. Adam and Eve did not die immediately, but they did eventually die.

⚬ *Did Adam and Eve die*
⚬ *like everybody else?*
⚬   —ABIGAIL, age nine

Critics of the Bible argue that the serpent was correct when he said, "You will not surely die" (Genesis 3:4). The skeptic's line of reasoning is this: "God said that eating the fruit would cause death. But when Adam and Eve ate the fruit, they weren't struck down. They *did not* die. They lived."

What Is Evil?

If you have older children or ones who are philosophically minded, this material may help you.

Some people assume that evil is a "thing," so if God created everything, then He must have created evil. The disheartening conclusion would then be that this world of suffering must somehow be the way God wants it.

Christian thinkers like Augustine and C. S. Lewis reasoned that evil is not a thing. Evil is not a tangible or physical object; it is a corruption of an otherwise good thing. Scholars use the word *privation* with regard to evil. Therefore, God was being truthful in His assessment of His entire creation, recorded in Genesis 1:31: "It was very good."

Evil is a parasite that feeds on a host. God did not "create" evil when He set the Tree of Knowledge of Good and Evil in the garden of Eden. Evil is the degradation and corruption of something that otherwise is good. God *allowed* evil to enter the equation; He allowed *privation*. But it's not accurate to say that He *caused* it or *created* it.

However, the wording in Genesis 2:17 literally means "When you eat of it, in dying, you shall die." Even though Adam and Eve did not keel over dead right that instant, physical death became a part of the human experience and a consequence of human sin. But the subtle reality of Genesis 2:17 is this: *Sin's entrance into the human experience meant that spiritual death would follow physical death.* "In dying, you shall die." Think of it: a double dose of death for every person. The implications of this are tragic beyond description.

"In Adam's Fall, We Sinned All"[1]

As a result of Adam and Eve's disobedience, sin was passed on to the rest of humanity. This bent for evil in humans is called sin nature. The onset of sin nature is where the question of evil turns personal and can present an opportunity to share the gospel. Most children (and many adults) think of evil as describing someone like Hitler, drug dealers, or Uncle Leroy who divorced six wives. When your children realize that they themselves are part of the world's evil and that a penalty of death is required of them, then the need for God's grace becomes apparent.

The Fate of the First Couple

Adam and Eve did die like everyone else. They were the first people to experience death. God had warned them not to eat of a certain fruit in the garden where they lived, but they chose to disobey Him and did it anyway. This caused Adam and Eve to begin growing older, and they eventually died. Because of their sin, the process of aging and death now happens to all people everywhere. Sin causes not only physical death but also that death within our souls, or what some call spiritual death. If it weren't for the forgiveness offered by Jesus, Adam and Eve—and you and I— would be separated from God forever because of sin.

If your children ask, "Couldn't God just snuff out all the wicked people in an instant?" you can explain that of course He could, but that would wipe out *all* of us. God defines evil as selfishness, anger, unforgiveness, untruthfulness, faithlessness, and so on. These "minor" sins are as odious to God as the things that most of us would say are "major" sins (such as murder, robbery, rape, torture, etc.). To understand salvation and to have a sound Christian worldview, it's essential that this important fact become ingrained in your children's hearts and minds: "*All* have sinned and fall short of the glory of God" (Romans 3:23).

The Parable of the Weeds

In the Parable of the Weeds, Jesus hinted at God's patience and plans as He told His disciples this story:

> The kingdom of heaven is like a man who sowed good seed in his field. But while everyone was sleeping, his enemy came and sowed

---

The Sugar Test

Younger children may need a concrete example of how high God's standard for purity is. A fun and simple way to illustrate this is with a cup of white sugar and one grain of salt. Show your children the sugar and then pour it into a bowl. Let them dip their fingers in the sugar and taste it. Next, take a pair of tweezers, pick up a grain of salt, and drop it into the sugar. Mix in the grain of salt. Let your children taste the sugar again. It should taste fine to them, since one grain of salt doesn't affect their taste experience, but they have seen with their eyes that it's not pure sugar anymore. Explain that God knows where that grain of salt is even if we can't detect it, and until that grain is removed, the whole bowl is impure (evil).

weeds among the wheat, and went away. When the wheat sprouted
and formed heads, then the weeds also appeared.

The owner's servants came to him and said, "Sir, didn't you sow
good seed in your field? Where then did the weeds come from?"

"An enemy did this," he replied.

The servants asked him, "Do you want us to go and pull them up?"

"No," he answered, "because while you are pulling the weeds,
you may root up the wheat with them. Let both grow together until
the harvest. At that time I will tell the harvesters: First collect the
weeds and tie them in bundles to be burned; then gather the wheat
and bring it into my barn." (Matthew 13:24–30)

This parable is easy for most children to understand. It demonstrates
the patience of God to endure evil people but also shows that there will
be consequences later. Simply put, delayed justice is not the same thing
as the absence of justice.

As a result of Adam and Eve's disobedience, humans were no longer
allowed in Paradise. Genesis 3:23 says, "So the LORD God banished him
from the Garden of Eden to work the ground from which he had been
taken." In fact, God told Adam that he and all of his descendants were
going to have difficult lives, a truth that continues to this very day:

To Adam he said, "Because you listened to your wife and ate from
the tree about which I commanded you, 'You must not eat of it,'

Cursed is the ground because of you;
    through painful toil you will eat of it
    all the days of your life.
It will produce thorns and thistles for you,
    and you will eat the plants of the field.
By the sweat of your brow
    you will eat your food
until you return to the ground." (Verses 17–19)

The Answer Continues in the New Testament

So, are we stuck with evil forever? No. God does have a plan to rid the world of all the evil. He's just waiting for the perfect time to do it. The final step will be the re-creation of the world as described in the book of Revelation—but we're getting ahead of ourselves. The *first* step toward ridding the world of evil was sending Jesus Christ to earth in human form.

Children understand the concept of second chances. We've all heard them ask for a do-over when they play games. Jesus Christ is called the "last Adam" because He was humankind's do-over—the way to get rid of the problem of evil. In 1 Corinthians 15:45, the relationship between Adam and Jesus is explained: "So it is written: 'The first man Adam became a living being'; the last Adam, a life-giving spirit." Because God knew that one day His Son, Jesus, would pay the price for sin and evil, He allowed humankind to live.

God Is Merciful

If your children question how God could allow so many evil people to go on living, ask them to consider Romans 3:25:

> God gave [Jesus] as a sacrifice to pay for sins. So he forgives the sins
> of those who have faith in his blood. God did all of that to prove that
> he is fair. Because of his mercy he did not punish people for the sins
> they had committed before Jesus died for them. (NIrv)

According to this verse, God allowed humans to live because He knew that Jesus Christ would pay the death-penalty debt that was outstanding. Before Jesus came to earth, God established a sacrificial system so His people could offer a payment for their sins against Him. In fact, the Old Testament describes many different types of sacrifices—bulls, lambs, goats, and even birds. However, all these sacrifices were temporary;

they were not a complete payment for sin. Additionally, these sacrifices symbolically pointed toward the need for Christ. The one perfect sacrifice would be God's Son, Jesus Christ, who would have no sin nature and would live a perfect life of obedience to God. Because of His special pedigree and holy life, Jesus would be the One who could take the punishment for everyone else.

God's Son (and as such, the "perfect man") could do what the animal sacrifices could not. Hebrews 10:4 points out that "it is impossible for the blood of bulls and goats to take away sins." Hebrews 10:10 explains how the relationship between God and fallen, evil people is restored: "We have been made holy through the sacrifice of the body of Jesus Christ once for all."

Jesus implied that children have, well, childlike faith (Matthew 18:3; Mark 10:14–15). (He said that adults need this type of faith every bit as much, but that's a separate story!) Simple concepts like the Sugar Test or parables like the Parable of the Weeds will resonate with children. And we need to tell our children that God is good. God is delaying punishment to give us a chance to accept His sacrificial offer of Jesus. In the end, there is a way home—and children can appreciate that.

Why Does God Allow Suffering?

*God whispers to us in our pleasures, speaks
in our conscience, but shouts in our pains:
it is His megaphone to rouse a deaf world.*

—C. S. Lewis, *The Problem of Pain*

Some nonbelievers point to suffering in this world and conclude that God (at least a good God) must not exist, because suffering is evil. It's a fairly popular idea that your children may absorb from the culture. The rationale goes something like this: "If I were God and I were all-powerful and good, I would eradicate suffering. Since there is indeed suffering, there must not be an all-powerful, good God."

To answer this charge, you and your children will need some logic training—this may seem like wordplay at first, but stick with me. This line of thought is essential in developing a Christian worldview that includes the concept of absolute truth.

Here's the basic principle: If there were no God, pain and suffering would not be a *moral* problem. The fact that there is pain and suffering is partial proof that there is a moral God. Keep in mind that if God didn't exist—if the universe consisted only of physical matter and natural forces—there would be no "problem of pain." There would be no good or bad, just "stuff."

Why is this? *Because God is the ultimate standard of good.* The fact that we may look at something and rightly conclude "This is good and

QUESTION RECAP: Why does an all-powerful and loving God allow pain and suffering to exist in this world?

1. By noting that suffering and pain exist and are bad, the questioner is expressing a moral judgment that there is a standard of good and bad—moral absolutes.
2. God is good and has His reasons for allowing pain and suffering, and though we may not understand them, we can trust that those reasons are for our ultimate good.

HOPE-FILLED ANSWER: God has a plan to eliminate pain and suffering from this world. Until then, Christians are to turn to Him for comfort and learn the qualities of patience and endurance through the tough times.

• •

that is bad" establishes that moral awareness exists. Such lines of thinking indicate that humans are able to discern when something conforms more closely to an *ultimate standard of good.* God is not only the Creator and Sustainer of the universe, He is also the ground (or foundation) of moral reality.[1]

In a universe with no ultimate standard of good, there could be no "good, better, and best." There could be no "bad, worse, and unconscionable." Remember that in Genesis 1:31 God looked over His creation and called it "good." But our world today has plenty in it that is inarguably "bad." All people and most circumstances fall short of goodness. In order for the concepts of evil or suffering to exist, there must be a fixed, unchanging, absolute standard (or measuring stick) of goodness, love, purity, justice, beauty, and truth. According to the Christian worldview, this standard of measurement comes from God. In commenting on the rightness or wrongness of any action or circumstance, we are expressing where something falls in relation to the ultimate standard. Take God, who is the measuring stick, out of the equation, and there is no right or wrong, no heroism or wickedness. There's just stuff. The fact that we rightly praise virtue or condemn evil is proof that all persons intuitively believe in some ultimate standard, if not God Himself.

So when your children come to you with questions about pain and suffering, give them praise for understanding and acknowledging that there is a standard, a measuring stick for good versus evil. Reinforce that their desire for a world without evil and suffering, a world that is filled with beauty and the absence of pain, comes from and is shared by the God who created everything to be "very good." Help your older children understand that even an atheist who complains about the pain and suffering in this world is in some way seeking after God's heart.

Once the concept of an absolute standard for good is established in your children's minds, you can look at why God allows pain and suffering to continue through events like earthquakes and cancer.

Why Does God Allow Bad Things to Happen?

It's easy to ponder how the world might be better, if only _____ (insert the suggestion of your choice). But the fact is that we live in the world that *is*. As we've seen from the texts in Genesis, the world is cursed and filled with evil. You might be thinking, *Okay, sure. Humans have sinned, and sin brings spiritual consequences (such as death and separation from God). But how do things like natural disasters and cancer fit into the picture? Why does God allow these?*

One of the reasons bad things happen is the fact that every created thing is subject to decay and death. Romans 8:21 says that the "creation itself" is in "bondage to decay." To give a tangible, concrete example of this concept, it may be helpful to show your children a perfectly ripe apple and put it out on the porch or windowsill where they can see it every day. You could even take a picture of it at the same time every day to document how it decays. Explain to your children that the earth is just like that—not only physically but also spiritually. Because we live in a world that's decaying, sometimes "good" people, even Christians, get hurt or killed.

Related to this discussion is a discovery announced in 1850 by scientist Rudolf Clausius. His second law of thermodynamics (called the law of entropy in 1865) was hailed as perhaps the high-water mark of nineteenth-century science.[2] It also affirms what the Bible predicts in several passages.

Clausius explained his law of entropy in "the following simple form: 1. The energy of the universe is constant. 2. The entropy of the universe tends toward a maximum."[3] Bottom line: The amount of *unusable* energy in the universe is increasing, and this increase is irreversible. The universe is moving from order to disorder. And this law of entropy is recognized as one of the most proven realities in all of science.

But what does the law of entropy have to do with questions about pain, suffering, and natural disasters? The answer is *plenty.* This is because sin introduced death and judgment into this formerly all-good creation. The fall of man resulted in spiritual and physical consequences such that *all* of creation is touched in some way.

As anyone over twenty-five years old knows, physical bodies also decay. We know that people suffer through illness. Biologists can explain how and why the human body ages and cancers start and grow. But many question why God allows disease and natural disasters. Your children will question this too, especially when a relative or friend becomes terminally ill or after a hurricane destroys the homes of a million "innocent" people. We're not in paradise anymore, that's for certain.

Could There Be a Purpose for Suffering?

Could God have a reason for allowing suffering? The answer, of course, is yes. Whether we are talking about moral evil (sin) or natural evil (the result of living in a fallen, decaying world with sinful, decaying bodies), let's ask the question the way many Christian scholars have done: Could God

have had a *morally sufficient* reason for allowing _____?"
(Fill in the blank with the tragedy of your choice.)

The answer to the question of moral sufficiency is yes. Sin happened, but God had patience with Adam and Eve. The flood was a judgment on a God-hating world, but God preserved the family of righteous Noah, and his line of descendants would one day lead to the birth of Christ. When God sent His Son to earth to be the Savior, He began the process of redeeming humankind, which is currently bound by the consequences of moral evil. God even brings good out of the natural disasters that result from this long chain of events that trace back to the fall of humankind.

> *I have read the last page of the Bible. It's going to turn out all right.*
>
> —BILLY GRAHAM, evangelist

Scientists believe that hurricanes and tropical storms help distribute the earth's heat. Violent weather disruptions help balance temperatures between the earth's poles. Severe storms bring copious amounts of rain, which are a natural part of the earth's water cycle (which contributes to agriculture and to the replenishing of wells and water tables). Earthquakes on the ocean floor can cause catastrophic waves. But the waves result in gases being released into the earth's atmosphere, which enhances plant growth. Lightning often causes fires that damage property and lead to loss of life. But lightning also releases nitrogen into the atmosphere, which is needed by plants and foliage. Fire can actually help enrich soil, since burned land frequently becomes more fertile than it was before an unplanned fire.[4]

Consider the ultimate good that came from Joseph's troubles in the Old Testament account. Joseph told his brothers, who had treated him badly years before, "As for you, you meant evil against me, *but* God meant it for good in order to bring about this present result, to preserve many people alive" (Genesis 50:20, NASB).

God *does* bring good out of evil. Therefore, He indeed has morally sufficient reasons for allowing such things.

God's Promises for this Life and the Life to Come

Ever notice a Construction in Progress sign posted in front of a building site? As I write this, a highway near my house is undergoing some repair and expansion. There is a large flashing sign by the road that scrolls through this message: "Repair in process. Stay alert. Expect delays."

God's Word flashes the same types of messages to us. This world is undergoing major renovation. In fact, it's more than this. We are in the process of *redemption*. And one day we'll understand that the scars we've accumulated along the journey—painful and perplexing as they seemed at the time—were worth it. We have God's promise that in "the ages to come," we will know that whatever price we endured for following Jesus during our earthly lives was well invested—in fact, God will show us "exceeding riches" in that future age (Ephesians 2:7, KJV).

Paul offered this perspective on suffering in light of the future God has promised:

> I consider that our present sufferings are not worth comparing with
> the glory that will be revealed in us. The creation waits in eager ex-
> pectation for the sons of God to be revealed. For the creation was
> subjected to frustration, not by its own choice, but by the will of the
> one who subjected it, in hope that the creation itself will be liberated
> from its bondage to decay and brought into the glorious freedom of
> the children of God. (Romans 8:18–21)

Children need to know that in life and in our walk with God, endurance is essential. And they need to acknowledge that life in this present age is difficult, even with the Holy Spirit to comfort us. As is often said, "It's not how you start but how you finish." We have the promises of God that we will be rewarded for standing firm for Him—and that means continuing to live according to His Word even when it's not convenient or easy.

God's Word encourages us to reflect on the good that suffering produces in our lives:

We also rejoice in our sufferings, because we know that suffering produces perseverance; perseverance, character; and character, hope. And
hope does not disappoint us. (Romans 5:3–5)

The God of all grace, who called you to his eternal glory in Christ,
after you have suffered a little while, will himself restore you and
make you strong, firm and steadfast. (1 Peter 5:10)

Our children's questions in these areas deserve thoughtful, logical
responses. It's not sufficient to simply write off disasters or hardships
by saying, "God works in mysterious ways." Use these times or events
to teach your children that while we live in a fallen world inhabited by
sinful people, it's only temporary, and that compared to eternal life with
Jesus in paradise, it will all be worth it. Encourage them with these words
from Revelation 21:4: "[God] will wipe every tear from their eyes. There
will be no more death or mourning or crying or pain, for the old order
of things has passed away."

3

Why Is God So Unfair?

*As flies to wanton boys are we to the
gods. They kill us for their sport.*

—The Earl of Gloucester, in Shakespeare's *King Lear*

The Shakespeare quotation is certainly pessimistic, isn't it? It makes God
out to be a cruel, capricious Being who treats us like lab rats. I've talked
with more than a few children who've expressed similar negative views
about God. Perhaps you have too.

They see God as "unfair" because of the pain and evil in this world,
the disappointments and losses in life, or broken family relationships.
This viewpoint isn't always prompted by the sense that God has been
unfair to us personally. Often, children question God's fairness when they
note poverty, war, and atrocities in other countries or throughout history.
Sometimes people wonder why God was so harsh to the Canaanites in
the Old Testament. In a way, the question of God's fairness is an exten-
sion of the problem of evil that we examined in the previous two chapters.

Children also have a sense of fair versus unfair that can often be set
on hyperdrive. How many times have you heard your kids say, "That's
not fair!" "I saw it first!" "Take that back!" And don't forget the ever-
popular declaration (make a menacing expression before you say this):
"It's *mine!*"

Are we just lab rats to God? Would He swat us as if we were annoying
insects? No. In fact, out of love He took the burden of "unfairness" on

Key Concepts

QUESTION RECAP: Why is God so unfair? Why was He so mean in Old Testament times? Why does it seem as if God doesn't care?

1. If God were truly fair, we would all deserve death. But we can be glad that He is "unfair" and gives us mercy and patience.
2. God wasn't "fair" to many of His most faithful followers, including the apostle Paul. Yet Paul used his weakness and trials to glorify God. He looked at trials as temporary and focused on the heavenly kingdom to come.
3. God's character hasn't changed over time, though circumstances have. Those circumstances include Jesus' sacrifice on the cross. Therefore, *despite appearances*, God will act only in ways that are ultimately good.

HOPE-FILLED ANSWER: God's actions are sometimes harsh and may seem unfair on the surface. However, a close examination of Scripture will reveal that He is eternally good, and His actions are always for our benefit within an eternal time frame.

• •

Himself by offering Jesus, His only Son, as a sacrifice for our sins. How "unfair" is that?

If God were only fair without the love and mercy that define His character, then there would be no grace. God would snuff out the evil in this world—and we would all perish.

> *How can I believe in God when just last week I got my tongue caught in the roller of an electric typewriter?*
>
> —Woody Allen, *Without Feathers*

So, "Is God fair?" The answer is no, and how grateful we should be for it! How fortunate we are that God isn't merely *fair*, quickly giving us the cosmic justice we deserve. God is *merciful*. God is *full of grace*. God is *loving, patient*, and *kind*.

In the previous chapter we saw that although evil happens in this life, in the end God will redeem the human race; He will sort it all out. Life's apparent "unfairness" will also be sorted out and redeemed. In the here and now, however, there's also something to be learned when we experience "unfair" treatment or trials.

God Wasn't "Fair" to the Apostle Paul

Many servants of God had an "unfair" life situation. The Old Testament prophet Hosea was commissioned by God to seek after an unfaithful wife. The prophet Jeremiah was attacked, beaten, and imprisoned: his nickname is the Weeping Prophet. And Jesus, who deserved to be treated like the God He was, did not have great riches and lots of popularity. His lot was a violent death on the cross.

Let's look at the apostle Paul for an example of how God turns "unfair" treatment into something beautiful. Paul's second epistle (or letter) to Timothy was written after his last missionary journey and shortly before his last imprisonment in Rome. A year or so after 2 Timothy was written, Paul was executed by the emperor Nero. We know from the other epistles that Paul had gone through many hardships. Paul was falsely accused and wound up in prison, but he also experienced numerous calamities, including shipwrecks and beatings (see 2 Corinthians 11:23–28).

This description of Paul's life doesn't seem very glamorous, does it? While Paul stood faithful throughout his life of Christian service, he prayed for help, only to be told by God, "My grace is sufficient for you, for my power is made perfect in weakness" (2 Corinthians 12:9).

So we see from Paul's writings that he didn't expect "fairness" in this life, but that didn't stop him from asking for help. In fact, he went on to note that those difficult times helped shape his character, and he seemed to be praising God for letting him go through those times:

Therefore I will boast all the more gladly about my weaknesses, so that Christ's power may rest on me. That is why, for Christ's sake, I delight in weaknesses, in insults, in hardships, in persecutions, in difficulties. For when I am weak, then I am strong. (Verses 9–10)

How did Paul process life's pains and "unfairness"? By reflecting on God and the reward that would come from faithfully following Him: "The Lord will deliver me from every evil work and preserve me for His heavenly kingdom" (2 Timothy 4:18, NKJV).

Telling Children the Truth about God and Life

So, what do we tell children about unfair suffering? Depending on the age of the child, I lean toward the straightforward truth that life is dif-

A Note about Job

Older children and teens would greatly benefit from a study of Job. Job thought that God had afflicted him for no reason. Job said, "He crushes me with a tempest; / And multiplies my wounds without cause" (9:17, NKJV). Despite Job's low moments (like that one), one of the main themes of the book is that God can allow pain and suffering *and still care for someone.* He can even do great things in a person's life *after* or *through* the suffering. The whole book is about the sovereignty of God.

The presence of trials and inequities in life in no way means that God has dropped the ball. The book of Job will help your children understand this. In complete confidence we may reflect on the reality that we know the end of the story. We know that eventually we will be rewarded for staying faithful through difficult times, and ultimately we will all say, "I know that my Redeemer lives, / and that in the end he will stand upon the earth" (19:25).

ficult. And at times life can be downright excruciating and emotionally painful.

Romans 8:28 is often quoted to comfort people in times of distress: "We know that all things work together for good to them that love God" (KJV).

But consider the way the New International Version translates this verse: "We know that in all things God works for the good of those who love him."

You may notice the difference between the two renderings: In the King James Version, the implication is that no matter what happens in this life, no matter how violent, sad, perverse, painful, or cataclysmic— somehow everything will "work together for good." In perhaps a better translation, the New International Version states that in all of those same circumstances, God will be working *for the good* of those who love Him, but there is no guarantee that in this life everything will *be* good. Bad things happen, even to devout Christians.

Why Was God So "Mean" in the Old Testament?

A quick comparison between the gorier parts of the Old Testament and the loving, healing Jesus of the Gospels could leave your children wondering if God has two faces. For centuries, people of all ages and backgrounds have pondered the nature of God's violent actions in the Old Testament and how those line up with the words of Christ, such as "Come to me, all you who are weary and burdened, and I will give you rest. Take my yoke upon you and learn from me, for I am gentle and humble in heart, and you will find rest for your souls" (Matthew 11:28–29). Some have theorized that God changed or adapted over time, interacting with and approaching His creation differently at different times. Others promote the idea that there was a *progressive* revelation of God, meaning that He described only parts of Himself, little by little, to be pieced together later.

However you choose to approach it, the premise of the question is quite relevant: Why does God appear to be at times merciless (or in a child's eyes, "mean") in the Old Testament and "kinder and gentler" in the New Testament? Was He being unfair to those people who lived before Christ?

Historic Christian orthodoxy denies that God's nature or ultimate plans change. Rightly so. The Bible clearly establishes that God doesn't

Old Testament Warm Fuzzies and New Testament Judgments

The Old Testament shows the wrath and judgment of God. But it also depicts a loving God. Consider these examples:

Hagar (Genesis 16)—This Egyptian woman was Abraham's concubine and mother of his son Ishmael. Abraham's wife, Sarah, badly mistreated Hagar. At Hagar's lowest point, God rescued her in the desert and gave her a new life.

Hannah (1 Samuel 1, 2)—This woman was barren and wept bitterly before God. God heard her prayer and gave her a son, whom she dedicated to God and gave to Eli the priest to be trained. The boy lived with Eli and would later become the great prophet Samuel. After Hannah gave Samuel to the Lord, God blessed her with five more children (1 Samuel 2:21).

Hezekiah (2 Kings 20)—The prophet Isaiah told Hezekiah to get his house in order, for he was to die. Hezekiah pleaded with God for mercy and received it. God allowed him fifteen more years of life. Not only that; God promised to "deliver you and this city from the hand of the king of Assyria" (verse 6).

Noah (Genesis 6–9)—Consider that while the flood did happen, and all but eight people on the earth were wiped out, the Bible tells us that Noah was a "preacher of righteousness" (2 Peter 2:5). Who was he preaching to? All of those around him, trying to save them from the impending flood! It was always change: He is said to be *immutable*, the One "who is, and who was, and who is to come" (Revelation 1:8). Take a look at these texts for examples:

> [Samuel said,] "He who is the Glory of Israel [God] does not lie or change his mind; for he is not a man, that he should change his mind." (1 Samuel 15:29)

God's desire to save more than just those eight people.

The New Testament reveals God's love, but it also shows God's righteous judgment:

Ananias and Sapphira (Acts 5:1–11)—This married couple thought they could sell their property and pretend to give all their proceeds to God's church, when they secretly held back some. It's actually quite a shocking New Testament story: God struck them dead on the spot for lying to the Holy Spirit.

King Herod (Acts 12:20–23)—This king was in a position of power and knew it. He had the apostle James beheaded and the apostle Peter arrested (Acts 12:1–3). Later, a mob of people praised him as "a god, not . . . a man" (verse 22). When Herod did not shift the glory to God, but kept it, an angel struck him down "immediately." He must have died of a horrible intestinal disease, because verse 23 says, "He was eaten by worms and died."

Jesus (Matthew 23)—Some of the most scathing words spoken by any biblical character or prophet came from . . . Jesus. Read Matthew 23 and judge for yourself whether Jesus was always just warm fuzzies, kindness, and gentleness.

Jesus (Matthew 21, Mark 11, John 2)—Next time you think Jesus was always just a gentle lamb, consider going into an open-air market, using a whip, and overturning all the sellers' tables, including money and materials, and driving out the animals. I'm pretty sure I'd lack the courage to pull that one off!

Every good and perfect gift is from above, coming down from the
Father of the heavenly lights, who does not change like shifting shad-
ows. (James 1:17)

I the LORD do not change. (Malachi 3:6)

So if we read that God doesn't change, how do we account for the
times where God says He did change His mind? (Genesis 6:6, for example.) What are we to make of the apparent different personalities we
see exhibited between the Old and New Testaments? The answer to this
issue can be found when we understand that what changes are *circumstances*, not God.

God is the same "yesterday and today and forever" (Hebrews 13:8).
The generalization that Scripture presents two Gods—a violent, warlike
deity in the Old Testament, and a gentle Jesus in the New—relies on too
simplistic a view of each testament. There are plenty of passages depict-
ing the love of God in the Old Testament, and there are vivid examples
of God's judgment in the New Testament. Check out the sidebar on
the previous page "Old Testament Warm Fuzzies and New Testament
Judgments" for examples.

Why Did God Kill So Many People in the Old Testament?

This answer requires some background information and a look at the
scope of the entire Old Testament and God's relationship with the nation of Israel.

From Genesis we learned that one of the fundamental principles
in the Old Testament is that every descendant of Adam deserves death.
God has never had a moral obligation to save anyone because of his
or her own "righteousness," since no one except Christ is righteous.
(Genesis 15:6 says that Abraham's faith was "credited . . . to him as
righteousness." But God wasn't obligated to do that—He did it out of
grace.) During the times recorded in the Old Testament, much of the

human race was rebellious and unredeemed. In Noah's day, sin got so bad that God almost wiped out humanity with the flood, leaving only eight people alive.

Enter Father Abraham and the nation of Israel. God created a special people set apart to worship and serve Him. This people group was supposed be an example to the other nations. Through the nation of Israel, salvation would come to the world via the birth, death, and resurrection of Christ Jesus. God gave the nation of Israel special attention as well as special responsibilities. The Jews have always been "the apple of [God's] eye" (Deuteronomy 32:10), but when the Israelites disobeyed God, they experienced discipline too. The Israelites weren't given a pass when they sinned. God allowed them to wander in the desert for forty years, afflicted them with plagues, and had them carted off to Babylon in captivity, as just a few examples.

> *Saints are sinners who keep on trying.*
> —Chinese fortune cookie

When your children hear the accounts of Israel killing off rival nations, their simplistic, concrete thought patterns and their overzealous fairness meter will sound an alarm. The questions really come pouring forth when young people learn that the Israelites were *following God's orders* when they killed the Canaanites, the Jebusites, and the Philistines.

A youth once asked me, "Did God tell Israel to wipe out the Canaanites just because they were different?" Because of the way the asker phrased the question, I wondered if he felt as if he were more compassionate than God. The multicultural thinking would go like this: "If I were God, I would have had mercy on non-Jews; it's not their fault they were living in the best land around, and their culture was different. However, God did not have mercy on the heathen people, and so I must be more compassionate than God."

When evaluating the morality of the battles between the Israelites and their enemies, we must look at the biblical record with three realities in mind: (1) God doesn't change; (2) God is carrying out what is for the greatest good; and (3) God is sovereign over all of creation.

Let's face reality here: This is God's universe. He made it. He is free to do what He wants with it. But it makes sense that He will act in accord with His nature—and His nature is good. Therefore, *despite appearances*, God will act only in ways that are ultimately good. We aren't more righteous or compassionate than God. As difficult as it is for our modern minds to accept, the killing of the Canaanites was for the ultimate good.

Their cultural practices included such things as child sacrifice and bestiality. (See Leviticus 18 for the whole sordid list of defilements; it's definitely adult-only material.) The people of Canaan violently opposed the nation of Israel. Would it really have been preferable if God had allowed the Canaanites to exterminate the nation that would bring forth the Savior? God's authorization of Israel to kill the pagans wasn't some flippant crime of passion. More than four centuries had gone by during which the Canaanites could have changed their corrupt and murderous ways.

We have evidence that had Israel's enemies repented (turned away from their sin), they would have been spared. Aliens were allowed to live with the Israelites as long as they obeyed God's laws (Deuteronomy 31:12), and so God wasn't doing an ethnic cleansing merely because the foreigners were "different." And remember the story of Jonah? The land of Nineveh was going to be destroyed because of the great sins of its inhabitants, but Jonah preached to the people of who lived there, and they repented (Jonah 3:10). When the enemies of the Israelites changed their ways, God showed them mercy.

4

How Do We Know
That God Loves Us?

Amazing love! How can it be that Thou,
my God, shouldst die for me?

—Charles Wesley, "And Can It Be?"

I love musician Chris Tomlin's recent adaptation of the classic hymn "And Can It Be?" As I travel and speak in America's churches, it thrills me to see a new generation being exposed to the timeless truths of Wesley's song. The full lyrics of the original hymn contain powerful lines such as these:

No condemnation now I dread;
Jesus, and all in Him, is mine!
Alive in Him, my living Head,
And clothed in righteousness divine,
Bold I approach the eternal throne,
And claim the crown, through Christ my own.[1]

It's incredibly moving to hear a crowd sing the refrain's famous question, "Amazing love! How can it be that Thou, my God, shouldst die for me?"

People of all ages have asked themselves, "How do I know that God loves me?"

Key Concepts

QUESTION RECAP: How do I know God loves me when I don't feel it or when bad things happen in my life?

1. All evil present in this world is traceable to Adam and Eve's fall into sin. That means every human is part of the world's evil. Sin and evil are virtually the same thing.
2. God is patient and loving, however, and He has a plan that will rid the world of evil and evil people. Part of that plan involves Jesus' death on the cross.

HOPE-FILLED ANSWER: The New Testament teaches that nothing can ever separate the Christian from God's love. God's love has been proven on the cross. Parents are in a good place to model unconditional love to their children.

• •

Jesus' Death Is the Greatest Proof of God's Love

If your child desires to love God, that is *indirect proof* that God loves your child. Think about the implications of this verse: "We love him, because he first loved us" (1 John 4:19, KJV).

When your child understands that God gave His "only begotten Son" out of love (John 3:16, KJV), then your child (in response to this love) will begin to love Him in return. As children begin to walk in God's promises and desire His will, they will grow in their daily experience of the fullness of His love.

The Bible is replete with examples of God's love shown to the world. Here are two familiar verses:

> For God so loved the world that he gave his one and only Son,
> that whoever believes in him shall not perish but have eternal life.
> (John 3:16)

God demonstrates his own love for us in this: While we were still sinners, Christ died for us. (Romans 5:8)

The word *demonstrates* in Romans 5:8 means "tangibly proves." God has demonstrably revealed His love for us by sending His Son. In Jesus we see that God is the great Initiator of the love relationship available to all: "This is love: not that we loved God, but that he loved us and sent his Son as an atoning sacrifice for our sins" (1 John 4:10). (*Atone* basically means "reconcile.") Think again about the growing seeds, or the sunset. We may not see growth, or change, all the time, but it is happening. Assure your child that a seed is changing, spreading, expanding—growing—even before it shoots out of the soil. A sunset moves a little faster, but you can still watch one for some time and notice only very small,

Growing a Strong Faith

Growing a plant or flower with your younger children can teach them the importance of patience and how the seeds of love and good works are just like the seeds you're planting together. All you need are a pot, planting soil, and a package of seeds. After you've planted the seeds according to the directions on the package, water the soil and then check it daily with your children. During this process, assure your children that the seeds are still there even though they can't be seen underneath the soil. Remind your children that their love and obedience to the Lord are like that: they may not be visible to other people, but they will in time bear fruit. As the first shoots of the plants appear, point out how vulnerable the little plants are and how important it is to protect them from the elements and bugs or other things that might hurt them. Remind your children that like these tiny plants, their love for God needs to be nurtured and cared for as well, so that it will grow stronger each day.

incremental changes. In the same way, God's love is happening, even when we don't see it.

In a concrete way, God showed His love by giving us Jesus, the living Word; that's the greatest example of His love for us. Another proof of God's love is the Bible; God cared enough to give us His written Word.

Love, then, isn't mere emotion, or feelings. These may accompany love. But biblically speaking, love is the commitment to meet other people's needs.

Our greatest need was forgiveness of sin. So God sent us a personal Savior, Jesus.

The Loving Judge

Walk your child through the following scenario, which explains that God shows love through forgiveness. You may have heard it before, but that's because it's one of the all-time best illustrations of God's love.

This faith alone, when based upon the sure promises of God, must save us.

—MARTIN LUTHER, "On Faith, and Coming to Christ"

Imagine for a moment that one day you were driving your car, and you didn't notice how fast you were driving as you entered a thirty-five mile-per-hour speed zone. A police officer stopped you and gave you a ticket for driving sixty miles per hour. The ticket carried a two-hundred-dollar fine, plus court costs.

The day comes for you to go to court. The officer presents the evidence against you—the record of the radar reading and his own account of the events. Despite your pleas for mercy, the judge pronounces you guilty and orders you to pay the fine plus the court costs.

Suddenly you realize that you are in big trouble; you don't have the money to pay your fine or the court costs. It looks as if you're going to spend some time in jail!

Then something wonderful and unexpected happens: The judge steps down from the bench, removes his robe, and pulls out his wallet. He invites you to walk with him to the office of the court clerk, where he pays your fine in full.

That would be awesome, right? Well, what if the judge not only paid your fine but also ordered the court clerk to expunge your record? As far as the state is concerned, you never broke the speed limit.

God—the ultimate Judge—paid the penalty for our sins by sending Jesus to die on the cross in our place. We were the ones who deserved to be on that cross because of our sins. And yet, not only did He pay our fine; He expunged the record! We are now considered righteous in His sight.

Helping Children Understand God's Love

When our hearts turn to God and we truly accept Jesus as our Lord and Savior, we are saved. At that moment we receive the gift of the Holy Spirit that the book of Ephesians says "seals" us:

> Having believed, you were marked in [Christ] *with a seal*, the promised Holy Spirit, who is a deposit guaranteeing our inheritance until the redemption of those who are God's possession. (1:13–14)

The word *seal* is indicative of the permanence of our salvation. In olden days a king would seal an official letter that he didn't want opened until it reached its intended destination. He would melt wax and then press his signet ring (hence the word signature) into the wax, officially sealing the letter. When we accept Christ as our Savior, we receive the gift of the Holy Spirit as His "seal" on our lives.

> *God loves each one of us as if there were only one of us.*
>
> —SAINT AUGUSTINE, *The Confessions of St. Augustine*

The book of Ephesians also mentions the indescribable love of God that is part of the salvation package. When your children struggle with the question "Does God love me?" it may comfort them to remind them what Scripture says about their standing with God:

> I pray that you, being rooted and established in love, may have power, together with all the saints, to grasp how wide and long and high and deep is the love of Christ, and to know this love that surpasses knowledge—that you may be filled to the measure of all the fullness of God. (Ephesians 3:17–19)

In order to explain God's love and model it to your children, it's vital that you have experienced that love firsthand. The first step to explaining God's love is to live in it and enjoy it yourself—and then to make sure that you lead your children into the joy of salvation as well.

When Your Children Don't Feel Lovable

Because I travel so much, I meet kids from all over the United States. I speak to cutters, drinkers, poor students, and overweight young men and women. I counsel those whose friends or family members have committed suicide. I hang with students who claim to be hard-core atheists. Every teen I meet probably feels flawed or scared in some significant way. Many of them feel unlovable.

Being the preacher that I am, I encourage them by falling back on the promise that God loves us even when we sin—that He loved us while we were "yet sinners" (Romans 5:8, KJV). I tell them that He loves us so much that He allowed His Son to die on a cross to save us from those sins. When we sin, we need to turn away from our sin (repent) and ask Him for forgiveness.

I encourage them with words from the apostle Paul:

> Who shall separate us from the love of Christ? Shall trouble or hardship or persecution or famine or nakedness or danger or sword? . . .
> No, in all these things we are more than conquerors through him

who loved us. For I am convinced that neither death nor life, neither angels nor demons, neither the present nor the future, nor any powers, neither height nor depth, nor anything else in all creation, will be able to separate us from the love of God that is in Christ Jesus our Lord. (Romans 8:35, 37–39)

But my words of encouragement can go only so far. Most of all, your kids need to see God's love in *you*. Again, love is "caught, not taught." If they see parents who faithfully love and support each other, and who patiently love their children (because it does take patience!), they'll come to believe more and more in Christ's love, which is insurmountable.

John 15:9–17 encourages believers to abide in Christ. Read the following passage to your children, and then ask them what they think and feel about it. You can ask them questions such as "How can I show you better that I love you?" and "What things do you need me to do so you know that I care?" You'll be wonderfully surprised at their responses.

As the Father has loved me, so have I loved you. Now remain in my love. If you obey my commands, you will remain in my love, just as I have obeyed my Father's commands and remain in his love. I have told you this so that my joy may be in you and that your joy may be complete. My command is this: Love each other as I have loved you. Greater love has no one than this, that he lay down his life for his friends. You are my friends if you do what I command. I no longer call you servants, because a servant does not know his master's business. Instead, I have called you friends, for everything that I learned from my Father I have made known to you. You did not choose me, but I chose you and appointed you to go and bear fruit—fruit that will last. Then the Father will give you whatever you ask in my name. This is my command: Love each other.

I have one last idea if you have a child who feels as if he or she isn't lovable. Help your child develop ways he or she can show love to others, which is the command at the end of the Romans passage: "Love each other." I've seen kids' self-esteem and self-confidence flourish because they turned the question around from "How can I be sure God loves me?" to "How can I be sure others see the love of God through me?"

5

Why Doesn't God Make My Life Easy?

*God who made the lion and the lamb, you
decreed I should be what I am. Would it spoil
some vast eternal plan, if I were a wealthy man?*

—Tevye, "If I Were a Rich Man," *Fiddler on the Roof*

Most of us can relate to those lines from the song "If I Were a Rich Man."
At one time or another, we've all wanted to be rich. American author
Dorothy Parker once said, "I don't know much about being a millionaire,
but I'll bet I'd be darling at it." Whether the craving is for money, fame,
leisure, power, or something else, it's easy to tell ourselves how right life
would be if only we had this or that.

In the first part of this chapter, we'll discuss the concept of trials and
tribulations. In the second part, we'll look at the feelings of confusion,
rejection, and disappointment children may feel when God doesn't answer their prayers the way they want Him to.

Trials Build Character

Humans tend to seek earthly things over God, and children are no excep-
tion. C. S. Lewis observed, "If I discover within myself a desire which
no experience in this world can satisfy, the most probable explanation

Key Concepts

QUESTION RECAP: Why doesn't God make my life easy? Why aren't I popular? Rich? Smart? Good looking? Why did my parents have to get divorced? Why isn't my life perfect? God has the power to help me—so why doesn't He?

1. Seeking after God is more important and satisfying than finding short-term happiness in worldly things.
2. Suffering encourages us to lean on God and develop character.

HOPE-FILLED ANSWER: God wants us to be free from selfish attitudes *and* have the full assurance that we can trust Him to do everything He has promised. We are to bring our needs to God in confidence, but He sometimes expects us to do without so we can develop endurance and patience.

● ●

is that I was made for another world."[1] We are prone to quest after _____ (fill in the blank with the desire of your choice), oblivious to the fact that what our hearts truly desire is not found on earth. We continue to long for *something* even after getting that new car, achieving the promotion at work, or buying the dream house. It's important for Christian children to understand that the things of this world don't ultimately satisfy. However, seeking after God does satisfy.

Unless children understand the long-term benefits of seeking after God in the midst of trials, their faith may become passive, or they may come to believe that God doesn't care about them if He doesn't make their lives easy.

One of life's paradoxes is that we often seek the easy, convenient, or less costly path in life, and yet struggles and challenges build our character. The paradox intensifies when an individual becomes a believer. We hold citizenship in heaven; yet for our time in this world, we have orders from God to make a positive Christian impact (see Matthew 10:16; Philippians 2:14–16). The Christian actually has God's permission to experience life to the fullest (see John 10:10; 1 Timothy 4:4). But the inevitable hard times come, and the upside is that such tough experiences teach us to trust in God. Trials and persecution provide opportunities for the Christian to respond as Jesus would.

We are never promised an easy life, but we do know that God will walk with us through our ups and downs (Hebrews 13:5). We also know that sometimes He is disciplining us out of love (Proverbs 3:11–12; Hebrews 12:10–11).

A Life of Perseverance

Perseverance in the New Testament is denoted by a Greek word that means "steadfastness" or "endurance."[2] The apostle James spoke of it in this way:

Why the Not-So-Easy Life Can Be Good

Encourage your children that while they can't avoid tough spots all the time, God can turn difficult times into learning experiences. God allows us to experience discomfort . . .

- to destroy reliance on self rather than on God—purging pride (Philippians 3:7–10)
- to draw us back into God's will through discipline (Job 5:17; Psalm 119:71)
- to build our character—perseverance (Romans 5:3–5; Hebrews 12:11)
- to teach us more about God—instruction (Psalm 94:12; Hebrews 12:6–11)
- to guide us in our walk with Him—following Jesus' example in suffering (2 Corinthians 1:3–5)

Consider it pure joy, my brothers, whenever you face trials of many kinds, because you know that the testing of your faith develops perseverance. Perseverance must finish its work so that you may be mature and complete, not lacking anything. (James 1:2–4)

These verses harmonize beautifully with the passage we read earlier from Romans that indicates the reward that Christians of all ages can expect when passing the test of trials we encounter:

We also rejoice in our sufferings, because we know that suffering produces perseverance; *perseverance [produces] character*; and character, hope. And hope does not disappoint us, because God has poured out his love into our hearts by the Holy Spirit, whom he has given us. (Romans 5:3–5)

The Greek word for *character* means "tried, approved character."[3] Character is the moral or ethical quality of a person that signifies that the outside is the same as the inside. The word *character* means basically the opposite of the biblical concept of a *hypocrite*, which means, "one who wears a mask." We are not to appear one way on the outside but really be someone else on the inside.

When we endure pressure-filled situations with godliness, truly putting our faith in God and His promises, we persevere. Perseverance produces character—proven integrity—and shows that we are who we say we are. Modeling this for our children and teaching them to respond in like manner are essential in helping them develop "proven character."

Best of all, we see that proven character produces hope. It's important to realize that biblical hope is different from today's concept of hope. Biblically, *hope* is the "joyful and confident expectation" of a future event,[4] whereas the modern definition indicates mere wishful thinking.

Did you know that it's possible to become proficient in one's ability to trust God consistently? As we respond to God in obedience, we can develop a knack for it. That's called perseverance. Rather than pining for the "good life" as we define it, steadfast Christians learn to allow God to chart their journeys. The continual passing of tests by being godly (despite the temptation to react in a worldly manner) develops character.

"Character" implies that the inside (the real us) and the outside (how we act and appear) agree. God wants this for His children. First

---

They Won't Care How Much You Know Until . . .

Yeah, it's a cliché I'm sure you've heard hundreds of times from preachers' pulpits: People won't care how much you know until they know how much you care. It may be a cliché, but . . . it's true!

And the best way to care, of course, is to listen—really listen—and *to share your own struggles*. Yes, even as a parent, share your struggles with your children so they can learn to trust God in the midst of their own struggles:

- Share the struggles you've had with understanding how God is working. You've had them, so be real about them. But then tell your children that you decided to trust God through the situations anyway.
- Share your struggles you've had getting close to God—the dry periods in your life. You've had them, so be real about them. Then share how you kept fighting through those struggles.
- Share your struggles with temptation to sin. But when you do, remember that it's important to *share only what's appropriate for your child's developmental stage*. That said, share when, for example, you've been tempted to give in to laziness or to be angry in unrighteous ways. You've struggled with those things, so be real about them. Then share how you battled through those temptations by confessing them to God and asking for His help.

Timothy 4:8 explains that character is valuable: "Godliness has value for all things, holding promise for both the present life and the life to come."

Teaching these lessons in the early part of our children's lives is essential. Childhood is referred to as "the character-forming years" for a reason. If we don't implement consequences for disobedience or encourage godly behavior at an early age, it will lead to greater struggles for our children later on. When they ask, "Why doesn't God make my life easy?" we need to be able to tell them that there is a better life coming. It's a certainty, but until we meet Jesus in person, we must be obedient to Him and His Word and follow His example. By obeying Him now, we are demonstrating that our value system is based on eternity, not on this temporary life.

When I was a youth pastor, I would light a match and tell my teenage students to watch the smoke carefully as I blew out the flame. I would then read James 4:14: "What is your life? You are a mist that appears for a little while and then vanishes."

When children are young, it's easy for them to believe they'll live forever. We all *will* live forever in either heaven or hell. Consider 2 Corinthians 4:17–18:

> Our light and momentary troubles are achieving for us an eternal
> glory that far outweighs them all. So we fix our eyes not on what is
> seen, but on what is unseen. For what is seen is temporary, but what
> is unseen is eternal.

Young people often assume they'll be perpetually youthful and alive *in this world.* Teaching your children learn about eternal rewards for their earthly obedience can help them grasp the beauty of the apostle Paul's words.

Why Does God Say No to Some Prayers?

Children can become confused, frustrated, and discouraged when God doesn't seem to answer their prayers. It's important to remind them that

God may not answer prayer right away because the timing isn't right, or He may say no because what we're asking for isn't in our best interests. (For more on prayer and why some prayer answers are delayed, see chapter 12.)

Now we'll focus on the book of James and its reminders to consider the motives behind our prayers:

> You want something but don't get it. You kill and covet, but you cannot have what you want. You quarrel and fight. You do not have, because you do not ask God. When you ask, you do not receive, because you ask with wrong motives, that you may spend what you get on your pleasures. (4:2–3)

God recognizes wrong motives, and He doesn't seem inclined to answer prayers that are about our pleasures or lusts. Many a preacher has rightly pointed out that God is responsible to meet your *need*, not your *greed*!

So many things that we consider essential are luxuries. We may think that computers, smartphones that can text and access the Internet, lattes, nice cars, a beautiful home, and so on, are vital to our existence. In reality, most of the people who have ever existed did not enjoy these benefits.

Even God's own Son didn't have some things that *truly are* necessities of life: "Jesus replied, 'Foxes have holes and birds of the air have nests, but the Son of Man has no place to lay his head'" (Matthew 8:20).

> *Aim at heaven and you will get earth thrown in. Aim at earth and you get neither.*
> —C. S. LEWIS, *Mere Christianity*

Should we demand things Christ Himself was willing to go without?

At times when we're challenged in the physical world, we need to take a step back and ask if what we're "suffering" is persecution, or whether our worldly desires have burdened us with debt and addicted us to "stuff." Your children might be asking why God won't get them the latest video game or a nice bicycle, but in reality you might not be able to afford it. Perhaps God might bless them with the item they're praying for by inspiring someone else to buy it for them, but sometimes you'll need to teach them patience or how to work or save up for something. Other times, you might have to teach them one of life's more valuable lessons—learning to do without!

The apostle Paul was born into a well-to-do, respected Jewish family. In Philippians 3, he extolled all of his worldly credentials (education, rank, commitment to the Law), and then he went on to state that they meant nothing to him. He parted with his worldly resources to pursue his spiritual calling. Look at the character Paul exhibited in the following verses, and see if you'd like your children to emulate this attitude:

> I have learned to be content whatever the circumstances. I know what it is to be in need, and I know what it is to have plenty. I

Rewards Worth Waiting a Lifetime For

Help your children see that heaven really *is* worth waiting for:
- Sin and guilt will be taken away forever, never to return (Hebrews 10:17, 18).
- Everything will be made new—no more friends or relatives dying or having pain (Revelation 21:5).
- No more tears, sadness, unexplained tragedy, or death (Revelation 21:4).
- Jesus will have special rewards for those who have stayed faithful to the end (Revelation 22:12).
- Greatest of all, of course, is this: being with God forever, basking in His eternal light, and worshipping Him (Revelation 2:7; 3:5; 4—5).

You can find many other eternal blessings throughout the New Testament. Add to this list!

have learned the secret of being content in any and every situation, whether well fed or hungry, whether living in plenty or in want. I can do everything through him who gives me strength. (4:11–13)

Another reason that God sometimes doesn't answer prayer is because we don't *really* believe that He will answer. We may not be fully trusting Him. Consider this verse from the book of Hebrews: "Without faith it is impossible to please [God], for he who comes to God must believe that He is, and that He is a rewarder of those who diligently seek Him" (11:6, NKJV).

When you ask, you must believe. You must not doubt. People who doubt are like waves of the sea. The wind blows and tosses them around. A man like that shouldn't expect to receive anything from the Lord. He can't make up his mind. He can never decide what to do. (James 1:6–8, NIrV)

On the flip side of faith, there is fear, doubt, worry, and anxiety. God wants us to be free from these attitudes and have the full assurance that we can trust Him to do everything He has promised.

These commandments that I give you today are to be upon your hearts. Impress them on your children. Talk about them when you sit at home and when you walk along the road, when you lie down and when you get up. Tie them as symbols on your hands and bind them on your foreheads. Write them on the doorframes of your houses and on your gates. (Deuteronomy 6:6–9)

Pursue these things—and pass them on to your children.

God's design is not to always make life easy. Life is designed to make us *godly.* The Lord arranges circumstances and answers prayers in ways that will facilitate this.

One day we will be able to thank Him appropriately for it.

Part 2

Questions about Jesus, the Son

Is Jesus Really God?

*Alexander, Caesar, Charlemagne, and
I myself, have founded great empires:
but upon what do these creations of our
genius depend? Upon force. Jesus, alone,
founded His empire upon love, and to this
very day millions would die for Him. . . .
I think I understand something of human
nature; and I tell you, all these were men;
and I am a man: none else is like Him. . . .
Jesus Christ was more than a man.*

—Napoléon Bonaparte,
nineteenth-century French emperor

Jesus asked Peter the most important question of life. I would say that this question is the most significant matter in history and in your children's hearts:

> "But what about you?" [Jesus] asked. "Who do you say I am?"
> Simon Peter answered, "You are the Christ, the Son of the living God." (Matthew 16:15–16)

You may not be able to do much about how the world responds to the question of Jesus Christ's divinity, but you can influence your children's

QUESTION RECAP: Is Jesus really God? Why does it matter? Who do you say Jesus is?

1. The New Testament describes Jesus as the Son of God, who was born to a virgin. God the Father also claimed that Jesus was His Son.
2. The New Testament records Jesus as saying that He can forgive sins and that He has conquered death's sting. Jesus used special names for Himself that referred to deity. Jesus also claimed to have divine attributes, to be like the Father, and to perform the same work as His Father.
3. The resurrection is proof that Jesus is really God.

HOPE-FILLED ANSWER: The New Testament offers the testimonies of Jesus' disciples, of God the Father, and of Jesus Himself that Jesus is God. In every sense, Jesus' life was authentic, and the details of His life confirmed that He is God.

• •

response to Him. After reading this chapter, you'll know how to explain to your children in clear and compelling terms that Jesus is the Son of the living God. We'll examine two types of evidence that support the claim that Jesus is God. First, we'll look at what the New Testament says about Jesus. Second, we'll study the evidence of the empty tomb and Jesus' resurrection.

> *The divinity of Christ is the one question on which everything in the world depends.*
>
> —FYODOR DOSTOYEVSKY

More discussion about Jesus as Savior and Messiah comes in the next chapter and will include a close look at Old Testament prophecies. Jesus' role as a member of the Trinity or Godhead will be discussed in chapter 11.

Before we take a look at the biblical and historical facts relating to Jesus' status as God, let's define some terms. The first word is *deity*, which in our context means "a holy, supernatural, all-powerful, supreme, and sacred being." The term *deity incarnate* refers to the human form of Jesus or God's indwelling of a human body; it's also simply called the *Incarnation*, which I've capitalized in reference to Jesus' humanity joined with His deity. *Divinity* is another word for "from or of God," or deity.

The New Testament Describes the Deity of Jesus

The Bible is a Christian's main source of evidence for establishing that Jesus is God, and your children should become familiar with the key verses that point to Christ's deity. (If you first need to establish the New Testament's credibility, see chapter 14.) These verses often crop up around Christmas and Easter, but their theological significance can get lost in the holiday trappings. Let's take a fresh look at the key verses through a single lens focused only on establishing the deity of Jesus Christ.

What Did God the Father Say about Jesus?
First, let's look at the testimony of God the Father concerning Christ as recorded in the New Testament. In the account of Jesus' baptism, Matthew 3:16–17 says,

> As soon as Jesus was baptized, he went up out of the water. At that moment heaven was opened, and he saw the Spirit of God descending like a dove and lighting on him. And a voice from heaven said, "This is my Son, whom I love; with him I am well pleased."

This account contains many phrases of noteworthy theological significance, but right now our focus is on the term *Son*. God, as a voice from heaven, proudly called Jesus His Son and proclaimed His approval.

The second passage we'll examine, called the transfiguration, comes later in the same gospel account:

> Jesus took with him Peter, James and John the brother of James, and led them up a high mountain by themselves. There he was transfigured before them. His face shone like the sun, and his clothes became as white as the light. Just then there appeared before them Moses and Elijah, talking with Jesus.
>
> Peter said to Jesus, "Lord, it is good for us to be here. If you wish, I will put up three shelters—one for you, one for Moses and one for Elijah."
>
> While he was still speaking, a bright cloud enveloped them, and a voice from the cloud said, "This is my Son, whom I love; with him I am well pleased. Listen to him!" (Matthew 17:1–5)

We'll jump right over the miraculous apparitions of Moses and Elijah and again look at the word *Son*, as a voice from a cloud proclaimed. Not only did God again claim Jesus as His Son, but He also gave Jesus heavenly approval once more.

Many of you may be shaking your heads and saying, "But Alex, we're all children of God. I already teach my family that we're all sons or daughters of God." That's true in a sense according to Romans 8:14–17—but Jesus is the special, divine Son, as we'll discover in the next section.

The Virgin Birth

The New Testament records that Jesus' birth was miraculous, which is another sign of His deity. We should make it clear to children that Jesus was literally God's Son and that He did not have an earthly father. Joseph helped Mary raise Jesus and was, in that sense, his "dad." But the following passage shows us that the Holy Spirit (or God, as we will see in chapter 11 on the Trinity) was Jesus' *Father*:

This is how the birth of Jesus Christ came about: His mother Mary was pledged to be married to Joseph, but before they came together, she was found to be with child through the Holy Spirit. Because Joseph her husband was a righteous man and did not want to expose her to public disgrace, he had in mind to divorce her quietly.

But after he had considered this, an angel of the Lord appeared to him in a dream and said, "Joseph son of David, do not be afraid to take Mary home as your wife, because what is conceived in her is from the Holy Spirit. She will give birth to a son, and you are to give him the name Jesus, because he will save his people from their sins." (Matthew 1:18–21)

Each parent needs to decide how much biology to reveal about the phrase "found to be with child through the Holy Spirit," but at the end of the discussion, a child or teen should come away with the conviction that Jesus' birth was one of a kind and miraculous.

The virgin birth, added to God's claim that Jesus was His Son, builds a solid foundation for the case that Jesus was deity.

Deity Incarnate

Some people claim that the human Jesus wasn't God. Others claim that Jesus was God, but He wasn't human. It's important to explain that God took on a human body and why. Jesus didn't come to hang out with humans or to rule them in the way the Greco-Roman gods like Zeus did. The Incarnation was necessary for salvation, and in chapter 8 we'll explore why Jesus, the Son of God, had to die on the cross. But for now, let's look at a New Testament passage that points to a man—Jesus—who was also God: "In the beginning was the Word, and the Word was with God, and the Word was God. He was with God in the beginning" (John 1:1–2).

The writer of the gospel of John is traditionally thought to be John the apostle. For our purposes in this chapter, note that John used the term *Word*, which is a theologically charged term and important for establishing Christ's divinity. *Word* is another name for Jesus, and John 1:1 says "the Word was God." (Pack that away for our talk on the Trinity in chapter 11.)

We've studied the passages in which God the Father called Jesus "my Son" and examined the circumstances surrounding Jesus' miraculous birth, and now we can add to our biblical evidence for Jesus' deity the testimony of an apostle, who wrote that Jesus was God.

Jesus Was Fully God and Fully Human

We also need to establish that Jesus was both 100 percent God *and* 100 percent human, which is important for our upcoming discussions in chapters 7 and 8, "Did Jesus Ever Sin?" and "Why Did Jesus Have to Die on the Cross?" First John 4:2 says, "This is how you can recognize the Spirit of God: Every spirit that acknowledges that Jesus Christ has come in the flesh is from God." And Colossians 2:9 provides additional support: "For in Christ all the fullness of the Deity lives in bodily form." (More on this topic appears in chapter 7 in the section "What Can Your Children Learn from a Sinless Man?")

Who Did Jesus Say He Was?

The words of Jesus Himself are a compelling line of evidence that also points to Jesus' status as God. Jesus presented Himself not as a mere *representative* of God (though He was that), but He claimed to *be* God. The claims of Jesus establish that He had divine attributes and was equal to God the Father. These statements can be grouped into five categories, and they add up to more than a powerful case for Jesus' deity. They point to an unavoidable conclusion: Jesus is God.

1. Jesus claimed He can judge and forgive sins and grant eternal life.
    - Jesus claimed that He had authority to forgive sins (Mark 2:10).
    - Jesus told people to repent or perish (Luke 13:3).

- Jesus warned that those who reject Him will die in their sins (John 8:23–30). Jewish leaders knew that being able to forgive sins and judge people for their sins were divine attributes.
- Jesus said that those who keep His word will never see death (John 8:51).

2. Jesus claimed the right to use special names for God.
   - Jesus said that He was "Lord . . . of the Sabbath" (Mark 2:28). The Sabbath was created by God, and so being Lord of the Sabbath meant that Jesus was equal with the Creator or God.
   - Jesus called himself "I AM" (John 8:58). This was the name God used of Himself in Exodus 3:14.
   - More than eighty times in the Gospels, Jesus called Himself the "Son of Man." This name is from Daniel 7:13–14, a title reserved only for the One who approaches the Ancient of Days and is given great authority to rule over the earth.
   - Jesus claimed to be Israel's promised Messiah (John 4:25–26).

3. Jesus claimed He had the authority to perform the functions of God.
   - Jesus said He was sending prophets to Israel (Matthew 23:33–34). God is the only One who has the authority to designate and send prophets.
   - Jesus said that He can truly set people free from sin (John 8:34–36).
   - Jesus said that He can give people life (John 5:21).
   - Jesus said that He will raise up believers "at the last day" (John 6:38–40).

4. Jesus claimed to be like His Father.
   - Jesus claimed to be of the same nature as the Father (John 10:30).

- Jesus said that He was the only way to God (John 14:6), that He came from God (8:42), and that "anyone who has seen me has seen the Father" (14:9).

5. Jesus claimed to have divine attributes.
   - Jesus referred to Himself as being eternal (John 8:53–58).
   - Jesus claimed to know the reason for His birth (John 18:36–37). This shows omniscience.
   - Jesus had all authority on heaven and earth, which shows omnipotence (Matthew 28:18).

Think about the specific details in this list. Did Jesus make these claims because He had an incredibly inflated sense of His origin, identity,

---

Resurrection Rolls

These treats are for Easter, but they can be made any time of year. Gather your family in the kitchen and teach them about Jesus' burial and resurrection with this tasty dessert. Each ingredient symbolizes something that was used during Christ's burial. You may think these are just for younger kids, but teens love them too.

Ingredients

- 8 large marshmallows
- Melted butter or stick margarine (less than 1/2 stick)
- A mixture of cinnamon and sugar (1/4 cup sugar with 1 tablespoon powdered cinnamon spice)
- 1 can of refrigerated crescent rolls (makes 8)

Directions

1. First open the can of crescent rolls and separate into triangles. The rolls represent the linen used for covering the dead.
2. Roll one marshmallow into the melted butter. Each marshmallow represents Jesus' body. In New Testament times,

and abilities? No. When you couple such facts with the realities that Jesus did miracles only God could do, the conclusion is clear: Jesus must really be God.

The Resurrection—Further Proof That Jesus Is God

Jesus performed many miracles while He walked on earth. But so did the apostles and some Old Testament prophets. The miracle of the resurrection sets Jesus apart from all other miracle workers. (For more on this topic, see "Why Believe in the Resurrection Miracle?" in chapter 15.) If Jesus isn't God and if He didn't rise from the grave, then there's no point

> oils were used to anoint the body. The melted butter represents the oil.
>
> 3. Then roll the marshmallow in the cinnamon-sugar mixture. The cinnamon-sugar mixture represents the spices used to prepare the body for burial.
> 4. Place the marshmallow in the center of one crescent triangle.
> 5. Fold the crescent around the marshmallow and pinch the edges tightly together, leaving no openings.
> 6. Place the crescent-wrapped marshmallows on a lightly greased cookie sheet.
> 7. Place the cookie sheet in the oven (which represents the tomb) and bake according to the package directions for the crescent rolls. Close the "tomb" tightly and wait . . .
> 8. When it's time, open the "tomb" and check to make sure the marshmallows have disappeared! The marshmallows melt while baking, leaving only the puffed crescent rolls. This represents how Christ rose from the dead. All that remained in the tomb were the linen burial wrappings.

to Christianity. As the apostle Paul summarized it, "If Christ has not been raised, our preaching is useless and so is your faith . . . you are still in your sins" (1 Corinthians 15:14, 17).

The Details Make the Difference

When a 1933 US $20 gold coin sold for $7.5 million dollars in 2002, it instantly set a record as the highest price ever paid for a coin. The coveted double-eagle gold piece is a type of coin shrouded in mystery, due to the fact that the US government supposedly melted down all the 445,000 coins that were minted. Amazingly, the $7.5 million-dollar double-eagle coin narrowly escaped destruction in 2001. It had been stored in a vault in New York City's World Trade Center and was transferred to another location just two months before the tragic attacks of 9/11. It had been estimated that as few as twenty ever made it into public hands, and fans of collectible money debate the accuracy of that number.

Not surprisingly, coins this valuable have been counterfeited by several enterprising minters over the past eighty years. More than a few excited (but likely inexperienced) coin collectors over the years have thought that they had an authentic double eagle. Trained experts had the skills to tell the true double eagles from the false ones.[1]

But even more important than being able to recognize an imitation coin is the ability to spot a counterfeit *God*. Your child's eternal soul is safe only in the care of the authentic Lord and Savior—and the evidence affirms that this is who Jesus is.

Did Jesus Ever Sin?

God had only one Son without sin,
but not one without suffering.

—James Wells, *Bible Images:*
A Book for the Young

One day a fourth-grade Sunday school teacher asked the class, "Do you know someone who is perfect?"

The kids in the class sat silently. The teacher, hoping someone would answer "Jesus," asked again, "Are you perfect, or do you know someone who is?"

One student slowly raised his hand. His hair was wild, he had punch stains around his mouth, and his Sunday clothes were already disheveled fifteen minutes into class time. He was all boy, a rough-and-tumble kid.

The teacher raised an eyebrow. "Trevor, do you think you're perfect?" she asked.

"Oh no," Trevor replied, "but from how my mom goes on, I think my older sister is."

Was Jesus Sinless?

Most of us have sinned in one way or another each day before breakfast. In light of the fact that we all sin, and sin a lot, it's amazing to think that Jesus never committed even the smallest of sins.

QUESTION RECAP: Did Jesus ever sin? Why is it important that Jesus was sinless?

1. Jesus' enemies couldn't find fault with Him. Scripture teaches that He was without sin.
2. The fact that Jesus was sinless means that God's wrath should not be turned toward Him. Jesus wasn't part of the sin problem that damaged all of creation. Jesus' sinlessness made Him the perfect candidate for the atonement.
3. Animal sacrifices were used for a time, but they're no longer needed now that Jesus has died on the cross to atone for our sins.
4. Jesus was fully human, but He wasn't a fallen human. He had both a human nature and a divine nature. Jesus demonstrated His sinless perfection by withstanding temptation.

HOPE-FILLED ANSWER: Jesus was and is sinless, and He is our example today. He understands our temptations because He is human, but He can also forgive us because He is God.

• •

What about the heart sins, the ones that stay inside and no one sees except God? For example, in the Sermon on the Mount, Jesus said that if you harbor anger in your heart against someone, then you have committed murder against that person (Matthew 5:21–22).

Did Jesus ever sin? Did He envy? Did He disrespect His parents? Did He hate Judas Iscariot for betraying Him? Did He covet His neighbor's ox, house, or wife? No, no, no, no, and triple no.

How do we know this? Our primary source for the answer is the New Testament. The Bible tells us that indeed Jesus lived a perfect life—totally without sin:

Since we have a great high priest who has gone through the heavens, Jesus the Son of God, let us hold firmly to the faith we profess. For we do not have a high priest who is unable to sympathize with our weaknesses, but we have one who has been tempted in every way, just as we are—yet was without sin. (Hebrews 4:14–15)

Two of Jesus' Disciples Wrote That He Did Not Sin

Eyewitnesses confirm that Jesus did not sin. The apostle Peter spoke of Jesus' sinless life when he wrote, "He committed no sin, / and no deceit was found in his mouth" (1 Peter 2:22). The apostle John wrote, "He appeared so that he might take away our sins. And in him is no sin" (1 John 3:5). Keep in mind that these two men were Jesus' disciples and spent at least three years with Him, day in and day out. They traveled with Him, ate with Him, and prayed with Him. Peter and John knew Jesus well and still vouched for His sinless life.

Witnesses at the Crucifixion Said That Jesus Did Not Sin

Even those who weren't followers of Jesus admitted that Jesus did no wrong. In the gospel of Luke we find the two thieves who were crucified alongside Jesus. Both mocked Him at first, but one had a change of heart right before his own death:

One of the criminals who hung there hurled insults at him: "Aren't you the Messiah? Save yourself and us!"

But the other criminal rebuked him. "Don't you fear God," he said, "since you are under the same sentence? We are punished justly, for we are getting what our deeds deserve. But this man has done nothing wrong." (Luke 23:39–41)

After the crucifixion, when darkness had fallen over the land and Jesus had drawn His last breath, we hear the words of one of the Roman centurions who had stood guard at the cross: "Surely this was a righteous man" (Luke 23:47). The testimony of this Roman soldier lends credence to Christ's righteousness.

Jesus' Enemies Couldn't Find Fault with Him

Even those who opposed Jesus were unable to successfully find any fault in Him, despite the numerous times they tried to entrap Him. Jesus asked a group of people: "Can any of you prove me guilty of sin? If I am telling the truth, why don't you believe me?" (John 8:46).

Their silence was deafening. No one in the crowd that day could pin anything on Jesus. It's interesting to note that the word Jesus used in the original language for "sin" refers to sin in general rather than any specific sin. In other words, this question, which received no answer from His critics, was referring to Jesus' sinlessness.

The clear teaching of Scripture is that Jesus never sinned. In fact, those who wanted to hand Jesus over to Pontius Pilate, the Roman governor, to be crucified had to find people who were willing to lie under oath. But when Pilate interrogated Jesus, he could find no evidence of any crime Jesus had committed. Finally Pilate said to the Jews, "I find no basis for a charge against him" (John 18:38).

Jesus Was Sinless, So What's the Big Deal?

Now that we've established the answer to "Did Jesus ever sin?" the next question an intelligent kid will ask is, "Why is it important that Jesus was sinless?" The answer is that despite the way our culture tends to dismiss sin, God sees sin as a serious matter that warrants His wrath and judgment. The Scottish pastor and teacher Oswald Chambers is reported to have written, "Sin is not weakness, it is not a disease; it is red-handed rebellion against God and the magnitude of that rebellion is expressed by Calvary's cross."

God must do something about this widespread rebellion called sin. His righteous and holy nature demands judgment. This is often called "the wrath of God." The word *wrath* isn't used much these days. Years ago there was a Star Trek movie titled *The Wrath of Kahn*. And sports-writers may colorfully describe losing teams as having felt "the wrath" of some stronger opponent. But in a biblical sense, *wrath* describes the appropriate divine repercussions that come about because of the evil we humans do. God's wrath is fearful, yet deserved; thorough, yet appropriately measured; severe, yet absolutely just. Such contrasts represent the realities of God's wrath.

Holy wrath isn't an angry, uncontrolled tantrum from heaven. Biblical references to wrath aren't descriptions of an arbitrary rage into which God lapses. Humanitarian worker Linda Falter, responding to questions about God's justice in light of human suffering, writes,

> God's anger is not like ours. It is infused with holy purpose. . . . Is God angry over sin? Yes. Why shouldn't he be? But his holy rage is under the perfect control of limitless love. He suspends final judgment for a time, until every good purpose is fulfilled.[1]

God's wrath against sin is necessary and appropriate, because sin is an affront to His nature and even to creation. God is holy, just, sovereign, and loving. The effects of sin stand in opposition to all of these attributes. Further, sin has damaged all of God's creation: angels, humans, and nature. Sin brings death; yet God is life.

Try to imagine the love, power, and justice necessary for God to cast His wrath on Jesus so that we might be saved. Humans are accountable for the choices we've made; yet God lovingly diverted His wrath away from us and onto . . . *Himself*. God the Son took on a human body capable of feeling the pain of divine wrath. And as sin bearer for all humanity, Jesus didn't go to the cross with shoulder pads and a helmet on. Completely satisfying the requirements of God's holy law—and yet vividly displaying perfect compassion—Jesus suffered in our place. He felt all the wrath that we deserved for all our sins.

Think about this: Jesus experienced the pains of hell that you would feel if you died without Him. Absolute love led Him to do that for you,

for me, for everyone. The fact that Jesus is sinless made Him an acceptable sacrifice for the sins of the world. Before we discuss "Why Did Jesus
Have to Die on the Cross?" in the next chapter, we need to first establish
why a sin-free sacrifice was needed.

"Without Blemish"

As we look at the Old Testament, we see that God established animal sacrifices to deal with sin and His consequent wrath. There were numerous
regulations on how sacrifices were to be presented and how the priests,
who were offering the sacrifices on behalf of the people who had sinned,
were to handle them. In every instance, God required that the animal
being offered be "without blemish" or spotless or without defect. This
innocent animal had to represent the very best that a person had to offer
God. And the sacrifice had to cost the sinner something. Let's look at
Leviticus 4 as just one example:

> Now the LORD spoke to Moses, saying, . . . "If anyone of the com-
> mon people sins unintentionally by doing something against any of
> the commandments of the LORD in anything which ought not to be
> done, and is guilty, or if his sin which he has committed comes to
> his knowledge, then he shall bring as his offering a kid of the goats, a
> female *without blemish*, for his sin which he has committed. . . . And
> the priest shall burn it on the altar for a sweet aroma to the LORD.
> So the priest shall make atonement for him, and it shall be forgiven
> him." (Verses 1, 27–28, 31, NKJV)

Note the words "without blemish" because this aspect of the Old
Testament law becomes very important in chapter 8, "Why Did Jesus
Have to Die on the Cross?"

A Life for a Life

It wasn't about blood so much as the offering of a life. In Old Testament
times, blood represented life, as Leviticus 17:11 states: "The life of a crea-

ture is in the blood, and I have given it to you to make atonement for yourselves on the altar; it is the blood that makes atonement for one's life."

Sin is so great an issue to God that death was required of Adam and Eve when they first sinned. (Reread the section "Moral Evil—the Answer Begins in Genesis" in chapter 1 if you need a review.) And God's allowing for an animal to be sacrificed as a substitute wasn't "mean"; it was an act of grace.

If the concept of sacrificing an animal still seems primitive to you, remember that before electronic refrigeration, seeing an animal die or seeing a recently killed animal wasn't uncommon. People in earlier cultures (as well as those living today in developing countries or in rural communities) understood the cycle of life in a survival sense. For a person to eat and live, often an animal had to die. In North America, technology has distanced us from that life-death connection, because our chicken meat comes wrapped in plastic or cooked in a can. We can buy our beef already ground and shaped into round patties or dried as jerky. We enjoy the life-giving qualities of our groceries, but we don't fully appreciate the fact that something had to die for us to survive.

In the Old Testament, animal sacrifice was meant to make amends or atone for the sin of the one on whose behalf it was offered. At set times during the year—on the Day of Atonement is one example—the high priest made a sacrifice for all the people. So instead of the sinning person being put to death for sin, an animal was substituted on his or her behalf. The shedding of the blood of an innocent animal was meant to satisfy the wrath of God for that year. For "without the shedding of blood there is no forgiveness" (Hebrews 9:22).

The Problem with Animal Sacrifices

The problem with these animal sacrifices to atone for human sins is elaborated in the book of Hebrews:

> For the law, having a shadow of the good things to come, and not
> the very image of the things, can never with these same sacrifices,

which they offer continually year by year, make those who approach
perfect. For then would they not have ceased to be offered? For the
worshipers, once purified, would have had no more consciousness of
sins. But in those sacrifices there is a reminder of sins every year. For
it is not possible that the blood of bulls and goats could take away
sins. (10:1–4, NKJV)

The animal sacrifices prescribed in the Old Testament were not
enough to purge the conscience of the sinner. These sacrifices served
only as a temporary covering for the offenses of the sinner for that year.

But Jesus' death on the cross became the ultimate and final sacrifice
for sin: "So Christ was sacrificed once to take away the sins of many

---

Do Christians Value Animals?

Absolutely, Christians should value animals and all of God's created work. When I'm caring for my pet, a blind Doberman named
Samson who needs special eyedrops every day, Proverbs 12:10
often comes to mind: "A righteous man cares for the needs of his
animal." Below is a little chart that shows some of the core differences between humans and animals.

Humans	Animals
Reflect God's image	Reflect God's creativity
Were created to reason and think abstractly	Operate on instinct to survive
Can make ethical choices	Not capable of ethical decisions
Are morally accountable	Are not morally accountable
Have three parts: physical (sarx), mental (psyche), and spiritual (pneuma)	Have only two parts: physical (sarx) and mental (psyche)
Can be redeemed	Will one day be restored with the rest of the natural world

people; and he will appear a second time, not to bear sin, but to bring salvation to those who are waiting for him" (Hebrews 9:28).

So in order for Jesus to be that ultimate sacrifice, He had to be perfect, without blemish or defect, spotless.

What Children Need to Grasp

November 9, 2009, marked the twentieth anniversary of the fall of the Berlin Wall. I remember back in 1989 when news reports around the world carried the announcement that the Berlin Wall would be destroyed. I was entering graduate school at the time, and the classrooms were abuzz with the news that for the first time in twenty-eight years, citizens would be free to travel from East Germany to West Germany. On November 10, 1989, bulldozers began to tear down the wall that for three decades had symbolized conflict, communism, and state control. (You can show your kids news clips on YouTube of the wall coming down.)

An even greater "wall removal" was accomplished more than two thousand years ago on the cross! Ephesians 2:14 proclaims the great news that "[Jesus] Himself is our peace, who has made both [Jew and Gentile] one, and has broken down the middle wall of separation" (NKJV). In Jesus, Jew and Gentile were brought together as one, and God and humanity were reconciled.

What Can Your Children Learn
from a Sinless Man?

It's important to recognize that the Bible doesn't say that Jesus was able to live without sin because of His deity. In fact, it says the opposite. Jesus was "tempted in every way, just as we are—yet was without sin" (Hebrews 4:15). You see, God can't be tempted by evil, but the man Jesus Christ was. Bear with me here; I know this is deep!

In the single person of Jesus dwelt *two* natures—a divine nature and a human nature. When Jesus came to earth, this wasn't made possible by the *subtraction* of His divinity, though He voluntarily limited it (Philippians 2:6–8). By the *addition* of humanity, the second person of the Godhead became a man. (More on Jesus as the second person of the Trinity in chapter 11.) God took on a human body. Jesus was fully human, but He was not a *fallen* human. Therefore, in relation to His divine nature, sin was no temptation at all. But in relation to His humanity, Jesus felt hunger, pain, loneliness, fear, and, yes, temptation. This is why the Incarnation—the God-man, Jesus—is so unique. There is nothing else like it in any other belief system.

The following illustration isn't perfect, but it'll give your kids something concrete to ponder. A dishonest person walks up to an off-duty law-enforcement officer and says, "I have a truckload of stolen merchandise out back. There are brand-new computers, stereos, game consoles, and plasma-screen TVs. I'll sell you anything in this truck for only twenty dollars per item! Interested?"

> *Professing that Jesus was sinless can be viewed as a way of portraying his unconditional openness to the Spirit and his loving and complete dedication to the work of God.*
> —WILLIAM E. REISER, *Jesus in Solidarity with His People*

Now, the off-duty cop appreciates a good deal as much as any of us would. As a consumer he might be tempted by the thought of buying expensive electronics at only twenty dollars apiece. But as an officer sworn to uphold the law, he knows that his only response to a thief fencing stolen goods is to whip out the handcuffs! A servant of the people, whose career has been built upon integrity and sacrifice, would never give in to this kind of temptation. In the face of temptation, he would stand firm. As a human, Jesus faced temptation, but He never gave in to it.

When we read about Jesus' temptations in the wilderness, it should inspire us. Too often we read the account and think, *Oh, that was Jesus.* Instead we should realize that He was setting an example for us, and it was being recorded for our benefit so that we could draw strength from it. There are many lessons to be learned in these passages, not only about Jesus, but also about ourselves. We not only see that Jesus didn't sin when He was tempted, but we also see how He overcame temptation. We, too, can overcome temptation and resist sin if we follow His example.

Undoubtedly, while Jesus was in the desert, He was very weak emotionally and physically from a period of extended fasting. It is often during our moments of weakness that we are most vulnerable to temptation. First Peter 5:8–9 tells us there are also times when the Adversary—the devil—will come at us, and his tactics with Jesus were no different.

Let's examine the famous temptation passage together:

> Jesus was led up by the Spirit into the wilderness to be tempted by
> the devil. And after He had fasted forty days and forty nights, He
> then became hungry. And the tempter came and said to Him, "If
> You are the Son of God, command that these stones become bread."
> (Matthew 4:1–3, NASB)

Despite His hunger, Jesus wasn't about to be goaded by the devil into abandoning reliance on the Father. Jesus always relied on God to provide for His needs. The Bible says that "He answered and said, 'It is written, "Man shall not live on bread alone, but on every word that proceeds out of the mouth of God"'" (verse 4, NASB).

Next, the devil tried to get Jesus to do something foolish and needlessly put Himself in a dangerous position:

> Then the devil took Him into the holy city and had Him stand on
> the pinnacle of the temple, and said to Him, "If You are the Son
> of God, throw Yourself down; for it is written, 'He will command
> His angels concerning You'; and 'On their hands they will bear
> You up, so that You will not strike Your foot against a stone.'"
> (Verses 5–6, NASB)

Notice how the devil was quoting Scripture out of context to Jesus! In all these temptations, the devil twisted Scripture, whereas Jesus correctly handled "the word of truth" (2 Timothy 2:15).

After spending forty days and nights fasting and communing with God, Jesus probably wished the angels would carry Him aloft. However, He knew better than to put Himself in a dangerous and foolish position—and certainly not at the request of God's arch-nemesis.

In our lives, we too can be tempted to take foolish risks in the hope that God will bail us out. Sometimes we deliberately ignore His Word, hoping that His grace and mercy will keep us from experiencing the consequences of our disobedience. Notice how Jesus handled the situation, and draw wisdom from His response: "Jesus said to [the devil], 'On the other hand, it is written, "You shall not put the LORD your God to the test"'" (Matthew 4:7, NASB).

The next temptation seems ludicrous to most Christians:

> Again, the devil took [Jesus] to a very high mountain and showed Him all the kingdoms of the world and their glory; and he said to Him, "All these things I will give You, if You fall down and worship me." (Verses 8–9, NASB)

Originally, Adam and Eve were given dominion over the earth (Genesis 1:28), but they disobeyed God's command, were cast out of the garden of Eden, and lost whatever authority they once enjoyed (Genesis 3). That there are evil principalities and powers at work in the world is made clear in Ephesians 6:12:

> Our struggle is not against flesh and blood, but against the rulers, against the authorities, against the powers of this dark world and against the spiritual forces of evil in the heavenly realms.

These "authorities" and "powers" and "spiritual forces of evil in the heavenly realms" were no doubt in full strength when the devil offered

Jesus "all the kingdoms of the world." The offer may or may not have been a bluff, but Jesus knew that the Word of God forbade Him from even considering worshipping the devil. Here is Jesus' response: "Be gone, Satan! For it is written, 'You shall worship the Lord your God and him only shall you serve'" (Matthew 4:10, ESV).

Jesus Christ: Our Example

So, what is the point of sharing these events in answer to the question "Did Jesus ever sin?" Simply to illustrate that we may overlook the power that comes from emulating Christ's example. In fact, some people use tradition or catchphrases to excuse their sin. They lament, "We're just sinners saved by grace," as though they have no defense against sin. However, Christians can look at Jesus' example, as one weapon against sin, and be encouraged by it:

> Let us fix our eyes on Jesus, the author and perfecter of our faith,
> who for the joy set before him endured the cross, scorning its shame,
> and sat down at the right hand of the throne of God. Consider him
> who endured such opposition from sinful men, so that you will not
> grow weary and lose heart.
>
> In your struggle against sin, you have not yet resisted to the point
> of shedding your blood. (Hebrews 12:2–4)

Believers are called to follow Jesus' example enabled by the power of the Holy Spirit. The true battle is to stand for God through all of life's experiences—whether in the midst of challenges or in times of prosperity—and to have our lives echo Jesus' response: "It is written"! (And we need to know what is written too.)

While we are called to model holiness, we also need to model humility. Only Jesus was sinless; we are not. Children (and their parents) will be comforted to know that when we do sin, however, God's free and full forgiveness is ours when we sincerely repent: "If we confess our sins, he is faithful and just and will forgive us our sins and purify us from all unrighteousness" (1 John 1:9). While Jesus will always remain the only person to live a lifetime without sinning, grown-ups should set an example for children in that we should strive to imitate Jesus Christ.

This task can seem overwhelming; however, we are not alone. The Holy Spirit will help us by bringing Scripture to our minds (John 14:26) and by keeping us holy (1 Corinthians 6:11).

What good is having someone who can walk on water if you don't follow in his footsteps?

—AUTHOR UNKNOWN

Why Did Jesus Have to Die on the Cross?

*And now brothers, I will ask you a terrible
question, and God knows I ask it also of myself.
Is the truth beyond all truths, beyond the stars,
just this: that to live without him is the real
death, that to die with him the only life?*

—Frederick Buechner, *The Magnificent Defeat*

One of our family's Christmas traditions is displaying a ceramic manger scene that has been in our family for generations. As a child, my niece Allie was always eager to come and help arrange the crèche, carefully studying the placement of every angel and shepherd. She painstakingly set out the pieces, frequently stepping back to evaluate her work.

Over the years this tradition has prompted Allie to ask many questions. "Did the baby Jesus get cold in the manger?" "Did Mary and Joseph have a blanket to cover him, or were the swaddling clothes warm enough?" "Do they sell swaddling clothes at the mall?" One Christmas my niece asked her most profound question yet: "Uncle Alex, why did Jesus come?"

"That's a great question," I said. "A *really* great question." Before I could fully answer, Allie asked another question that paved the way for an answer to the previous one: "Why did Jesus have to die on the cross?"

Key Concepts

QUESTION RECAP: Why did Jesus have to die on the cross? Why did He come at all?

1. Scripture tells us that sin entered the world through Adam and Eve. Sin came with the consequence of spiritual death. The penalty for sin needed to be paid.
2. Jesus was the only person who could pay the penalty for sin, because He was sinless and holy. Jesus was not only qualified to pay the debt, but He was also willing to do it.
3. By understanding the events of Passover, children can better understand why Jesus was the perfect sacrificial Lamb.

HOPE-FILLED ANSWER: Jesus had to die on the cross to pay the penalty for sin that every human owes. Jesus came to save the world from sin, and His death resulted in eternal life for those who believe.

● ●

Jesus: The Man Born to Die

In chapter 1 we looked at "Why Does God Allow Evil?" and saw that sin invoked a death penalty that all of humanity had to pay. Really "bad" people as well as those seemingly "good" folks have all sinned and deserve death. That includes me, the pastor of your church, you, your child, and everyone on Facebook. It includes everyone from the past, present, and future.

Hebrews 9:27 explains the ultimate judgment event that will come about, in which we will all appear before God. Sin will one day be finally reined in by a reckoning: "It is appointed unto men once to die, and after this the judgment" (KJV).

Holiday Theology

The complex implications of the God-man concept can be a tough one for kids to understand. They need to be exposed to it several times before it can sink in. Holidays are a great time to focus on family traditions and to also key in on biblical texts. Like my niece Allie, most kids are curious about Jesus during holiday seasons. Take advantage of Easter and Christmas celebrations to emphasize the dual nature of Jesus. Not only should you emphasize the miraculous virgin birth at Christmas, but you should also point out that Jesus was born to a woman and belongs to the human race. At Easter, focus on the joy of the resurrection while noting Jesus' human frailty. His human body literally died on the cross on Friday, which makes His Sunday resurrection so meaningful. (Visit Focus on the Family's websites *ClubhouseJr.com*, *ClubhouseMagazine .com*, and *ThrivingFamily.com* for great spiritual holiday material for Christian families.)

Take note of the two phrases, "once to die" and "after this the judgment." Here we see allusions to physical death and to the possibility of irrevocable spiritual death. How sad it would be if verse 27 were the end of the story. Had Jesus not died on the cross, *this* would be the chronology of existence for every human:

Sin → Death → Judgment → Damnation

But because of God's infinite love, our story doesn't end this way, and Hebrews 9 doesn't end with verse 27! Verse 28 reads, "So Christ was offered once to bear the sins of many. To those who eagerly wait for Him He will appear a second time, apart from sin, for salvation" (NKJV).

Jesus was born to die. God sent His Son to pay the ultimate price for the world's sins: for Adam's, for Eve's, for mine, for yours.

The Perfect Death

Preachers, songwriters, commentators, and poets have all said much about Christ's "perfect" sacrifice. And it was exactly that. Because Jesus was fully God and yet fully human—deity incarnate—He was not only *qualified* to be humanity's sin bearer; He was also *willing*. Jesus could have been *able* but *unwilling*. Or He might have been *willing* but *unable*. Fortunately, this one person in the entire universe who could save humanity was willing to do it.

> We know life and death only through Jesus Christ. Apart from Jesus Christ, we do not know what is our life, nor our death, nor God, nor ourselves.
>
> —BLAISE PASCAL, *Thoughts*

Think about all that was accomplished in Jesus' suffering on the cross, His death, and His resurrection. The appropriate measure of punishment for all of humankind's sin was poured out on Jesus. Some catechisms, or statements of faith, rightly speak of God's "just displeasure" or "wrath." It must have been agonizing for the heavenly Father to bring the justice of heaven down on Jesus, and it was agony for Christ to endure it. The word *perfect* becomes the only apt description of Christ's sacrifice for us: The justice of God

Family Statement of Faith

Throughout history, Christians have developed catechisms or statements of faith. I like them, but most people find them stuffy and unclear. Why not write your own family statement of faith? (You can find examples on the Internet. Just search for the term "statement of faith.") You can add to it with every chapter in this book. That way you can put the answers to these questions in easy-to-understand language for your family. You can occasionally recite parts of it with the blessing before dinner.

was satisfied, the holiness of God was maintained, the laws of God were observed, and the grace of God was manifested. Volumes could be written on any of these points.

Romans 3:25–26 explains it succinctly:

> God presented [Christ] as a sacrifice of atonement, through faith in his blood. He did this to demonstrate his justice, because in his forbearance he had left the sins committed beforehand unpunished—he did it to demonstrate his justice at the present time, so as to be just and the one who justifies those who have faith in Jesus.

Jesus, Our Passover Lamb

Christian kids can better understand the need for Jesus' death on the cross if they understand what the Jewish Passover celebration is all about. God instituted the observance of Passover to commemorate a dramatic historic event that is also a foreshadowing of Jesus Christ. The Passover story is also an excellent way to demonstrate to children in a way that's more illustrative than conceptual why Jesus needed to die on the cross.

Passover is best understood when some background information is provided. Joseph (also symbolic of Jesus) was sold by his brothers into slavery. After numerous events took place, Joseph wound up bringing his entire family to Egypt. While there, the Israelites grew exponentially in number, and the Egyptians—somewhat afraid of them—made them slaves. At a certain point, God heard the cries of His people and sent Moses to deliver them from bondage.

A familiar series of events followed: Moses and Aaron became the "spokespersons" to Pharaoh on behalf of the Jewish people. Pharaoh refused to allow God's people to leave Egypt and worship Him in the desert. With increasingly severe repercussions, God sent numerous plagues to get Pharaoh's attention. God turned the Nile River to blood; sent frogs, gnats, flies, and locusts; and afflicted the livestock with a terrible disease.

He afflicted the Egyptians with boils (physical sores), sent hail raining down on them, and plunged the land into darkness.

If Pharaoh refused to free the Israelites following these plagues, God would send a final plague that would kill the firstborn son of every household in Egypt. The Lord gave Moses and Aaron specific instructions about what the Jews should do to prepare for this most severe of all the plagues. Every Israelite household was to kill a perfect lamb and wipe some of the blood of this lamb on the posts of their front door. If the blood was applied as God instructed, the angel of death would "pass over" that house. God's instructions for Passover were very clear:

> The animals you choose must be year-old males without defect,
> and you may take them from the sheep or the goats. Take care of
> them until the fourteenth day of the month, when all the people
> of the community of Israel must slaughter them at twilight. Then
> they are to take some of the blood and put it on the sides and tops
> of the doorframes of the houses where they eat the lambs. (Exodus
> 12:5–7)

To Pharaoh and the Egyptians, God issued a final warning:

> I will pass through Egypt and strike down every firstborn—both men
> and animals—and I will bring judgment on all the gods of Egypt. I
> am the LORD. (Verse 12)

To Moses and the Israelites, God issued comforting promises:

> The blood will be a sign for you on the houses where you are; and
> when I see the blood, I will pass over you. No destructive plague will
> touch you when I strike Egypt. (Verses 13)

This story of the Israelites' exit from Egypt was so important to God that He instructed Israel to observe it for generations to come (verse 14).

The Passover was emblazoned on the minds of the Israelites, and every succeeding generation of Jewish people has learned of the miraculous deliverance of God. But I believe that God also preserved the memory of the original Passover because the event foreshadowed not only the crucifixion of Jesus Christ but also the deliverance from sin and death that God offers each of us in Christ.

You can help your children understand in a much deeper way the significance of what Jesus accomplished on their behalf by pointing out the similarities between the Passover and Jesus' death on the cross. Just like the Israelites, who were enslaved to the Egyptians, all of humanity is (apart from Jesus) in bondage to sin. Just as the Jewish people needed to put the blood of a perfect lamb on the doorposts of their homes, we are to put the blood of God's Lamb—Jesus Christ—upon our hearts.

Everyone who put the lamb's blood on the doorposts of their homes before the last plague struck would be protected. The angel of death would pass over them. Those who did not obey would, like the Egyptians, experience the death of every firstborn son in their families. This illustrates the need for us to share the gospel about the true Lamb of God with everyone: our children, our families, those we work with, anyone who will listen.

Your children may find it odd that God instructed the Israelites to put the blood of a spotless lamb on the doorposts of their homes. But consider the staggering consequences of disobedience: the death of every firstborn son. Likewise, without the blood of Jesus on the "doorpost" of our souls, every one of us would face the dire consequences of refusing God's offer of salvation: eternal separation from God. The "angel of death" will visit those whose hearts are not protected by the blood of Jesus, and they will experience spiritual death.

In the Passover and in Jesus' death on the cross, we see the seriousness of sin. Hebrews 9:22 says that "without the shedding of blood there is no forgiveness of sins" (ESV). Why would God allow His Son to be executed on the cross? Because there was no other way. It was either this solution or destroying the entire human race. In love, God did the hardest thing of all. Pondering this gives us a glimpse not only of the seriousness of sin but also of the seriousness of rejecting God's magnanimous offer.

Even prior to creation and the fall of humankind, God knew that Jesus would go to the cross. Revelation 13:8 speaks of "the Lamb slain from the foundation of the world" (KJV). Even before the Serpent tempted Adam and Eve, even before Adam and Eve disobeyed God, and even from you and I were born and embarked on life's sin-tainted journey, God's plan of salvation was as good as done. Satan's attack and Adam's rebellion did *not* take God by surprise. Jesus was en route to Calvary to rescue us even before we needed to be rescued. Yes, God really is that much in control. Jesus' death on the cross illustrates that God truly is the Lord of Life.

Isaac

A spectacular comparison between Jesus and Isaac is found in Genesis 22:1–14, the account of Abraham offering his son Isaac in obedience to God. I am always moved by the words of verses 13–14:

> Abraham looked up and there in a thicket he saw a ram caught by its horns. He went over and took the ram and sacrificed it as a burnt offering instead of his son. So Abraham called that place The LORD Will Provide. And to this day it is said, "On the mountain of the LORD it will be provided."

Abraham's offering of Isaac was a picture of God the Father offering His Son, Jesus. The place where Jesus was crucified is part of Mount Moriah. True to Genesis 22:14, on that same hill years after Abraham's time, another Lamb would have thorns around His "crown" (or "head"). On that mountain, God provided Jesus, "the Lamb of God" (John 1:29).

Why Is Jesus the Only Way to Heaven?

Know Jesus, know peace. No Jesus, no peace.

—Bumper sticker

Jesus made it clear that to be saved, we need to *know* Him personally (Matthew 7:21–23). But in order to have this relationship, we must first *know about* Him. We must understand that He truly was God come to earth. More than just a good man, He was the God-man. In John 8:24, Jesus declared, "If you do not believe that I am the one I claim to be [God in the flesh], you will indeed die in your sins."

Not long after completing seminary, Robert Pierce (now in his late fifties) found himself serving a small church. Robert had been in full-time ministry only a few weeks when he was asked to officiate at a funeral service.

A minister from another local church called, explaining that the grieving family had requested the two ministers perform the funeral together for the deceased. A conflict arose as the two men met to plan the service. The other minister asked Pastor Pierce to read a passage from a book that clearly taught all people go to heaven.

Pastor Pierce told the minister that he would gladly read from the Bible, or from a book that complemented what the Bible taught. But the mourners at the funeral would not hear him read something that contradicted the Bible.

QUESTION RECAP: Why is Jesus the only way to heaven? Why can't other religions be true too?

1. Today's society embraces *pluralism*, which allows that there is truth in all religions. Pluralism asserts that "it's all true." Tolerance is seen as the highest virtue. Pluralism stems from Eastern philosophies, but pluralism is not biblical.

2. Jesus Himself taught that "no one comes to the Father except through me" (John 14:6). Christians need not be embarrassed or defensive about Jesus' claim.

3. The New Testament teaches that Jesus is the only way to heaven. The Gospels and the Pauline Epistles espouse this view.

4. The fact that Jesus is the only way to heaven is not exclusive. Anyone of any race, age, religion, culture, or gender can repent and believe.

HOPE-FILLED ANSWER: There is a way to heaven! God desires that all should be saved, and He sent Jesus to die for all. The fact that Jesus is the only way to heaven is the good news. This news should spark celebration, not apologies.

• •

"The other minister seemed dumbfounded at first, and then slightly angry with me," Pastor Pierce told me. "When I told him I believed that Jesus is the only way to heaven, he said, 'Well, I surely thought we were past those days.' "

Jesus Says He's the Only Way

Over the past fifty years, tolerance has come to be viewed as the greatest virtue. For many, it has become the default position regarding religion and faith. Even many church members chafe at the idea that Jesus is the only way to heaven.

This is the main worldview your children have been exposed to through the media and public education.

The assumption today is that what you believe is not as important as how sincerely you believe it. Your children may grow up with the impression that sincerity of heart somehow validates one's beliefs and opinions. Couple that with the idea that all paths to God are equally true (pluralism), and you can see how our culture would believe that a loving God would never set before humanity an either-or, once-for-all ultimatum. Many people believe that God will forgive them or simply cut them a break because He is compassionate.

The exclusive claims of the Christian faith may sound narrow-minded, bigoted, or intolerant to your children's ears. A question asked not just by children but also by many adults is "Why is Jesus the only way to heaven?" It's a very legitimate question. The most obvious answer is that this is what Jesus taught. He said, "I am the way and the truth and the life. No one comes to the Father except through me" (John 14:6).

When discussing the exclusive claims of Christ, it's important to reframe the question so that God is glorified, as He should be. To begin to frame an honest, accurate answer, we first need to see the "trap" in the question. Like most of the things God's enemy—the devil—does, the question sounds more like an accusation than a search for truth.

> *One of the mistakes that human beings make is believing that there is one way to live. . . . There are many paths to what you call God.*
>
> —OPRAH WINFREY, talk-show host

This doesn't mean that well-meaning Christians or sincere seekers don't sometimes question how it is that Jesus is the only way to God. It's a great question if it comes from a sincere heart. However, many

Christians become defensive or ashamed when answering this question. And yet the fact that there is any way to heaven at all should be cause for dancing, not shame!

Followers of Jesus needn't be ashamed or embarrassed by the exclusive claims of Jesus. He is the Lord who rightly demands our allegiance. Our highest command is to love Him with all our heart, mind, soul, and strength (Mark 12:30). Jesus is the way to eternal life! That's why it's called the Good News and *not* the Embarrassing News.

When you're equipped with truth and package the response in love, you'll often see questions like these as open doors to share the true faith with your children and anyone else who brings up the subject. In fact, as you embrace the truth, you'll probably find yourself seeking ways to work the gospel into conversations, and you'll be emboldened and encouraged to share about the saving work of Jesus Christ!

And hopefully, your children will follow your example.

The Bible Tells Me So

Does the Bible teach that Jesus is the only way to heaven? The simple answer is yes. In the gospel of John, we find the context of Jesus' exclusive claim:

> [Jesus told His disciples,] "Let not your heart be troubled; you believe in God, believe also in Me. In My Father's house are many mansions; if it were not so, I would have told you. I go to prepare a place for you. And if I go and prepare a place for you, I will come again and receive you to Myself; that where I am, there you may be also. And where I go you know, and the way you know."
>
> Thomas said to Him, "Lord, we do not know where You are going, and how can we know the way?"
>
> Jesus said to him, "I am the way, the truth, and the life. No one comes to the Father except through Me." (John 14:1–6, NKJV)

Pay careful attention to Jesus' words. These were explosive statements then, and they still are! Jesus not only told His disciples that He was going to prepare a place for them in heaven, but that He was their only ticket for admission!

Jesus made similar statements elsewhere in Scripture, claiming that access to God the Father and eternal life are found in Him alone, e.g., Matthew 11:27. Not only did Jesus make these bold claims, but His followers also taught that He was the only way to heaven. After Jesus was raised from the dead and had ascended into heaven, the apostle Peter declared publicly that Jesus was the only way for people to be saved:

> Then Peter, filled with the Holy Spirit, said to [the Jewish leaders], "Rulers of the people and elders of Israel: If we this day are judged for a good deed done to a helpless man, by what means he has been made well, let it be known to you all, and to all the people of Israel, that by the name of Jesus Christ of Nazareth, whom you crucified, whom God raised from the dead, by Him this man stands here before you whole. This is the 'stone which was rejected by you builders, which has become the chief cornerstone.' Nor is there salvation in any other, for there is no other name under heaven given among men by which we must be saved." (Acts 4:8–12, NKJV)

The apostle Paul, who was once an enemy of Jesus and His followers, also affirmed the exclusive claims of Christ in a letter to Timothy, his son in the faith:

> There is one God, and there is one mediator between God and men, the man Christ Jesus, who gave himself as a ransom for all. (1 Timothy 2:5–6, ESV)

Paul stated that there was only one mediator between God and humans—Jesus Christ. A mediator is a middleman whose job is to reconcile two parties who are at odds with each other. Jesus' death on the cross made reconciliation possible between God and humankind.

An honest reader of the Bible has to admit that Scripture declares Jesus as the only way to heaven—even if they don't agree that the statement is true.

God Doesn't Own a Country Club

Rather than being an exclusive club, Christians are a family that extends an open invitation to everyone to join. That invitation is found in one of the most well-known verses in the Bible: "For God so loved the world that he gave his one and only Son, that *whoever* believes in him shall not perish but have eternal life" (John 3:16).

This verse is probably ingrained in the minds of the vast majority of Christians. And yet we often get perplexed when we're asked about the exclusivity of our faith. Our response should be to quote this verse and remind people that God wants *everyone* to be part of His family.

Jesus is such a complete Savior and the cross accomplished such a comprehensive salvation that there is no need for any other way to heaven. The Bible is a love story about a God who went to heroic lengths to save a planet full of rebellious peoples: "The Lord is not slow in keeping his promise, as some understand slowness. He is patient with you, *not wanting anyone to perish*, but everyone to come to repentance" (2 Peter 3:9). Out of His great love for humanity, God wants to save as many as possible!

> *Let us therefore yield ourselves and bow to the authority of the Holy Scriptures, which can neither err nor deceive.*
> —SAINT AUGUSTINE OF HIPPO

God doesn't own a fancy country club where only select people are welcome. On the contrary, He makes His appeal over and over for everyone to receive Jesus into their hearts and be saved. The Bible says that "God our Savior . . . desires all men to be saved and to come to the knowledge of the truth" (1 Timothy 2:3–4, NKJV). The Scriptures also remind us that "Christ's love compels us, because we are convinced that [Jesus] died for all" (2 Corinthians 5:14).

What does Scripture say? That Jesus "died for all." He gave His life for the rich, the poor, people of color, young people, the elderly, male, female—it doesn't matter. He laid down His life for *all*.

Paid in Full

A second way you can answer the question "Why is Jesus the only way to heaven?" is by responding, "Because Jesus paid the price in full. There doesn't need to be any other way!" To illustrate the point, you could then ask your children, "If you had a bill for fifty dollars, would you pay sixty dollars?" Their answer, of course, would be no; they would pay only the fifty dollars because that would pay the bill in full. Likewise, Scripture says, "[Jesus Christ] is the propitiation [*payment*] for our sins, and not for ours only but also for the whole world" (1 John 2:2, NKJV).

God has provided the perfect Savior for humankind through the person of Jesus Christ. He is the only way to heaven because there only needs to be one way. The key is to shine the light into the darkness so that anyone and everyone who wants to be a part of the kingdom has an opportunity to believe.

What about Those People Who Have Never Heard of Jesus?

This brings us to the inevitable question, "What about those people who have never heard about Jesus?" Perhaps you've heard this question phrased as it was recently posed to me by a student on a university campus: "Alex, do you mean God is going to send some people to hell simply because they haven't heard the name of Jesus? Would a person be lost because their only crime is that they were born on the wrong continent?"

Parents, some of this will probably be over the heads of your kids, but it's important to know the history on how the church has handled that question. Then we'll recap in an easy-to-understand way for you to tell your kids.

William Carey's Legacy

The English church of the eighteenth century didn't have much zeal for evangelism. Like . . . none. Maybe it was a feeling of resignation—that Christ's command to "make disciples of all nations" was impossible to fulfill (Matthew 28:19). Maybe it was spiritual complacency—"My family and I are saved; the souls of faceless masses on foreign continents are not my responsibility." For some, the absence of missionary zeal was due to less-than-biblical theological ideas called *hyperpredestination* or *double predestination*. People who held that view thought that God created some to be saved and some to be damned; it wasn't the church's place to interfere with His sovereign plans.

Going against the conventional wisdom of his day, young William Carey believed that it really was the church's responsibility to take the message of Jesus to all people. Carey—often called "the father of modern missions"—was convinced that the unevangelized peoples of the world needed the gospel and would be lost forever without it. Consequently, he insisted that it was the church's responsibility to deliver the message.

Dealing with this issue led Carey to write *An Enquiry into the Obligations of Christians to Use Means for the Conversion of the Heathens*.[1] The word *means* is a reference to going to great lengths, attempting to reach people with the gospel by any available methods. Published in 1792, Carey's work ignited a missionary revolution that continues to this day.

If a child is worried about those who have never heard of Jesus, the issue of evangelism cannot be ignored. The souls of tribespeople on remote continents should not be shoved to the back of your children's minds.

Carey, and countless faithful missionaries who would follow, acted on what we find in the Bible. Your kids should be able to understand William Carey's clear Christian worldview: *People are lost and need Jesus. Period. So get moving.*

Bad Answers

A biblically inaccurate answer to questions about those who have never heard will certainly cause your children to wonder if the Bible is true or not. Some theologians solve the dilemma by concluding that people aren't *really* lost and in need of salvation—*everyone* will go to heaven. But such a universalist belief (that all will go to heaven) begs the question, "Why, then, preach the gospel in the first place?"

Others conclude that it just must be God's will for some to be lost. But to believe that some people were created for the express purpose of being condemned, with no recourse or chance whatsoever to be saved, certainly seems counter to numerous biblical assurances of God's goodness and mercy.

God's General Revelation

God created humans with free will, and He offers them truth and light. While not everyone has heard of Jesus in an explicit way, God has revealed Himself in a general way to everyone, so that everyone is accountable to Him. Psalm 19 speaks poetically about this created world, which points to a Creator: "The heavens declare the glory of God; / the skies proclaim the work of his hands" (verse 1). It also speaks of God's perfect law (verses 7–11) and that voice within each of us (our conscience) that convicts us when we've violated it (verses 12–14).

The point? No one is innocent before God, because we have each violated moral standards that we really are aware of. God has shown Himself to *everyone* through creation and conscience: "There is no speech or language / where their voice is not heard" (verse 3).

Romans 2:14 points out that non-Jews (Gentiles) proved their own guilt when they did the things mandated by the Scriptures, even though they didn't have the law of God as the Jews did. In the first two chapters of Romans, the apostle Paul argued that all humans stand guilty before God. He pointed out that Jew and Gentile, whether or not they have God's written Word, strive to do the things God's law demands. And their conscience convicts them when they violate that law (1:22–32).

The sins listed in Romans 1 and 2 aren't confined to people living in unreached foreign lands but are celebrated and encouraged by twenty-first-century Westerners. Whether in a remote village of thatch-roofed huts or in a modern urban setting, pagan people *can* find God . . . if they want to.

You Are Accountable for What You Know

Those who haven't heard about Jesus do know about God. And deep down, they know they've done things they shouldn't have. They are accountable for the lives they've lived, and they will eventually face the God who created them. Multitudes have confessed to knowing that the religion they were practicing was insufficient to put them in right standing with almighty God.[2]

Most Christian scholars would agree that people will be judged not by what they didn't know but by what they did with the light they had.

C. S. Lewis on Heaven, and Those Who Truly Desire It

In his classic work *Mere Christianity*, C. S. Lewis wrote, "If I find in myself a desire which no experience in this world can satisfy, the most probable explanation is that I was made for another world. If none of my earthly pleasures satisfy it, that does not prove that the universe is a fraud. Probably earthly pleasures were never meant to satisfy it, but only to arouse it, to suggest the real thing. If that is so, I must take care, on the one hand, never to despise, or be unthankful for, these earthly blessings, and on the other, never to mistake them for the something else of which they are only a kind of copy, or echo, or mirage. I must keep alive in myself the desire for my true country, which I shall not find till after death; I must make it the main object of life to press on to that other country and to help others to do the same."[3]

Yet the tension still lies in the timeless truth that "salvation is found in no one else [but Jesus], for there is no other name under heaven given to men by which we must be saved" (Acts 4:12). The real issue isn't that God sends people to hell because they lived in the wrong place at the wrong time and never heard about Jesus. The issue is that everyone knows the truth on some level, but many choose to "suppress" it (Romans 1:18).

Abraham asked, "Will not the Judge of all the earth do right?" (Genesis 18:25). The answer is yes. God's holy nature assures us that He will always do the right thing. God is fair. In fact, He's more than fair; He's "rich in mercy" and love (Ephesians 2:4). He offers everyone the opportunity to know Him, but He won't force Himself on us. Yet when we truly seek Him, God promises that we'll find Him (Jeremiah 29:13).

Ask a Different Question

You can tell your kids with confidence that the Bible is crystal clear that anyone who wants to go to heaven must be born again (John 3:3). What will happen to those who have never heard about Jesus? Will God extend special grace to them at the final judgment? I don't know, but I do know that God will be merciful and fair.

Rather than asking whether God will send people to hell who haven't heard about Jesus, perhaps the better question to ask is "Who are some people I can tell about Jesus?"

As a family, practice sharing the gospel. You can visit my website—*alexmcfarland.com/How-Do-I-Become-A-Christian.html*—for ideas on what to say. Another idea is to memorize a short set of scriptures from the book of Romans, commonly called the Roman road to salvation:

- Romans 3:23—All have sinned and fall short of the glory of God.
- Romans 6:23—The wages of sin is death, but the gift of God is eternal life in Christ Jesus our Lord.
- Romans 5:8—God demonstrates his own love for us in this: While we were still sinners, Christ died for us.

- Romans 10:13—Everyone who calls on the name of the Lord will be saved.

I believe every Christian should be able to clearly share the gospel with others. You and your children have been given a light for the world; plan now on how you'll use that knowledge to impact your community.

When Is Jesus Coming Back?

> *The Queen said, "The rule is, jam*
> *tomorrow and jam yesterday—*
> *but never jam to-day."*
> *"It MUST come sometime to 'jam to-day,'"*
> *Alice objected.*
> *"No, it can't," said the Queen. "It's jam*
> *every OTHER day; to-day isn't any*
> *OTHER day, you know."*
> *"I don't understand you," said Alice.*
> *"It's dreadfully confusing."*
>
> —Lewis Carroll, *Through the Looking Glass*

"Alex, when do you think Jesus will come back?" A student posed this question to me during an open-mic Q-and-A session at a summer camp.

"That's pretty much one of the biggest questions of all, isn't it?" I responded. "Well, get ready for the answer."

The room became amazingly quiet as several hundred teens listened for my take on this important question. I said, "Jesus will return just as He arrived: at *precisely* the right time."

Galatians 4:4 says that "when the [fullness] of the time was come, God sent forth his Son, made of a woman" (KJV). The verse literally means that Jesus came "at exactly the right time." He will come back to earth at the right moment as well.

Key Concepts

QUESTION RECAP: When is Jesus coming back? Why are there differing viewpoints about the end times?

1. The Bible teaches that no one except the Father knows the day or hour when Jesus will come back. Not even Jesus. Those who have made false predictions about Christ's return have become laughingstocks, and they give nonbelievers a negative impression of Christianity.

2. Famines and earthquakes are among the signs of the end times, but Jesus said these are just the "birth pangs." He also warned that wars and rumors of wars would take place before His return, but they aren't necessarily a sign that the end has come.

3. Christians are to take comfort that we'll be reunited with believing loved ones who have "fallen asleep" in Christ. Christians are also to persevere to the end and be ready when Jesus does come back.

4. Because prophecy is difficult to interpret, Bible scholars disagree on the order of events of the end times. If someone has a differing viewpoint on the end times, don't let that create tension in your relationship.

HOPE-FILLED ANSWER: Jesus is coming back, but no one except God the Father knows the date, and Christians shouldn't focus on predicting it. Instead, Jesus expects us to use our time wisely until He returns. That means sharing the gospel and encouraging one another.

• •

It's just that no one here on earth knows when that will be, though plenty of people have made predictions that turned out to be wrong. For example, in 1843, after spending fourteen years studying the Bible,

William Miller became convinced that Christ would return that year. Miller began to proclaim that April would be the month, leading his growing band of followers (called Millerites) to gather on mountaintops, hoping for a head start to heaven. Some gathered in graveyards, planning to ascend in reunion with resurrected loved ones. Near Philadelphia, upper-crust society ladies gathered together outside of the city to avoid entering God's kingdom amid the common herd.

April came and went, and the Millerites were saddened that their promised dates turned out to be incorrect. The Millerites became the butt of jokes for many years. Revising his calculations and setting more dates, William Miller retained many of his followers. He expanded the range of dates during which Christ would return. March 21, 1844, was publicized, then October 22 of that same year. Yet, as with other groups who have participated in such movements, the Millerites ended up sorely disappointed.[1]

Yet not everyone learned from Miller's mistake. In 2011, a well-publicized group, led by radio talk-show host and Bible teacher Harold Camping, predicted that the Lord would return on May 21.[2] (You and your kids can watch a YouTube video of the Associated Press news release about Camping's prediction: "Believers: World to End May 21.") The date came and went uneventfully.

Save the Date?

One unfortunate result of failed attempts at predicting the date for Christ's return is that it often leaves nonbelievers with a negative impression of Christianity. Many unkind and insulting comments were posted at the end of online stories about the Harold Camping predictions. Some people outside the faith assume that Christians are irrational, easily convinced dupes. When masses of otherwise-sane believers ignore the clear teachings of Scripture and set a date for the end of the world or follow a leader who has done so . . . well, the results are never good.

The date setters of 2011 included some people who sold their homes and businesses in preparation to leave this world. Others gave away life savings prior to the predicted end-of-time date—some to good causes, but a few lavishly spent entire bank accounts over a period of weeks. None of these behaviors are representative of how disciples of Christ should conduct themselves, and the impression bad behaviors give the world is certainly not positive.

But wanting to know about the end times is natural for us. Even the disciples, when they met with Jesus in His resurrected body, tried to glean details about His return. But the secret remained hidden in the heart of the Father:

> So when [the disciples] met together, they asked [Jesus], "Lord, are
> you at this time going to restore the kingdom to Israel?"
>
> He said to them: "It is not for you to know the times or dates the
> Father has set by his own authority." (Acts 1:6–7)

In Matthew 24 Jesus warned about the misleading teachings of those who claimed to have insider knowledge about the end of time:

> This gospel of the kingdom shall be preached in the whole world . . .
> and then the end will come. . . . If anyone says to you, "Behold, here
> is the Christ," or "There He is," do not believe him. For false Christs
> and false prophets will arise and will show great signs and wonders,
> so as to mislead, if possible, even the elect. Behold, I have told you
> in advance. So if they say to you, "Behold, He is in the wilderness,"
> do not go out, or, "Behold, He is in the inner rooms," do not believe
> them. . . . But of that day and hour no one knows, not even the an-
> gels of heaven, nor the Son, but the Father alone. (Verses 14, 23–26,
> 36, NASB)

Bottom line for your kids: No angel or human knows when Jesus is coming back, *not even Jesus!*

Signs of the End Times

The question "When is Jesus coming back?" may be the tip of an eschatological iceberg. (Eschatology is the study of end times.) Your kids could be wondering if Jesus is coming back before Friday's big test so they won't have to study. Or they may have heard something on the news that sounds as if planet Earth is going to be destroyed, and they're wondering

---

Key End-Times Terminology
Your Child Should Know

- *Eschatology*—the study of the end times and Christ's return; it literally means "last things."
- *The great tribulation*—a period in which there is devastation and turmoil as never before in history, according to Matthew 24:21–29 and Revelation 7:14.
- *The judgment*—also referred to in the New Testament as "the day of judgment," "the judgment to come," "God's judgment," "God's judgment seat," and "the eternal judgment." All the people who have ever lived will be judged, as will Satan and his followers. (See Revelation 14, 16, and 20.)
- *The millennium* or *thousand-year reign of Christ*—A thousand-year period when Satan will be bound, and Christ and some of His dedicated followers will rule the earth (Revelation 20:1–7).
- *The rapture* or *the second coming*—the moment when Christ comes back to earth in the clouds, and Christians are gathered to Him (Matthew 24:30–31; 1 Thessalonians 4:13–18). Some dispensationalist teachers believe the rapture is the secret coming of Christ before the visible second coming.

if that unrest is an indication of the end times. Today as I'm writing, the headlines are all about Hurricane Sandy and the devastation she hurled upon the northeast coast of the United States.

It would be easy to believe that this hurricane was more significant than a mere weather event. However, there have been thousands of hurricanes since Christ's death—how would we know if any specific weather event was heralding Jesus' return? What about wars? Many people thought that World War I was surely a sign of the end times because never before had the whole world been fully at war. How do we know which events have significance in a biblical time line?

End-times prophecies can seem confusing to believers, but God doesn't want us to be as mixed up as Alice was in her "jam to-day" conversation with the queen in the chapter-opening quote. There are answers. Since we've already looked at what we can't know about Christ's return, let's look at the things we can know.

"Many Will Come in My Name"

Matthew 24 contains the most detailed information that Jesus provided us concerning the end times:

> As [Jesus] was sitting on the Mount of Olives, the disciples came to Him privately, saying, "Tell us, when will these things happen, and what will be the sign of Your coming, and of the end of the age?"
>
> And Jesus answered and said to them, "See to it that no one misleads you. For many will come in My name, saying, 'I am the Christ,' and will mislead many." (Verses 3–5, NASB)

Many people over the years have professed to be Jesus, or the true Christ. Note that Jesus didn't tell His disciples *when* He would come again, but rather He cautioned them about false messengers who would claim to be the Messiah. Jesus went on to say, "You will be hearing of wars and rumors of wars. See that you are not frightened, for those things must take place, but that is not yet the end" (verse 6, NASB).

Again Jesus wasn't saying that wars are necessarily a sign of the end; rather, He was saying the opposite: "That is not yet the end." During World War II, people claimed the end times had surely arrived because never before had there been enough weapons to fully wipe out earth's entire population. Not only had ships, aircraft, tanks, and firearms dramatically improved, but atomic warfare also debuted during this era.

Wars and rumors of wars will continue as long as we live in this world, but remember Jesus' words: "That is not yet the end."

The Birth Pangs

Jesus indicated that violence and war among the nations are the inevitable course of this fallen race: "Nation will rise against nation, and kingdom against kingdom, and in various places there will be famines and earthquakes. But all these things are merely the beginning of birth pangs" (Matthew 24:7–8, NASB).

During the past few years, we've seen what some call an unprecedented number of earthquakes and famines around the world. I already mentioned Hurricane Sandy and the destruction on the East Coast. A few years ago several hurricanes wreaked havoc upon Florida, and not long after that, Hurricane Katrina destroyed most of New Orleans and other regions around the Gulf of Mexico.

Famines have been going on in developing countries for all of known history. For the most part, the cause of famines has been drought or other severe weather patterns. But in the twenty-first century, the planet has become so interwoven economically and politically that monetary policy dictated by the US Federal Reserve can impact inflation to the point that it can cause a food shortage in undeveloped parts of the globe.[3]

These realities should be cause for sympathy and concern, but not cause for alarm. Instead, we should be alert and diligent in sharing the gospel. When your children ask when Jesus is coming back, remind them that we are experiencing the birth pangs Jesus spoke of in Matthew 24, and only the Father knows how long they will continue.

When Jesus Comes

In the book of 1 Corinthians, the apostle Paul shed some light on the events surrounding Christ's return:

> Behold, I tell you a mystery: We shall not all sleep, but we shall all be changed—in a moment, in the twinkling of an eye, at the last trumpet. For the trumpet will sound, and the dead will be raised incorruptible, and we shall be changed. For this corruptible must put on incorruption, and this mortal *must* put on immortality. So when this corruptible has put on incorruption, and this mortal has put on immortality, then shall be brought to pass the saying that is written: *"Death is swallowed up in victory."* (15:51–54, NKJV)

The ultimate victory of being a Christian is when Jesus returns for us, and we are given new bodies that are designed for eternal life. First Thessalonians 4:13–18 is a passage that has been much discussed by Christian believers of many different backgrounds. While several interpretations of this passage have been offered by scholars, it is clear that the overall importance of the passage is the comfort it offers concerning Christians who have died:

> Brothers, we do not want you to be ignorant about those who fall asleep, or to grieve like the rest of men, who have no hope. We believe that Jesus died and rose again and so we believe that God will bring with Jesus those who have fallen asleep in him. According to the Lord's own word, we tell you that we who are still alive, who are left till the coming of the Lord, will certainly not precede those who have fallen asleep. For the Lord himself will come down from heaven, with a loud command, with the voice of the archangel and with the trumpet call of God, and the dead in Christ will rise first. After that, we who are still alive and are left will be caught up

together with them in the clouds to meet the Lord in the air. And so we will be with the Lord forever. *Therefore encourage each other with these words.*

Notice that the promise of Jesus' return is to be an encouragement to those who have lost loved ones. When the Bible speaks of believers who "fall asleep," it is referring to those who have already died, but whom we will see again in heaven.

For many children who are facing the loss of a loved one, the promise of this reunion is a great comfort.

Are We in the Last Days?

When I'm cohosting the weekday radio show *Exploring the Word*, I often hear questions like these: "Are we in the last days?" "Is the Antichrist alive today?" "Can the book of Revelation help us pinpoint where we are in history right now?" "We can't know the day and hour of Christ's return, but what about the year or decade or century?"

Faithful, Bible-believing scholars from various groups within the body of Christ have different answers to these questions. And, I'm sad to say, some argue vehemently about eschatology, well beyond a healthy scholarly discussion.

I don't want to get into that fray; I'd rather focus on helping children understand the proper heart response to the good news that Jesus is coming back. It's possible to be knowledgeable and confident about our convictions and yet loving and respectful at the same time when we have different viewpoints about the end times. That's what I'd like to encourage your family to do.

If you need more direction, you and your children can talk with your pastor or research more about prophecies and the order of end-times events together. At the end of the chapter, I've provided some links to websites you can visit to learn more about the differing time lines.

Why Are There Differing Viewpoints about the End Times?

The Bible contains many details about the state of the world leading up to Jesus' return. The Bible's prophecies are complex, and the language is often obscure. Both Old and New Testaments contain many prophetic passages. One scholar has estimated that there are 1,845 references to the second coming in the Old Testament. In the 260 chapters of the New Testament, there are 318 references to the second coming of Christ. Amazingly, this amounts to a mention in one out of every thirty verses. Twenty-three of the twenty-seven New Testament books refer to Christ's return. For every prophecy in the Bible concerning Christ's *first* advent, there are approximately eight verses that allude to His *second*![4]

As we digest all this material, it's important to remember that a key approach to biblical interpretation is *balance*. We don't want to make the Bible and the verses about the second coming say *less* than what they say, as some do who dismiss prophecy as being all symbolic and nonliteral. But we shouldn't try to force the Bible to say *more* than what it really says either, like those who insist that their understanding of future events is the *only* correct interpretation.

Not Knowing Is a Good Thing

I teach kids that not knowing everything about end-times events can be viewed in a positive light. God has given us enough information about the future to instill hope and motivation. But prophecy isn't so cut-and-dried that we can know the exact date of Christ's return. If that were the case, Christians might become complacent and simply wait until just before the last day to start living for Christ.

Some liberal scholars scoff at the idea of Jesus' return or believe it will be merely a spiritual movement. But the Bible clearly asserts that Jesus' *second* visit to planet Earth won't be a quiet, timid affair. That's what your kids need to know.

His return won't be a subtle descent from heaven en route to a gentle manger. In stark contrast to His first coming, Scripture tells us that Christ's return will be accompanied by a loud shout and a trumpet blast (1 Thessalonians 4:16)! No one will miss this event! The Word of God declares that Jesus'

> *The question that all religious believers now face: Show me the evidence.*
> —DAVID BERLINSKI, *The Devil's Delusion*

second coming will be a spectacular event that everyone alive at the time will witness.

No Thumb Twiddlin' Allowed

Christians shouldn't just sit around idle, watching the world grow darker spiritually as they obsessively pore over Scripture to prove their end-times viewpoints and complacently wait for Jesus to return. *Jesus left the church here on earth to make a difference!* Your kids need to realize that Christ's return can be a wonderful motivator for faithful daily living. Christians are to stay busy until they meet the Lord, serving diligently by faithfully employing their particular gifts and callings. We are called to share Jesus with a lost world and contribute to the needs of the body of Christ (other believers around us), knowing that we will be rewarded in heaven for our service.

Your kids will be growing up in a world that cares little for what Scripture says is most important. Even the most dedicated Christian families struggle against the pull of modern-day culture. Matthew 6 tells us,

> Do not lay up for yourselves treasures on earth, where moth and rust
> destroy and where thieves break in and steal; but lay up for your-
> selves treasures in heaven, where neither moth nor rust destroys and
> where thieves do not break in and steal. For where your treasure is,
> there your heart will be also. (Verses 19–21, NKJV)

Caught Up in the Rapture

I grew up as a Presbyterian in the rural South, where outspoken Baptists and other diverse denominations congregated. Sure, we talked about our different views of baptism and communion, but I don't ever recall a discussion on the rapture or hearing disparaging remarks about a person's eschatological beliefs one way or the other. Making a person's belief about the rapture a litmus test for orthodoxy is a relatively new wrinkle in Christendom, introduced by the popular book *The Late Great Planet Earth* (1970) by Hal Lindsey and Carole C. Carlson. Before this book was published, there wasn't a whole lot of brouhaha over the topic. Today, however, the most heated discussions among believers are over end-times chronology and when the rapture will occur. Your older kids need to know about the differing views about the rapture, or they'll be "left behind" intellectually.

The term *rapture* isn't found in the Bible, but it refers to the moment when Christ descends from heaven and believers will be "caught up" with Him in the clouds (see 1 Thessalonians 4:13–18). A *premillennial* view of the end times posits that the rapture will occur *before* the thousand-year reign of Christ. Most Southern Baptist and evangelical theologians and seminaries hold to a premillennial rapture time line. Most Catholics, Lutherans, and Reformed churches take a different viewpoint called *postmillennialism,* which holds that the rapture will occur *after* the thousand-year reign of Christ. To further complicate things, there are a dozen or so variations within those two schools of thought, such as pretribulation and post-tribulation rapture sects and partial preterist, and so on.

My take on the rapture is this: If a person believes Jesus is coming back and sees that as a good thing, then that person is my brother or sister in Christ. Together we can echo the words of the apostle John in Revelation 22:20: "Amen. Come, Lord Jesus."

When we really believe that Jesus is coming back, our service for Him will flow freely. The apostle Paul was encouraged through tough times by relying on the knowledge that Jesus was coming back and would be rewarding those who had been faithful:

> I have fought the good fight, I have finished the race, I have kept
> the faith. Finally, there is laid up for me the crown of righteousness,
> which the Lord, the righteous Judge, will give to me on that Day,
> and not to me only but also to all who have loved His appearing.
> (2 Timothy 4:7–8, NKJV)

Note the phrases "on that Day" and "all who have loved His appearing." We should live each day in light of "that Day" when we will stand before God. For the believer, Christ's appearing is a source of joyful anticipation! Consider the words of 1 Thessalonians 1:3: "We continually remember before our God and Father your work produced by faith, your labor prompted by love, and your endurance inspired by hope in our Lord Jesus Christ."

The word *hope* used here is a translation of the Greek word *elpis*. As I mentioned in an earlier chapter, in today's vernacular, hope might imply wishful thinking or the notion of something that might possibly happen but isn't guaranteed. In the Greek language, however, the word *elpis* denotes looking forward to a event that was sure to happen. The English translation might leave one wondering about the possibility that an event won't happen, but the implication of the original language was that the promise was absolutely rock solid.

A similar level of certainty is implied by Hebrews 6:19: "We have this hope as an anchor for the soul, firm and secure."

The Christian's hope in Christ's physical return is what keeps us motivated and drives us to do our best for Him! Either by death or His promised return, we'll *all* one day report to King Jesus. So we should invest ourselves now in the things that will count for eternity and teach our kids the same.

The Book of Revelation

During a Christian conference I was attending, a young person came up to me and asked me about "all that scary stuff" in the book of Revelation. Revelation does indeed contain some pretty stunning imagery about future happenings on planet Earth, but Jesus' words in Matthew 24 inspire enough fear:

> When you see the abomination of desolation which was spoken of through Daniel the prophet, standing in the holy place (let the reader understand), then those who are in Judea must flee to the mountains. Whoever is on the housetop must not go down to get the things out that are in his house. Whoever is in the field must not turn back to get his cloak. (Verses 15–18, NASB)

There has been much speculation about what the "abomination of desolation" is, was, or will be. Most commentaries refer to Luke 21:20–24, which seems to point to the Roman army, which occupied Jerusalem and destroyed the Jewish temple in AD 70 (see also Luke 21:5–6). They say that the entire period since the destruction of the temple in the year 70 has been the end times. Others believe that the "abomination of desolation" is the Muslim mosque called the Dome of the Rock, which was built on the site where the Jewish temple once stood.

A full exploration of these various versions is beyond the scope of this book. But it's clear that a number of events in the Holy Land have ushered in the end times—the destruction of the Jewish temple, and before that, Christ's death on the cross and His victorious resurrection (Matthew 27:32–54; John 19:30—20:18).

As we discussed earlier in the chapter, one of the signs of the end times is the appearance of false teachers who would claim to be the Messiah, or "anointed one." Many well-meaning people have been duped by false teachers claiming to be the Christ. During my lifetime alone, false teachers have misled thousands of people. One who comes to mind is

David Koresh, who caused more than a hundred people to die prematurely near Waco, Texas, because they were following a false messiah. In 1978, followers of Peoples Temple committed ritualistic suicide at the command of their leader, Jim Jones. I remember riding on my school bus as reports of this tragedy played over a transistor radio. The normally noisy school bus became totally silent as we all listened to the horrific news report. Nine hundred and eighteen people died in Jonestown, Guyana. This disturbing record of human death resulting from religious fanaticism peaked on September 11, 2001, when Muslim terrorists hijacked passenger airplanes, two of which flew into the Twin Towers in New York City.

In contrast to the unfulfilled promises of history's false messiahs, Jesus Christ presented facts about His own return in detail:

> For just as the lightning comes from the east and flashes even to the west, so will the coming of the Son of Man be. Wherever the corpse is, there the vultures will gather.
>
> But immediately after the tribulation of those days the sun will be darkened, and the moon will not give its light, and the stars will fall from the sky, and the powers of the heavens will be shaken. And then the sign of the Son of Man will appear in the sky, and then all the tribes of the earth will mourn, and they will see the Son of Man coming on the clouds of the sky with power and great glory. And He will send forth His angels with a great trumpet and they will gather together His elect from the four winds, from one end of the sky to the other. (Matthew 24:27–31, NASB)

Many details regarding Christ's second coming aren't fully understood, even by the best of Bible scholars. But we definitely know this: Jesus Christ will return to earth one day, and everyone will see Him "coming on the clouds of the sky with power and great glory." Sadly, the Bible is clear in its warnings that some people won't be ready (Matthew 7:21–23).

Deep down inside, all people know that they will one day face God. And it's here, finally, that we come to the crux of the matter: The question your kids should be asking isn't "When is Jesus coming back?" but "Am I ready to meet Jesus one day, and how can I help others be ready as well?"

We don't know when Jesus is coming back, but we do know that we need to tell others about Him. The fact that Jesus didn't know the exact time of His return should remind us that no one else on earth should claim to know either. The next time someone comes out with a fascinating timetable about the Lord's return, remember the biblical position on the subject: Leave specific times and dates to God and continue laboring for Christ as if every day might be *the* day! (See Matthew 24:43–50.)

To Learn More about the Timing of the Rapture . . .

Visit these websites to find out more about the differing time lines for the rapture, the millennium, the tribulation, and judgment day:

- *reformed.org/eschaton* (Center for Reformed Theology and Apologetics)—offers a good selection of articles on apologetics and the end times from a traditionally Presbyterian/Reformed perspective.
- *fivesolas.com/esc_chrt.htm*—presents four views on the end times for comparison.
- *gotquestions.org/questions_end-times.html* (GotQuestions.org)—posts end-times articles from a respected apologetics site, presented from a dispensational perspective. (Dispensational theology says that biblical history can be separated into a series of distinct time periods called *dispensations*.)
- *foigm.org* (The Friends of Israel)—a website that deals with the political issues in the Middle East from a Christian perspective. The site's search feature yields many articles about the end times from a dispensational perspective.

Let's face it—it's possible for equally God-fearing Christians to come up with different understandings of this complex content. While a passage's exact meaning might be in question, the love that Christians of differing opinions have for the Savior should not be.

A complete and accurate understanding of the Bible's prophetic works won't fully be possible this side of heaven. Yet various Christians have passionately argued for and against interpretations of Revelation that emphasized the past-tense, present-tense, and future-tense understandings.

So who has the right approach? Perhaps there is some truth in all three: There is at least some history in Revelation. There are spiritual principles from the unsettling events depicted that we can apply to our lives today. And everyone recognizes that at least some of the book's images belong to the future (just read Revelation 21:9—22:5).

The bottom line for your kids: Christ will triumphantly return to earth one day and will usher in an eternity of righteousness and joy to be shared with those who love Him. No matter how corrupt this world may get in the meantime, all past and present evils will one day be reckoned and accounted for. In short: No worries! God wins!

Part 3

Questions about the Trinity and the Holy Spirit

How Can God Be the Only God If There Is Also Jesus?

"I tell you the truth," Jesus answered,
"before Abraham was born, I am!"

—John 8:58

Not long after Saint Augustine had finished writing his theological treatise *On the Holy Trinity*, he was walking along the Mediterranean shore on the coast of North Africa. There he saw a boy who kept filling a bucket with seawater and pouring the water into a large hole in the sand.

"Why are you doing that?" Augustine asked the boy.

The boy replied, "I'm pouring the Mediterranean Sea into the hole."

"My dear boy, what an impossible thing to try to do!" chided Augustine. "The sea is far too vast, and your hole is far too small."

Then as Augustine continued his walk, it dawned on him that in his efforts to write on the Trinity, he was much like that boy: The subject was far too vast, and his mind was far too small![1]

You may feel much like Augustine did when considering the Trinity, but don't give up. While this topic isn't the easiest to teach, it can be done effectively.

QUESTION RECAP: The doctrine of the Trinity states that there is one God who eternally exists in three distinct persons: the Father, the Son, and the Holy Spirit. These three distinct individuals are one God. The Bible says, "Hear, O Israel: The LORD our God, the LORD is one" (Deuteronomy 6:4). By introducing Jesus and the Holy Spirit as being fully God along with the Father, there appears to be a math problem. How can 1 + 1 + 1 = 1?

1. It is difficult to explain the Trinity because there is nothing to compare God to—He is in a category all by Himself.

2. Object lessons about the Trinity can be useful for younger children. I recommend the three-note chord illustration. However, when examined closely, all object lessons eventually break down in describing the Trinity.

3. The Bible teaches the Trinity both directly and indirectly. Scripture shows that the Father is God, Jesus is God, and the Holy Spirit is God, and that the three work together in unity. The math can work too, if you use multiplication instead of addition because 1 x 1 x 1 = 1.

4. Because human understanding is finite and God is infinite, we can understand only a limited amount of God's nature. As a pet goldfish is limited in what it "knows" about the person who sprinkles food in its bowl daily, so we too are limited in what we "know" about the Source of our life and existence.

HOPE-FILLED ANSWER: The concept of the Trinity is accurately revealed in Scripture. However, there is much about the Trinity that we finite humans are unable to comprehend an infinite God.

The Trinity as an Object Lesson

In one way or another, all the concrete object lessons about the Trinity not only fail to depict God's triune nature, but the examples may also cloud biblical truth. I believe the illustrations about water (water, ice, steam), three-leaf clovers, a man (father, son, husband), and even eggs (shell, yoke, white) all break down theologically. I don't recommend using them for teens.

However, I don't want to portray God or the Trinity as a cumbersome problem. We can't just toss up our hands, shrug, and say, "Oh, well."

I understand that younger children aren't able to hold on to abstract ideas, and so, *with caution*, I recommend the three-note chord example. In a three-note chord, each note is distinct, but together the notes blend to make a unique, recognizable sound that is more beautiful and complete than each note individually. Likewise, each person of the Godhead is distinct, and yet when joined together, the three form a complete and beautiful God who is distinguishable from the three individual persons.[2]

> *Let us not be misled by the foolish argument that because the term Trinity does not occur in the Scriptures, the doctrine of the Trinity is therefore unscriptural.*
> —F. F. BRUCE, Bible scholar

What the Bible Says about the Trinity

To some people, the Trinity sounds like bad math. How can there be three persons and yet only one God? It just doesn't add up! But like Augustine, we must understand that there are some things God has revealed about Himself that are beyond our limited human understanding. This makes us uneasy, because we are rational beings plagued with insatiable curiosity. Our hearts desire understanding, especially when it comes to eternal matters. It's important to note, however, that the Trinity isn't a

About the Word Trinity

When used as a theological term, *Trinity* comes from the Latin word *trinitas*, which means "three-ness." Christian apologist and theologian Tertullian was one of the first leaders of the early church to use the term. He spoke of God as "a Trinity of one divinity—Father, Son, and Holy Spirit."

The concept of the Trinity has been a divisive issue throughout church history. Disagreements about the Trinity have resulted in many heresies as people have attempted to understand this vital doctrine. Here are a few:[3]

Modalism: The belief that God is one single person who has revealed Himself throughout history in three modes or forms. In the Old Testament, He was the Father. At the incarnation, He was the Son. Since Christ's ascension, He has been the Holy Spirit. (The United Pentecostal Church and the United Apostolic Church currently hold to this doctrine.[4]) Variations of modalism assert that at different times the one God wears a different mask, so to speak. When I warned of concrete analogies breaking down into false teaching, modalism is most often the result.

Arianism: The belief that God was too pure and infinite to appear on the earth, so He created the Son, Jesus, out of nothing. He is the first and greatest creation. Because of His exalted position, He is to be worshipped but is still a created being. Jehovah's Witnesses teach a variation of this heresy, as they consider Jesus to be the archangel Michael.[5]

Tritheism: The belief that God is actually three separate beings. Early Christians were actually accused of worshipping three gods. Even today, some cults and world religions, such as Islam, accuse Christians of this heresy.

It is beyond the scope of this book to deal with these heresies in detail. I simply want to make you aware of some of them.

contradiction, or even a paradox, but a beautiful mystery clearly revealed in Scripture. In this section we'll examine the biblical texts that comprise the doctrine of the Trinity.

There Is Only One God

First, the Bible says that there is only one God:

> I am God, and there is no other;
> I am God, and there is none like me. (Isaiah 46:9)

> There is one body and one Spirit—just as you were called to one hope when you were called—one Lord, one faith, one baptism; one God and Father of all, who is over all and through all and in all. (Ephesians 4:4–6)

Jesus Is God

The Bible also tells us that Jesus is God:

> In the beginning was the Word, and the Word was with God, and the Word was God. . . . The Word became flesh and made his dwelling among us. (John 1:1, 14)

One of the names ascribed to Jesus in the Bible is *the Word*. It comes from the Greek term *logos*, which was familiar to both Jews and Greeks of the first century. To the Jew, the Word of God is often personified. For example, in Psalm 147:15 we read, "He sends his command to the earth; / his word runs swiftly." To the Greeks, *logos* was used to represent the rational principle or mind that ruled the universe. So it's very appropriate that John would use this term to show the divinity of Jesus.

Colossians 2:9 tells us, "For in Christ all the fullness of the Deity lives in bodily form." This is a clear assertion that Jesus is equal with God the Father. He isn't inferior to the Father in any way.

We also see that after the crucifixion, Jesus began to appear to His disciples. Thomas, one of the twelve, wasn't with the others when Jesus appeared to them. They told him that they had seen the risen Lord.

Eight days later, Jesus again appeared to His disciples, including Thomas. Jesus told Thomas to touch the scars on His wrists and to put his hand in Jesus' side. Thomas cried out: "My Lord and my God!" (John 20:28, NASB). Thomas, the man who had a reputation for doubting, recognized that Jesus was his Lord and his God! This is one of the strongest references to the deity of Christ in the New Testament.

The Holy Spirit Is God
The Bible also reveals that the Holy Spirit is God:

> Peter said, "Ananias, how is it that Satan has so filled your heart that you have *lied to the Holy Spirit* and have kept for yourself some of the money you received for the land? Didn't it belong to you before it was sold? And after it was sold, wasn't the money at your disposal? What made you think of doing such a thing? *You have not lied to men but to God.*" (Acts 5:3–4)

Many of the believers in the early church were selling their lands and properties and using the money to help those in the church who had financial needs. Ananias and his wife sold one of their properties with the promise that they would give all the proceeds to the church. But when the time to give that money came, Ananias instead kept back some of the money and lied about it. Later, Peter told him, "You have not lied to men but to God." In this indirect way Peter equated the Holy Spirit with God.

The Three Persons of the Trinity
Finally, we see all three members of the Trinity presented in unity in the Great Commission:

> Go and make disciples of all nations, baptizing them in the name of the Father and of the Son and of the Holy Spirit. (Matthew 28:19)

When Jesus gave the Great Commission, He told His followers to baptize in *the name* of the Father, Son, and Holy Spirit. In other words, Jesus didn't tell the disciples to baptize in the "names" of the Father, Son, and Spirit as distinct entities but in the name, as one God or unified entity. Baptism was an act of public association not only with the church but also with all three members of the Trinity.

At the baptism of Jesus, we also see all three members of the Trinity present:

> As soon as Jesus was baptized, he went up out of the water. At that moment heaven was opened, and he saw the Spirit of God descending like a dove and lighting on him. And a voice from heaven said, "This is my Son, whom I love; with him I am well pleased." (Matthew 3:16–17)

The Holy Spirit was present in the form of a dove, and the Father pronounced His Son's approval from heaven in an audible voice.

Lessons from a Goldfish

When I talk about the Trinity and not being able to understand God, I find that comparing humans to a goldfish is helpful, especially for younger kids.

The analogy goes like this: Imagine that you are a pet goldfish. Your world is a bowlful of water, colorful rocks, a small pastel-colored ceramic castle, and food flakes that appear once a day. The large shape that delivers this food is reliable.

Here's what the goldfish knows—the shape is large and lives outside the bowl. The shape is giving it the food flakes. The shape probably won't hurt the goldfish and might even care for it. And that's it.

Here's what the goldfish *doesn't* know: The shape is a human male. It breathes air, not water, which is an altogether different biological paradigm. He's a green grocer, loves banana-flavored ice cream, has an IQ of

130, uses Aqua Velva aftershave despite his girlfriend's protests, and has always wanted to be a ventriloquist. There's a vast knowledge bank about the shape that the fish can't even begin to comprehend.

As humans, we have a limited view of the eternal God. We are like the pet goldfish. What we know about our divine Caretaker is accurate and true, but there's a vast amount we don't know about Him. Part of that vast unknown amount is how the intricacies of the Trinity work.

So while reason alone can't help us understand the Trinity and explain it to our kids, it's a good start. And surely it isn't unreasonable that an infinite God can exist in three distinct persons and yet be only one divine entity.

On tough concepts like the Trinity, sometimes we just have to teach our kids—and ourselves—to think outside the goldfish bowl.

When I Pray, Who Is Listening—God, Jesus, or the Holy Spirit?

This is going to take awhile. . . .
[I have] 1,527,503 unanswered prayer
requests? I'd better manifest some coffee.

—Bruce, in *Bruce Almighty*

Have you ever been walking through a store and seen someone carrying on a conversation—with no one? You look around for someone within earshot. Maybe the person is talking to you? No, you don't know anyone named Tristan, and you won't pick him up from school. Then you finally see it: tucked in the person's ear is the wireless headset for a mobile phone.

Prayer can seem like that to children. Whom do we talk to when we pray, and who is listening? Are we praying to God the Father, Jesus the Son, or the Holy Spirit?

If you're like me, the temptation is to answer this question with a simple yes and then close the chapter. But children—as well as many adults—truly want to know the godly order of prayer. Fortunately we do have biblical guidance. It's important that we understand the distinctions between God, Jesus Christ, and the Holy Spirit when it comes to prayer.

Key Concepts

QUESTION RECAP: Because our God has a three-part nature, the roles of each divine person sometimes overlap. So which of the eternal three is in charge of listening to prayers? Whom should we pray to?

1. Most often it's God the Father who is addressed in prayers in the Bible. Jesus Himself prayed to the Father.

2. Jesus said to pray to the Father in Jesus' name. This shows the eternal partnership between the Father and the Son.

3. There are no examples of people praying to the Holy Spirit in Scripture. However, the Holy Spirit intercedes for us in prayer, and that means He's listening as well.

4. There are different types of prayers recorded in Scripture. The phrase "in Jesus' name" is a key element to certain types of prayers.

HOPE-FILLED ANSWER: Prayer is a healthy activity. It's appropriate to pray to any member of the Trinity: Father, Son, or Holy Spirit. There are, however, specific guidelines in Scripture about different types of prayers and how to direct them.

• •

Along the way, we'll look at some of the unique qualities and functions that are part of a Christian's prayer life.

When we explore prayer in the Bible, we find that in most passages, the term *God* is referring to God the *Father*, and most of the prayers in Scripture are directed to the Father. In the New Testament, after Jesus' death and resurrection, the majority of prayers are offered to God the Father in the name of Jesus Christ. We'll look at examples of each.

God the Father and Prayer

There're few things in life sweeter than praying with children at bedtime. How we pray with them, when we pray with them, and how often we pray with them shape their attitudes and future prayer practices.

> **How does God choose which ones of our prayers He will answer?**
> —MICAH, age seven

Likewise, in His Sermon on the Mount, Jesus wanted to shape His disciples' prayer practices. He gave instructions on how to pray, specifically telling His followers to address their prayers to the Father: "When you pray, go into your room, close the door and pray to your Father, who is unseen. Then your Father, who sees what is done in secret, will reward you" (Matthew 6:6).

Jesus then modeled how to pray to the Father in what we now refer to as the Lord's Prayer:

> Our Father in heaven,
> Hallowed be Your name.
> Your kingdom come.
> Your will be done
> On earth as it is in heaven.
> Give us this day our daily bread.
> And forgive us our debts,
> As we forgive our debtors.
> And do not lead us into temptation,
> But deliver us from the evil one.
> For Yours is the kingdom and the power and the glory forever. Amen.
> (Matthew 6:9–13, NKJV)

Similarly, we see other passages modeling prayer. The early church members addressed their prayers to the Father. In Romans, the apostle

Paul began his epistle by reminding his fellow believers that he prayed faithfully for them:

> I thank my God through Jesus Christ for all of you, because your
> faith is being reported all over the world. God, whom I serve with
> my whole heart in preaching the gospel of his Son, is my witness
> how constantly I remember you in my prayers at all times. (1:8–10)

Since Paul referred to God distinctly from the Son, we know he was referring to God the Father. Likewise, Paul told the church in Ephesus that he was petitioning "the God of our Lord Jesus Christ, the glorious Father" on their behalf (Ephesians 1:17).

When we pray to God the Father, we can be assured that He hears us and answers our prayers "according to his will" (1 John 5: 14–15). Matthew 7:7 tells us that if we ask, "it will be given to you." That doesn't mean God answers all of our prayers with a yes. If we're seeking after God and our desires line up with His will, as 1 John says, we'll receive whatever we ask of Him. When our prayers don't line up with His will or His timing, God may not answer our requests with a yes. At those times it may seem that God hasn't heard our prayers. But God is always listening, and He does answer all of our prayers, even if sometimes the answer is no or "wait." We may not always understand why God answers our prayers the way He does, but we do know that He is sovereign (supremely in control) and has our best interests at heart.

Jesus Himself taught us to pray to the Father, asking Him to meet our needs. You can confidently encourage your children to pray as Jesus did, asking the Father to meet their needs and forgive their sins. But there are also other forms and types of prayers.

Jesus Christ and Prayer

Jesus continued to teach His disciples to pray. He began preparing them for the transition that was coming. Jesus told them that after He returned to the Father, they would begin to pray in a different way:

I tell you the truth, anyone who has faith in me will do what I have been doing. He will do even greater things than these, because I am going to the Father. And I will do whatever you ask in my name, so that the Son may bring glory to the Father. You may ask me for anything in my name, and I will do it. (John 14:12–14)

The Holy Spirit and Prayer

In the Bible we don't see any prayers addressed specifically to the Holy Spirit. However, we do find examples of Him *answering prayers* and responding to the needs of the believers. One example is found in Romans 8:

> The Spirit helps us in our weakness. We do not know what we ought to pray for, but the Spirit himself intercedes for us with groans that words cannot express. And he who searches our hearts knows the mind of the Spirit, because the Spirit intercedes for the saints in accordance with God's will. (Verses 26–27)

These verses show that the Holy Spirit is not just listening to our prayers but goes even further by interceding for us when "we do not know what we ought to pray for" (verse 26).

Jesus gave the Holy Spirit to be with believers when He could no longer be with them in the flesh. The Holy Spirit serves as our Counselor, Comforter, and Guide:

> But the Counselor [or Comforter], the Holy Spirit, whom the Father will send in my name, will teach you all things and will remind you of everything I have said to you. (John 14:26)

> When He, the Spirit of truth, has come, *He will guide you* into all truth; for He will not speak on His own authority, but whatever He hears He will speak; and He will tell you things to come. (John 16:13, NKJV)

Scripture shows that the Holy Spirit is a personal Being who communicates to believers and guides and inspires the people of God (Acts 13:2–3; 21:11). Since the Holy Spirit is our Comforter, Counselor, and Guide, it would be completely appropriate to address our prayers to Him when we seek comfort, counsel, and guidance.

There's Power in the Name!

There are numerous instances in the New Testament where people commanded things to happen in Jesus' name and they happened! But they weren't praying directly to God the Father, Jesus, or the Holy Spirit. How could this be?

When we're born again, we become Spirit-filled people who have

Praying Always

While we may not understand all the complexities of the relationship between the Father, Son, and Holy Spirit, we know that prayer is extremely important. Think of it: God invites us to be in constant communication with Him. What an immeasurable blessing!

Many Christians make the mistake of assuming that because God is omniscient (He knows everything), they don't have to pray. Some ask themselves, "Why tell God what I need if He already knows?" Jesus addressed this when He told His disciples to pray, but not to fill the air with empty words, "like pagans."

When you pray, go into your room, close the door and pray to your Father, who is unseen. Then your Father, who sees what is done in secret, will reward you. And when you pray, do not keep on babbling like pagans, for they think they will be heard because of their many words. Do not be the ability to see and experience God's power. Christians are indeed able to tap into God's great power. One of Paul's prayers to the Father for the Ephesians includes his desire "that you may be filled with all the fullness of God" (Ephesians 3:19, NKJV).

It's important to remember that we aren't God, and we're never to think that He has to act according to our demands. Far from it! But as Spirit-filled believers, we have authority and power on earth. This is the type of power the apostles exhibited when they ministered in the name of Jesus:

> One day Peter and John were going up to the temple at the time of prayer—at three in the afternoon. Now a man crippled from birth was being carried to the temple gate called Beautiful, where he was put

like them, for your Father knows what you need before you ask him. (Matthew 6:6–8)

Did you catch that? Jesus was telling His disciples that they still needed to pray, *even though* God already knew what they needed. We have bold access to the throne of God because of the redemptive price Jesus paid (Ephesians 3:12), and we're instructed in numerous places to *pray, pray, pray*:

> Be joyful in hope, patient in affliction, faithful in prayer. (Romans 12:12)

> Pray in the Spirit on all occasions with all kinds of prayers and requests. With this in mind, be alert and always keep on praying for all the saints. (Ephesians 6:18)

> Do not be anxious about anything, but in everything, by prayer and petition, with thanksgiving, present your requests to God. (Philippians 4:6)

> Pray without ceasing. (1 Thessalonians 5:17, NKJV)

every day to beg from those going into the temple courts. When he saw Peter and John about to enter, he asked them for money. Peter looked straight at him, as did John. Then Peter said, "Look at us!" So the man gave them his attention, expecting to get something from them.

Then Peter said, "Silver or gold I do not have, but what I have I give you. In the name of Jesus Christ of Nazareth, walk." Taking [the crippled man] by the right hand, [Peter] helped him up, and instantly the man's feet and ankles became strong. He jumped to his feet and began to walk. Then he went with them into the temple courts, walking and jumping, and praising God. When all the people saw him walking and praising God, they recognized him as the same man who used to sit begging at the temple gate called Beautiful, and they were filled with wonder and amazement at what had happened to him. (Acts 3:1–10)

Peter stated, "In the name of Jesus Christ of Nazareth, walk." He didn't say, "Heavenly Father, please heal this man," or "Dear Lord Jesus, please heal his crippled legs." Moved by the Holy Spirit, Peter simply made the declaration in faith, and the man was healed—and what a healing it was! The Bible says that he was "walking and jumping, and praising God."

Huge crowds gathered, wanting to know how such a miracle could occur. Part of Peter's response included this explanation:

By faith in the name of Jesus, this man whom you see and know was made strong. It is Jesus' name and the faith that comes through him that has given this complete healing to him, as you can all see. (Verse 16)

When I Pray, Who's Listening?

Prayer is a basic necessity for living in the world and becoming the men, women, and children God wants us to be. Even though God knows our needs and the Son and the Spirit are interceding for us (Romans 8:27, 34), He tells us to pray constantly.

Although we should generally be directing our prayers to God the Father in the name of Jesus Christ, based on the examples in the New Testament, it's also appropriate to address our prayers to individual members of the Trinity depending upon the request.

As we've seen, the three persons of the Trinity fill unique roles, so our prayers may be directed to each person based upon the specific need. For example, when we're praying for something extraordinary, or circumstances that require God's power, we should be making our requests to God the Father in the name of Jesus Christ. Decisions about when and where to move, where to fellowship, and with whom we should spend our time all seem to fall under the scope of Jesus' role as our head. Order within the church would be under His purview as well. When we're seeking guidance on where to witness or share the gospel, as well as seeking comfort, counsel, or an understanding of God's truth, these requests would be appropriately addressed to the Holy Spirit.

Sometimes, when we feel inspired, we can simply command away sickness (or even demonic powers) in Christ's name, exercising our authority as children of God! God may not always do our bidding, because He is sovereign and knows what's best. But it should encourage us to know that we can indeed call upon God and His great power, and at times He will respond with a definitive "Yes!"

We can approach the throne of grace boldly (Hebrews 4:16), and we should do so frequently. As we read God's Word, we learn about His will for our lives. Then we can pray confidently and effectively, as the apostle John encourages us to do:

> This is the confidence we have in approaching God: that if we ask anything according to his will, he hears us. And if we know that he hears us—whatever we ask—we know that we have what we asked of him. (1 John 5:14–15)

Will the Holy Spirit Leave Me If I Keep Sinning?

If the Holy Spirit was withdrawn from the church today, 95 percent of what we do would go on and no one would know the difference. If the Holy Spirit had been withdrawn from the New Testament church, 95 percent of what they did would stop, and everybody would know the difference.

—Attributed to A. W. Tozer

As a middle child, Beth Simmons was sandwiched between a near-perfect, straight-A-student older sister and a hopelessly cute, always-the-center-of-attention younger brother. Beth's presence was often overshadowed by her two siblings, but her quiet personality seemed well suited for her place within the Simmons family. But as the years progressed and she grew increasingly introverted, her parents felt concern for their middle child. They frequently worried over school progress reports that observed, "Shy; Beth doesn't make friends easily."

Her search for a secure sense of self was also impacted by the fact that of the three children, only Beth had been adopted. Her parents strove to raise their children with consistent love and impartiality, but by her late teens, Beth had come to greatly resent her siblings. In fact, she seemed to

Key Concepts

QUESTION RECAP: Will the Holy Spirit leave me if I keep sinning? What is blasphemy against the Holy Spirit? Can I act so badly that God will stop loving me?

1. Our salvation is based solely on Christ's work on the cross, not on our deeds. God forgives and unconditionally loves all of His children of faith.

2. The Pharisees committed blasphemy against the Holy Spirit when they rejected Jesus' deity. The religious leaders in Jesus' day had a front-row seat as they watched Jesus perform miracles—yet they still rejected Him, saying He was working for the devil. It's doubtful that blasphemy against the Holy Spirit as described in Mark 3:29 can occur today because Jesus is not walking the earth.

3. When Christians are confronted by atheists who malign the name of Jesus, we are to respond lovingly and kindly, exhibiting a Christlike response to evil.

HOPE-FILLED ANSWER: Like a parent, God is a loving Father who still loves us even when we sin. He wants us to return to Him and make things right, but no matter what we do, He will never stop loving us even though our sinful choices often have painful consequences. He promises forgiveness when we confess our sins to Him.

● ●

withdraw from all close relationships. By her senior year in high school, church and youth group, which had previously appeared to be sources of great enjoyment and stability in Beth's life, had lost their importance.

In fact, it was on her seventeenth birthday that Beth announced to her parents that she was now an agnostic. At this point, friendships from youth group had all evaporated. Healthy interaction with her siblings was all but gone. Ditto for her relationship with her parents.

"Raising Beth had always been a bit of a challenge," reflected Mrs. Simmons. "But when we tried to talk with her about friends, clothes, attitude, grades, and issues that were really concerning us—and especially about her relationship with God—what she said just broke our hearts." Quoting the 1960s band Jim Morrison and the Doors (a favorite retro band religiously followed by many of Beth's new friends), she told her shocked parents, "Cancel my subscription to the resurrection."[1] Beth, who had once been a standout in Bible-verse memory drills, was now more likely to quote her favorite atheist philosophers and writers.

The good news is that after about two and a half years of spiritual and emotional struggle, which included some time with a competent Christian counselor, Beth experienced a wonderful turnaround. Two brief failed attempts at college and a series of entry-level jobs contributed, in part, to the wake-up call. The crop of chic, antiestablishment, skeptic friends eventually lost their appeal. When Beth began to long for the relationships and environment she had abandoned, a patient family and church were ready to welcome her back.

During the darkest days of Beth's late-teen years, her parents were both prayerful and fearful. Interacting with them wasn't the first time a worried parent had asked me, "Has my child *lost* her salvation? Could my daughter have committed blasphemy against the Holy Spirit?"

Faith in Jesus Christ = Children of the Living God

Before we get to the question of whether the Holy Spirit will leave a believer, let's examine what happens when someone becomes a Christian.

The Bible says, "But as many as received [Jesus], to them He gave the right to become children of God, to those who believe in His name: who were born, not of blood, nor of the will of the flesh, nor of the will of man, but of God" (John 1:12–13, NKJV).

Through faith in Jesus Christ, we secure this new relationship with God. This relationship is so intimate and secure that the apostle Paul was inspired to write these moving words:

For I am persuaded that neither death nor life, nor angels nor
principalities nor powers, nor things present nor things to come,
nor height nor depth, nor any other created thing, shall be able to
separate us from the love of God which is in Christ Jesus our Lord.
(Romans 8:38–39, nkjv)

Notice how the Word of the Lord says nothing can separate us from
God's love, "which is in Christ Jesus our Lord."

True pride is thinking that our sin is too great that the blood of
Jesus can't cover it, or that we sin so frequently that we've exhausted His

If I Sin after I Accept Christ, Will God Still Love Me?

A related question that may arise when talking to young children
about sin is "If I sin after I accept Christ, will God still love me?"
The simple answer is yes! God's love is unconditional. As someone
has said, "You can't do anything to make God love you any more,
and you can't do anything to make God love you any less."

When children—or anyone for that matter—ask a question like
this, it lets me know that they understand just how serious their
sin is to God. It is also a good indicator that God is at work in their
life, drawing them to Christ. Or they may feel unlovable at the moment and need to confess something.

One way of illustrating God's unconditional love is to remind
your children of parental love. Most parents love their children unconditionally. There are some exceptions to this, but chances are
if you are reading this book, you're the kind of parent who loves
your child no matter what.

Do you still love your daughter when she doesn't clean her
bedroom? What about when your son doesn't tell the truth? What
if you had a teenage daughter who came home and told you she

patience. Jesus is our High Priest, and nothing we will ever do can get Him demoted. He is before the throne of God on our behalf twenty-four hours a day, three hundred and sixty-five days a year, year after year, pleading our case (Hebrews 7:24–25).

Can a Born-Again Person Blaspheme the Holy Spirit?

Now that we understand what happens to believers when they accept Christ and what that means, let's look at the question of blasphemy against the Holy Spirit.

---

was pregnant? Would you still love her? What if your son came home and said, "Mom, I think I'm gay"? You would no doubt be shocked, but would you still love him?

You may not like what your children do, but you still love them. You desire the best for their lives and want to see them do the right thing. Your heart may break when they rebel against all they've been taught, but you still love them.

Likewise, God is a loving Father who still loves us even when we sin. He wants us to return to Him and make things right, but no matter what we do, He will never stop loving us. He promises forgiveness when we confess our sins to Him: "My little children, these things I write to you, so that you may not sin. And if anyone sins, we have an Advocate with the Father, Jesus Christ the righteous" (1 John 2:1, NKJV).

The heart of God for His wayward child is seen in the parables of the prodigal son and the lost sheep in Luke 15. If a child is missing, He will seek her out. If a son is lost, He will receive him with open arms. Study these parables and others with your children. Pray that the Holy Spirit reminds them of the stories whenever they are feeling unloved or unlovable.

This question relates to Jesus' words in Mark 3:29: "Whoever blasphemes against the Holy Spirit will never be forgiven; he is guilty of an eternal sin." Skeptics treat this passage like some kind of theological flaw, faulting God for being either unable or unwilling to forgive this specific sin. But what exactly is blasphemy? Are there unforgivable or unpardonable sins? And how do we know if we've crossed the line and passed beyond the point of God's forgiveness?

Sometimes I get really mad at my sister. Okay, fairly often, but I do feel bad about it later. My question is this: Does God still love us even when we sin?

—SARA, age thirteen

Biblical examples of blasphemy imply irreverence or slander against God. But the term also means "to spurn." Scriptures alluding to blasphemy against the Holy Spirit imply a twofold indictment against the religious leaders who personally encountered Jesus while He was on earth: First, they refused to acknowledge Him as Messiah, *and then* they accused Him of being empowered by Satan. To say the least, they *spurned* Jesus.

Biblical scholar Barry Leventhal is director of the graduate school of ministry and missions at Southern Evangelical Seminary in North Carolina. Regarding passages dealing with blasphemy against the Holy Spirit, Leventhal notes that most scholars agree that Jesus' ominous warnings about blaspheming the Holy Spirit represented a situation unique to Christ's time on earth. "Jesus had presented Himself as Messiah to the Jewish leaders," Leventhal explains. "With irrefutable evidence, He had done everything necessary to validate who He was." Because the religious elite knew the Old Testament Scriptures intimately, Leventhal says, and the incarnate Lord was right in front of them, those Jewish leaders had been entrusted with unparalleled revelation that people today can't experience. "For them to stubbornly maintain that posture of unbelief and then to attribute Christ's work to the devil—[a clear] rejection of God's overtures—was the inexcusable, unpardonable blasphemy of the Holy Spirit."[2]

Sadly, some Christians struggle with a nagging fear that they may have committed an unforgivable sin. Such verses as 1 John 1:7 remind us that when people come to God in repentance and faith, "the blood of Jesus, his Son, purifies us from all sin." And Romans 8:1 assures believers that "there is now no condemnation for those who are in Christ Jesus."

Jesus said that part of the Holy Spirit's work in the world would be to reveal people's sinfulness and need for salvation (John 16:8–11). A healthy concern about sin is evidence that the Holy Spirit is still at work in a person's life. To feel contrite about sin proves that one *hasn't* committed some unpardonable sin.

Habitual Sin

Have you ever heard the phrase "Just because you can, doesn't mean you should"? It's a cheeky way of saying what the apostle Paul did in Romans 6:1: "Shall we go on sinning so that grace might increase?" The answer to this was, of course, "By no means!" (verse 2). This expression might also be translated, "may it never come to pass!" In today's language Paul might have said, "Are you kidding me?" Paul thought it absurd that believers could have such a flippant attitude toward sin. Paul reminds us that we have died to sin, which means that sin no longer has control over the believer. That does not mean that it no longer has influence over us or that we are no longer tempted to sin. The only control sin has over us is what we allow it to have. As Paul goes on to say:

> Therefore do not let sin reign in your mortal body so that you obey
> its evil desires. Do not offer the parts of your body to sin as instru-
> ments of wickedness, but rather offer yourselves to God, as those
> who have been brought from death to life; and offer the parts of
> your body to him as instruments of righteousness. For sin shall not
> be your master, because you are not under the law, but under grace.
> (Romans 6:12–14)

Just because God forgives sin, doesn't mean we should. But there are Christians who continue on a path of sin even after being impressed by God to stop. We've all experienced what the Bible calls *conviction*—that nudging by the Holy Spirit, that heaviness of conscience—as God calls on us to change our ways. But what happens when we won't obey the promptings of God? Many Christians have wondered, "Will the Holy Spirit continue to lead me if I keep on sinning?"

Let's be clear: All Christians commit sins. First John 1:9 promises God's forgiveness to those who confess their sins—and this verse was written to *Christians*. My understanding of Scripture leads me to believe that a born-again person doesn't lose salvation if he or she commits a sin. The Bible shows us that while we may struggle with temptations, weaknesses, and sins, Christ's followers must not willingly and repeatedly *yield* to them.

The consequences of choosing to habitually sin include loss of intimacy with God, interruption of progress in our spiritual growth, and anemia in our prayer life. Also common is a diminished ability to understand and apply God's Word, if one is reading the Bible at all. When a person has resisted the overtures of the Lord over a period of time, the New Testament speaks of their conscience (or heart) becoming "calloused." This callousness can be likened to tissue in the body that is devoid of feelings, such as fat around the heart or intestines (Psalm 17:10; 119:70).[3] The longer we remain in a state of disobedience, the more our ability to recognize the Holy Spirit's voice will be impaired (see Matthew 13:15; Ephesians 4:17–19).

Habitual sin can also bring bitter consequences into the relationships we have with others. Hurt feelings, loss of trust and respect—these are but a few of the emotional and personal repercussions. There can be measurable physical consequences, especially if a person indulges in substance abuse. Gambling, refusing to tithe, and lust for material things have left many Christians with financial consequences.

Some habitual sins can exist—for a time, at least—hidden from other people. I think of anger, lust, jealousy, pride, hatred, racial prejudice, and even unwarranted discouragement. But their *effects* eventually and invariably will be visible to others.

Romans 6:14 says, "Sin shall not be your master." First John 3:9 indicates that habitual sin should not be characteristic of the believer: "No one who is born of God will continue to sin, because God's seed remains in him; he cannot go on sinning, because he has been born of God." (See also Psalm 19:13; 1 Corinthians 10:13; James 4:7).

How do we coach our children so that they will recognize sin and with God's help overcome it? A first step is to help them understand that without the help of the Lord, sin *will* creep into (and throughout) their lives. Christians need to walk closely with God every day, which takes discipline and commitment.

Another key is to be mindful of the fact that Christian maturity does not happen automatically. Kids must learn to nurture their own spiritual growth. They can become so in love with Jesus that the lures of this world aren't so strong. Over time, their lives will benefit from years of intentionally making God-honoring choices.

Finally, kids (and grown-ups) need to know that bad habits must be replaced with good ones. Like Joseph, we have to run from the things that tempt us (Genesis 39:12–15). If we are serious about overcoming "the sin which doth so easily beset us" (Hebrews 12:1, KJV), we will stay far away from the things that can cause us to fall into its clutch.

The Blasphemy Challenge

Though only seventeen, high school senior Perry Frost has met more than her share of atheists and agnostics. For several years she has reached out to skeptical peers—including those who insult the Creator of the universe and post those videos online. "Some of the teens who seem most hostile toward God are the same ones who emphasize that they are rational thinkers," Perry says. "It seems odd [for a rational person] to want to insult Someone who supposedly isn't there."

Perry is referring specifically to the Blasphemy Challenge, an Internet campaign that encouraged people to post clips of themselves cursing God or renouncing the Holy Spirit's work in their lives. The more brazen examples invite the consequences of this rebellious act—including hell—should it turn out that God *does* exist.

The Blasphemy Challenge promoters admitted a desire to promote atheism among adolescents. One website offered teens recording a personal rejection of God a free DVD documentary belittling Christianity. During media interviews covering the story, project organizers were gleeful in their criticisms of Christianity and the attention (especially among young people) that it seemed to generate.

> No one can say, "Jesus is Lord," except by the Holy Spirit.
>
> —1 CORINTHIANS 12:3

Interestingly, the taunts of modern atheists are almost all directed at the God of the Bible. "The online atheists and teens who are into the Blasphemy Challenge are almost exclusively opposed to Christianity," says Perry. "There are almost no complaints against other faiths."

Whether Christian kids are on a playground or at a sporting event, taunts usually occur because someone's looking for a reaction. In this case, it's atheists. And young believers should give them one: a sincere, Christ-honoring witness full of appropriate expressions of love. The rise of spiritual skepticism and outright blasphemy is a vivid reminder that we must strive to be authentic as Christians. After listing the evidences of a Spirit-led life—love, joy, peace, patience, kindness, goodness, faithfulness, gentleness, and self-control—Galatians 5:23 says, "Against such things there is no law." We should answer the blasphemy of an unbelieving world with a tangible testimony of Christlikeness.

Part 4

Questions about the Bible

Is the Bible *Really* the Word of God?

The death of truth in our society has created a moral decay in which "every debate ends with the barroom question, 'Says who?' "[1]

—Francis J. Beckwith and Gregory Koukl,
Relativism: Feet Firmly Planted in Mid-Air

Have you ever seen the bumper sticker that reads "God said it. I believe it. That settles it!"? (It's usually available for about $3.99 at your local auto-parts store.)

Some Christians are satisfied with that explanation for the "Is the Bible really the Word of God?" question. "The preacher told me it was so," they confidently insist, "so it must be!" But to an unbelieving world or a questioning child, that's not enough.

Christianity comes under a lot of criticism for seemingly throwing logic and common sense out the window. Jesus was asked what the greatest commandment was. In His response He pointed out that we as humans are complex: We have a heart, a soul, and a mind.

"The most important [commandment]," answered Jesus, "is this: 'Hear, O Israel, the Lord our God, the Lord is one. Love the Lord your God with all your heart and with all your soul and with all your mind and with all your strength.' " (Mark 12:29–30)

Key Concepts

QUESTION RECAP: Is the Bible really the Word of God? Can we trust it? Did it really come from God? How can we know it's true?

1. There are hundreds of biblical manuscripts and thousands of fragments that have been found the world over, and many don't agree with each other. But that doesn't mean we can't figure out which manuscripts are trustworthy. Thanks to the Dead Sea Scrolls, we can be sure that we have reliable Old Testament manuscripts; they are especially trustworthy in the area of doctrine.

2. Scripture teaches that the Spirit of God worked through holy men so they wrote down exactly what God wanted written.

3. The more a person studies the Bible, the easier it is to comprehend that it's true. The Bible's words enlighten readers to a proper understanding of spiritual things.

HOPE-FILLED ANSWER: We have reliable Bible texts. The best way to test the words of the Bible is to live them. Christians who live out the Bible not only convince themselves that the principles and information are true, but they also show others that the Word of God is living and active because of the fruit that is developed in their lives.

• •

God wants our minds and our intellect involved in loving Him and worshipping Him. He doesn't want us to have blind faith—believing something just because someone else tells us to believe it without putting it to the test. Biblical faith, in contrast to blind faith, is based upon studying God's Word in a sincere quest to understand and believe it. Trust me. The Bible can bear any scrutiny we choose to give it and will stand up to any test. Second Timothy 2:15 says, "Be diligent to present yourself approved to God, a worker who does not need to be ashamed, rightly dividing the word of truth" (NKJV).

As we study (rightly divide) the Word of God and put it into practice, we'll have no further need for blind faith. Instead, we'll have biblical faith that has been proven to be true in real life.

Let's apply this quest for biblical faith to the Word of God, the Bible. Can we trust it? Did it really come from God? How can we know it's true?

Are Modern Bibles the Same as the Original?

If someone were to say, "The original biblical manuscripts have been lost, and all we have are copies of copies, and those have been translated and retranslated so many times, the Scriptures just aren't reliable," they'd be right. Sort of.

Well, a thousand years ago, they *might* have been right.

Unfortunately, we no longer have the original manuscripts that were written by the authors of the Bible. That means we can't make a 100 percent objective case for the accuracy of the Scriptures—we don't have that smoking gun. What we have are copies of copies, and within that process, mistakes can certainly be made no matter how careful the scribes were.

With these copies, however, we can make a strong rational, and trustworthy case that the Scriptures are accurate.

For a period in history, the Scriptures were in danger of possibly being corrupted depending on what political or social conditions existed in a particular region. If political or religious rulers were to get their hands on the first copy that came to their region, there's always the possibility that they could have had something changed, added, or omitted to fit their own beliefs or interests. In fact, history bears this out, since there are hundreds of manuscripts and thousands of fragments that have been found the world over, and many don't agree with each other.

> *If the Church has lost the Word, it is not simply ill, its throat is cut.*
> —John Calvin

Until the mid-twentieth century, the oldest surviving Old Testament manuscripts dated from around AD 900, hundreds of years after they were first written.

All of this would seem to confirm the inaccuracy of the Old Testament. But something happened in 1947 to change all that. Bedouin shepherds stumbled upon an ancient community called Qumran on the northwest shore of the Dead Sea and made the discovery of a lifetime.

There, a series of eleven caves were discovered that contained more than eight hundred separate scrolls that date from approximately 200 BC to AD 70. Fragments of every Old Testament book were discovered, except for the book of Esther. In some cases, multiple copies of individual books were found. It appears these scrolls were the library of a Jewish sect living in that area and were placed in the caves for safekeeping about AD 70.[2]

Scholars were anxious to learn whether these scrolls would show significant changes or errors compared to the Bible that had been handed down and copied through the generations. After intense study, they were astonished to find that they were nearly identical! In comparing the copies of the book of Isaiah, they found the following:

> The texts from Qumran proved to be word-for-word identical to
> our standard Hebrew Bible in more than 95 percent of the text.
> The 5 percent variation consisted primarily of obvious slips of
> the pen and spelling alterations. . . . Further, there were no major
> doctrinal differences between the accepted and Qumran texts. . . .
> This forcibly demonstrated the accuracy with which scribes copied
> sacred texts, and bolstered our confidence in the Bible's textual
> integrity.[3]

So there was a time when the Scriptures were getting more and more diluted, but in the modern era, scholars have used the texts from the Dead Sea Scrolls as well as gathered thousands of fragments and manuscripts to try to produce a manuscript that is as close as possible to the original text. The result is a text that is up to 99 percent accurate, according to some scholars.[4]

Are the Words in the Bible
Really the Words of God?

Even though scholars have been able to affirm the accuracy of later copies of Scripture based on ancient records, that still doesn't answer the question "Are the words in the Bible really the words of God?" For that, we have to look at Scripture as a starting point. Many people have argued over the years that the Bible was written by imperfect men, not God, and therefore it *must* contain errors. But why don't we let Scripture speak for itself on how it came into being?

The apostle Peter wrote, "No prophecy of Scripture came about by the prophet's own interpretation. For prophecy never had its origin in the will of man, but men spoke from God as they were carried along by the Holy Spirit" (2 Peter 1:20–21).

Notice that the text says, "Men spoke from God as they were carried along by the Holy Spirit." God was the Author, but He asked men to write down His words. There were approximately forty authors from diverse backgrounds who wrote the Scriptures over a period of fifteen hundred years in three languages. This accounts for differences in vocabularies and writing styles; however, even with all these authors, the essential message of Scripture is incredibly cohesive and unified.

In his second letter to Timothy, the apostle Paul echoed Peter's assertion that Scripture is divinely inspired: "All Scripture is God-breathed and is useful for teaching, rebuking, correcting and training in righteousness, so that the man [and woman] of God may be thoroughly equipped for every good work" (3:16–17).

Paul stated it even more emphatically to the church in Galatia: "I want you to know, brothers, that the gospel I preached is not something that man made up. I did not receive it from any man, nor was I taught it; rather, I received it by revelation from Jesus Christ" (Galatians 1:11–12).

We can see that Scripture itself clearly testifies that men didn't just sit down and write what they felt God might want them to say. Rather, the image we get from Scripture is that God chose these men to write down exactly what He wanted them to write, as the Holy Spirit worked through them.

Is the Bible True?

Critics argue that it's just circular reasoning to say that the Bible is true simply because it claims to be the inspired Word of God. That doesn't prove anything—and guess what? They're right! It is circular reasoning, and it isn't enough just to say, "Well, the Bible says it's God's Word, so it must be!" That doesn't win over skeptics, and again, God doesn't want blind faith!

It's clear from Scripture that God wants you to use the mind He gave you to discern His truth. And He wants you to test it through experience:

> Do not be conformed to this world, but be transformed by the re-
> newing of your mind, so that you may prove what the will of God is,
> that which is good and acceptable and perfect. (Romans 12:2, NASB)

If you are willing to renew your mind by thinking in a new way—looking at God's Word in a new way—you won't have to rely on the sinking sand of blind faith. You will live out the Scripture and, as a result, prove that God is real, that His Word is trustworthy, and that all the accomplishments of Jesus Christ are ours to enjoy.

Consider the verse "Prove all things, hold fast that which is good" (1 Thessalonians 5:21, KJV). The Greek word for "prove" is *dokimazo*, which means "to test . . . (to see whether a thing is genuine or not)."[5] As you read the Bible in a way that's intellectually honest and put its teachings into practice, you'll feel like the prophet Jeremiah, who said, "Your words were found, and I ate them, / And Your word was to me the joy and rejoicing of my heart" (Jeremiah 15:16, NKJV).

When the Word of God is put into practice, there's no denying its wisdom or source of power—God!

> My son, if you receive my words,
> And treasure my commands within you,
> So that you incline your ear to wisdom,
> And apply your heart to understanding;
> Yes, if you cry out for discernment,
> And lift up your voice for understanding,
> If you seek her as silver,
> And search for her as for hidden treasures;
> Then you will understand the fear of the LORD,
> And find the knowledge of God.
> For the LORD gives wisdom;
> From His mouth come knowledge and understanding.
> (Proverbs 2:1–6, NKJV)

Notice that the text says we must "seek [understanding] as silver" and search for it "as for hidden treasures." This goes way beyond the habit of most Christians, who pick up the Bible occasionally, casually flip it open, read a few verses, and then feel they've just done their spiritual duty. These words from Proverbs show that much effort must be put into our study of God's Word and our search for the truth.

This is learning about God that reaches your heart and soul. (Remember Mark 12:29–30?) You can't experience God solely through your mind. Investing your total person is required. Nothing less will yield true spiritual knowledge.

Consider the parable of the sower and the seed, as an example. Jesus taught about a farmer who scattered seeds on the ground. Some of the seeds fell on a path, some fell on stony places, some grew among weeds or thorn bushes, and some fell on good soil. Jesus explained that the seed represents the Word of God, and the different kinds of soil are the people who hear the Word:

Listen then to what the parable of the sower means: When anyone hears the message about the kingdom and does not understand it, the evil one comes and snatches away what was sown in his heart. This is the seed sown along the path. The one who received the seed that fell on rocky places is the man who hears the word and at once receives it with joy. But since he has no root, he lasts only a short time. When trouble or persecution comes because of the word, he quickly falls away. The one who received the seed that fell among the thorns is the man who hears the word, but the worries of this life and the deceitfulness of wealth choke it, making it unfruitful. But the one who received the seed that fell on good soil is the man who hears the word and understands it. He produces a crop, yielding a hundred, sixty or thirty times what was sown. (Matthew 13:18–23)

The Power of a Telescope

La Palma Island, part of the Canary Islands, is known for a world-famous telescope that is perched atop an extinct volcano. The *Gran Telescopio Canarias* is one of the most powerful telescopes in the world. It was commissioned by the king of Spain, Juan Carlos, and completed in 2009. Because its location is 7,870 feet above sea level, the telescope sits above cloud cover. This location provides astronomers with unobstructed sky views of the Northern Hemisphere and part of the Southern Hemisphere that are unrivaled anywhere else in the world.[6]

Just as that powerful instrument enables scientists to see things they wouldn't otherwise see, the Word of God is our "telescope," providing us with vision beyond our human abilities. The *Gran Telescopio Canarias* provides an unobstructed look at the heavens, but the Bible lifts our sights toward realities that we otherwise could not know. Above the fray of human perspective and changing opinions, the Bible presents the mind of God and eternal truth:

"The man who hears the word and understands it," Jesus said, "produces a crop." Unfortunately, it was only one out of the four different types of soil that actually went on to bear fruit. We and our children can be that good soil! When you're bearing fruit because you have a relationship with God, your life testifies that God's Word is true. No one can talk you out of it, because you see the results.

Is Thinking Overrated?

An objective belief in the truth of the Word is needed to gather the facts about Jesus and the gospel. But faith is more than an intellectual pursuit; it involves the heart as well. The apostle Paul gives us this warning:

> The word of God is living and active. Sharper than any double-edged sword, it penetrates even to dividing soul and spirit, joints and marrow; it judges the thoughts and attitudes of the heart. (Hebrews 4:12)
>
> The Greek word for "active" is *energeo*, which means "to be at work" or "to put forth power."[7] Our English words *energy* and *energetic* come from this word and related terms. When we believe the Word of God, we're filled with unmistakable energy and can often feel the power and excitement of eternal truths.
>
> Many people get excited at sports games or at concerts, or doing anything they're passionate about. But the Holy Bible provides a sacred energy from the inside out. When our thoughts and hearts embrace God's message, our finite minds connect with the infinite God through His Spirit. As we stay plugged in to the living energy of God's Word, no one will be able to convince us that it's not authentic, because we enjoy the fruits and benefits that come from trusting in the promises of God.

So I tell you this, and insist on it in the Lord, that you must no longer live as the Gentiles do, in the futility of their thinking. They are
darkened in their understanding and separated from the life of God
because of the ignorance that is in them due to the hardening of their
hearts. (Ephesians 4:17–18)

The Ephesian believers Paul was writing to in this letter were the
same believers he had previously described as "the faithful in Christ Jesus"
(Ephesians 1:1). The book of Ephesians contains many incredible and
glorious truths, and yet Paul also found it necessary to warn believers not
to become separated from the life of God.

When we make the wrong choices ("live as the Gentiles do") and
get our perspectives on life from the world ("the futility of their thinking") rather than from God's Word and through the Holy Spirit, we can
forget how spectacular life is: We have God as our Father! We have Jesus
Christ as our Lord, Redeemer, High Priest, and Forerunner to heaven!
We have been sealed by the Holy Spirit, "who is a deposit guaranteeing
our inheritance" (Ephesians 1:14)! We're looking forward to Jesus' return
so that we can live with Him forever in heaven! We're going to be given
new bodies that are designed for eternal life!

As our children see the fruit of the Spirit in our lives and learn to follow God for themselves, they will have a solid biblical faith—not a blind
faith—and will be "rooted and grounded in love" (Ephesians 3:17, NASB).

Are the Miracles in the Bible True?

*Miracles are like pimples, because
once you start looking for them
you find more than you ever
dreamed you'd see.*

—Lemony Snicket, *The Lump of Coal*

Have you ever thought about how many biblical miracles involve water?
The Israelites got drinking water from a rock. Jesus and Peter walked on
water. Elijah caused an iron ax head to float on water. He later soaked
a pile of firewood with water to demonstrate God's power, and the wet
mass exploded with fire. God, through Moses, caused the waters of the
Red Sea to part. And God caused Gideon's fleeces to become both wet
and dry.

Water-related miracles represent only a fraction of the biblical passages in which God directly intervened in the physical world. When it
comes to biblical accounts of the fantastical and miraculous, the stories
are definitely there. But are we to actually believe them? Should we accept
that the miracles of Scripture really happened?

My simple answer is yes.

I know, I know, many educated people would disagree—and so
might your children one day. So let's take a deeper look.

QUESTION RECAP: Did biblical miracles really happen? Or are they fairy tales like the tooth fairy and the Easter bunny?

1. God is all-powerful. When He performs a miracle He is simply being Himself. God miraculously delivered the Israelites from slavery in Egypt, demonstrating His love and provision for His people.

2. The Bible was recorded primarily by eyewitnesses. It is not an oral tradition in which the stories' details may have changed with each new storyteller. This strengthens the believability of the biblical accounts of history.

3. When you experience God working in your own life, it becomes easier to believe the miracles of the Bible. God rewards us for believing in Him. Abraham believed God and his faith was counted to him as righteousness.

HOPE-FILLED ANSWER: God has been and still is working in the lives of His children. We can trust the miracles in Scripture because we know that God is capable of such miracles and that they were recorded by eyewitnesses to the events. When we trust God, He blesses us and wants us to be witnesses to others of how God has changed our own lives.

• •

Stories or Lies?

Almost as many adults as children ask, "Are the miracles in the Bible true?"—and understandably so. Children ask the question out of curiosity, while adults ask because they're seeking the truth of not just the miracles but the Bible as a whole. After all, if the miracles in the Bible are true, then we have further evidence that the entire Bible is true, and if it is true, we would feel obligated to live according to all of its instructions and guidance.

When we truly believe that the miracles are true—that they are historically accurate and really happened—we understand that God is real and active not only in the past but also today in our lives.

While our kids are learning the miracles of the Bible—Noah and the flood; Daniel and the lions' den; Jesus walking on water, changing water into wine, healing the sick, rising from the dead after being in the grave for three days, and ascending to heaven, to name a few—many are also hearing that Santa Claus, the Easter bunny, and the tooth fairy are all real. The stories seem like harmless fun that amuse our kids and are downright endearing.

For children, though, it's difficult to tell the difference between the reality of Bible stories and the fantasy of the fairy tales. It doesn't help when we see many of the miracles "cute-ified" as they're morphed into cartoons and nursery rhymes. The danger comes when kids start to believe that Santa isn't real, and they also begin to question the authenticity of Bible stories and characters. When this happens, it can feel as if their belief system is crumbling.

At age seven, Jeffery heard from his friend that parents are the tooth fairy. He asked his mom, "Is the tooth fairy real?" She knew what his friend had told him and answered truthfully, "No. But it's a fun story, isn't it?" He agreed and walked away with a confused look on his face.

You could almost see his young brain following the line of reasoning: "If the tooth fairy isn't real, then how about the Easter bunny? And if the Easter bunny isn't real, then probably Santa isn't real either! And if Santa isn't real, how about Jesus? Mom told me about all of them, too! Was she lying about everything? What's real?"

As children mature they will become extremely defensive after feeling so gullible. "Fool me once," the old adage goes, "shame on you. Fool me twice, shame on me." We don't intend to lie to our children, but by telling them that these childhood fairy tales are true in one breath, and then telling them that Bible stories are also true in the next, we've set the stage for spiritual doubts.

We must be very careful to make sure our children understand that the stories of the Bible are true, and that they actually happened. Fairy tales are wonderful, so don't misinterpret what I'm saying here. I'm not telling you to burst your children's fantasy bubbles. But as they learn the truth about fantasy characters, help them see that fairy tales are wonderful, fun stories, but Jesus is real!

Miracles of the New Testament

The New Testament records at least three dozen miracles that Jesus performed. These miracles include demonstrations of His power over nature (Matthew 8:23–27), His power to heal (Matthew 9:20–22; Mark 1:40–45; Luke 13:10–17; John 4:46–53), His power to cast out demons (Luke 9:37–42), and His omniscience (John 1:48). Jesus demonstrated power over animals (Matthew 17:24–27) and even power over plants (Mark 11:20–26). He exerted power over evil spirits (Matthew 8:28–34), and He could even heal an entire group of people at once from an otherwise incurable disease (Luke 17:11–19). The miracles of Jesus blessed the recipients and no doubt amazed the witnesses present, but they were done to drive home one clear point: Jesus Christ is God.

Miracles continued to occur even after Jesus commissioned the disciples and sent them forth to preach the gospel. There were miracles of protection and deliverance (see Acts 5:19; 12:10; 16:26). There were miracles of healing, done by God *through* His apostles (Acts 3:7–11; 5:12–16; 14:8–18). There were miracles of resurrections from the dead (Acts 9:39–42; 20:8–12). There are also accounts of three individuals being miraculously *slain* by God (Acts 5:5–10; 12:21–23). There are examples of God miraculously revealing Himself to individuals (Acts 10:9–22), and miracles of deliverance from demons (Acts 16:18). The book of Acts even contains two accounts of God accomplishing His purposes by miraculously causing an earthquake (Acts 4:31; 16:26).

The lists above are not exhaustive, but the miracles mentioned remind us that God has (and does) act in history. The Lord reveals Himself, reminds us of His power and authority, and puts a supernatural stamp of approval on His messengers. The miracles also give us a glimpse of what things will be like in heaven, when the effects of sin and the fall are removed, and when there will be "no more death" (Revelation 21:4). In this sense, miracles serve to *restore*. God has reached into time and history, and has "turned back the clock," showing us how things were *before* the fall, and how things will be *after* His return. Miracles are like a glimpse of heaven here on earth—when "God himself will be with them" (Revelation 21:3).

The miracles described in the New Testament are not only *possible*, but we have every reason to believe they were *actual*.

Miracles in Egypt

As you may recall, we read about the exodus, as well as the plagues and the Passover, in chapter 8. But I'd like to revisit the story with a focus on the authenticity of the miracles. One of the most miraculous periods of biblical history took place when the Israelites were delivered from slavery in Egypt (Exodus 1—14). About four hundred years after Jacob (also known as Israel) lived, his descendants had become so numerous (about a million people) that the Egyptians were afraid of them and made them slaves (Exodus 1:7–14). The Israelites suffered in bondage for many years, until God called Moses to deliver them. God instructed Moses to confront Pharaoh and tell him, "Let my people go, so that they may worship me in the desert" (Exodus 7:16).

Pharaoh continually refused to allow his Hebrew slaves to go free, even for a short time to worship their God. After numerous warnings, God, through Moses and his brother, Aaron, told Pharaoh that Egypt would begin experiencing terrible plagues. Again, Pharaoh refused to let the Israelites go, so the plagues began. The Nile River turned to blood, and frogs invaded the land. There were gnats, flies, and pestilence. The Egyptians were covered in sores. There were hailstorms and swarms of locusts.

The last of the plagues would result in the death of the firstborn son in every household, unless the Jews followed God's command to kill, cook, and eat a spotless lamb and place its blood on the doorposts of their homes. The vast majority of Israelites followed the command, and the angel of death passed over them (instituting the Passover). But the Egyptians did not, and the prophesied consequence happened. The firstborn male in every Egyptian household died, including Pharaoh's own son.

Finally Pharaoh relented and let the Israelites go. But immediately after they departed, Pharaoh had a change of heart and decided to pursue them. The Israelites, showing their lack of faith, panicked and blamed Moses for leading them to their death. You can read their accusations in Exodus 14:10–12.

After all the miracles that the Israelites witnessed God doing on their behalf to get them out of Egypt, they still experienced a crisis of faith because of the life-and-death predicament they were in. They chose fear over faith—to believe what their senses were telling them instead of trusting in God's protection. As you read the account in Exodus, you can sense God's frustration with their unbelief in His power to deliver them:

> And the LORD said to Moses, "Why do you cry to Me? Tell the children of Israel to go forward. But lift up your rod, and stretch out your hand over the sea and divide it. And the children of Israel shall go on dry ground through the midst of the sea. And I indeed will harden the hearts of the Egyptians, and they shall follow them. So I will gain honor over Pharaoh and over all his army, his chariots, and his horsemen." (14:15–17, NKJV)

Moses acted on what the Lord asked him to do, and naturally (or *super*naturally) God fulfilled His promise.

Exodus 14 describes the amazing events in which God delivered the Israelites from the Egyptian armies. When Moses raised his hands over the sea, as the Lord instructed, God parted the waters. The Israelites were able to walk through the Red Sea on dry ground. As predicted, the Egyptians pursued them, but God was faithful to protect His children, and Pharaoh's army was drowned in the sea when the water came crashing down on them.

God's miraculous intervention through the plagues and the Red Sea deliverance forever changed the course of history for the Jewish people. They were finally going back to claim the Promised Land as their own country and to establish their nation and their faith in the God who had led them through difficult times. It was during this period that the Israelites were given God's laws to live by and base their faith upon. Because they had seen God's faithfulness in the exodus from Egypt, they knew that He could be trusted in the future.

> *[Childhood] was not merely a world full of miracles; it was a miraculous world.*
>
> —G. K. CHESTERTON,
> *The Autobiography of G. K. Chesterton*

Even today, millions of devout Jews, and even many Christians, celebrate Passover by holding seders (special dinners). This was actually the dinner that Jesus and His disciples were celebrating on the night before His death on the cross: the Lord's Supper. The Passover story is also a picture of a future story: Jesus, the perfect Lamb, who was sacrificed so that our sins might be "passed over." (See "Jesus, Our Passover Lamb" in chapter 8 for more about the Passover and seder celebrations.)

Oral Tradition Versus Eyewitness Testimony

Most religions have shared events orally that were handed down from generation to generation before they were written down. Most of the events of the Bible, however, were recorded in written form very soon after they happened. It is believed that the Passover story we just read about was recorded by Moses.

There is a huge difference between stories that are passed down verbally from generation to generation and those that are recorded by eyewitnesses. Even when great care is taken to pass them on intact, each time the story is retold, it could be changed slightly—exaggerated, confused, or even combined with other stories. In a court of law, this would be called hearsay.

But if the record of an event is written down by an eyewitness, we can go back to that document and read the same story to each succeeding generation. It's more trustworthy because the person who experienced the event is sharing it in a documented account.

The Effect of Belief

If people were to tell you that there is no such thing as the wind, you would tell them they were crazy. If they asked you to prove the wind is

Is It Rational to Believe That God Performs Miracles?

The question over biblical miracles could really be divided into *two* questions: We may question this or that miracle claim, but even before this is the consideration of whether God would or could do *any* miracles.

As C. S. Lewis pointed out in his book on the subject, if God exists, miracles are not only possible, but to be *expected*.[1] In reality, there is no *logical* reason to dismiss all claims of the miraculous. Could God reach into this finite world and perform a supernatural act? Of course. *He's God.* The more fundamental question is not "Are miracles possible?" but "Do we have good reason to accept this or that miracle claim?"

Why should we trust that the Bible's miracle accounts are trustworthy? Let me suggest three reasons:

1. The context warrants them. The Bible is the story of God working (against great odds, mind you, which included human wickedness and satanic opposition) to accomplish the following: raising up the nation of Israel, giving His

real, you'd want to take them outdoors and wait for a breeze so they could feel it for themselves. But if they insisted on staying indoors, in a room with no windows, and put the burden of proof on you to make them believe that the wind exists, you might be there for a long time with an unconvinced audience. However, you would still know in your heart that wind exists, even if you couldn't produce tangible proof on demand.

If you took those people to a place where a tornado had wreaked havoc, they still might have grounds to doubt and say that perhaps a bulldozer came through and uprooted the trees, turned cars upside down, and ripped the roofs and walls off the barns and houses. But if during that conversation, another tornado formed and they witnessed the power of

---

written Word, and sending His Son to initiate the plan of salvation for the world. Divine intervention seems appropriate for the enacting of these things.

2. The biblical miracles are not only possible but also *plausible*. God exists; therefore miracles are possible. The biblical miracles conform to what we know about God. In one way or another, they demonstrate His power, wisdom, and love. None of the biblical miracles undermine God's nature or logic. For example, we don't read of God miraculously making a "square circle" or a "one-ended stick." We do read of God performing miracles that have redemptive value and reveal His power and glory.

3. The biblical miracles are affirmed by credible eyewitnesses, and even by those *hostile* to what God was doing. For example, Pharaoh acknowledged and blamed Israel's God for the plagues that happened in Egypt. The resurrection of Jesus was also validated by ancient Christian, Jewish, Greek, and Roman sources.[2]

wind for themselves, they would suddenly become believers and would surely tell others about their experience. They would warn their children about the signs that precede a tornado, and they might even require that the next house they purchase have an emergency shelter.

The Gentiles (non-Jews) saw the hand of God protecting His children, the Jews, in miraculous ways. The Jewish people witnessed the miracles and therefore knew that God could be trusted with their future and that He deserved their worship and allegiance.

Did they forget? Absolutely—and God would remind them and rebuke them when they did. When they repented and returned to the Lord, He would again provide for them and protect them. The events that were recorded were for us to learn from and they were written down for our benefit—so that all the future generations could learn from them and walk in the awe and reverence of God (see 1 Corinthians 10).

Like the effects of a tornado—and please pardon the destructive nature of the example—the effects of God's interaction with people even today can be clearly seen. You may not be able to capture it in a bottle and open it at your command to show the doubters, but you have something better. Just as putting God's Word into practice convinces you that it's true, it can also convince you that the miracles recorded in Scripture are true, because you experience the hand of God in your own life. Once you have a firsthand relationship with the Holy Spirit, there is no denying it, and you can pass that trust and faith on to your children.

Some people have been drawn to Christianity because they saw that when they put the teachings of the Bible into practice, they could see the effect of God working in their lives. Likewise when they looked back on the times they acted against the sound wisdom of the Bible, they could trace the consequences to their disobedience—even if they didn't know they were disobeying God's will.

Julia Adelsperger had been addicted to crack cocaine and was homeless for many years. Her family, health, and entire life had been destroyed by her desire for one more fix. One day coming down from a high, she heard a friend of mine preaching about Jesus in a downtown park. God broke through her drugged haze, and she surrendered her life to Him that day. She left the park and entered a drug rehab program. Three years later, she is still clean and sober, has a job, and has a place to live. If you were to ask Julia if God can work miracles, you would get an earful! She knows that He works miracles because she experienced His work in her life. No one will ever convince her otherwise.

The Reward of Belief

Hebrews 11:6 states, "Without faith it is impossible to please God, because anyone who comes to him must believe that he exists and that he rewards those who earnestly seek him."

When we earnestly seek God, He will reward us! When you prove to yourself that God "exists and that he rewards those who earnestly seek him," you can experience more peace, less doubt, and less fear because your trust is securely anchored in Him. Such tangible proof is available if we will do our part. How do we do that? The beginning of the verse says that "without faith it is impossible to please God." Where does faith come from? Scripture tells us that "faith comes from hearing the message, and the message is heard through the word of Christ" (Romans 10:17).

Faith—which means trust and confidence—has to be based on something! God never asks for blind faith; rather, He tells us to pursue biblical faith, which is based on His promises *and* His character. Abraham is called the "father of all who believe" (Romans 4:11) because God asked him to sacrifice his son Isaac, and he obeyed (see Genesis 22). Abraham believed God's promise and reasoned that God was able to raise Isaac from the dead. Hebrews puts it this way:

> By faith Abraham, when God tested him, offered Isaac as a sacrifice. He who had received the promises was about to sacrifice his one and only son, even though God had said to him, "It is through Isaac that your offspring will be reckoned." Abraham reasoned that God could raise the dead, and figuratively speaking, he did receive Isaac back from death. (11:17–19)

Why Believe in the Resurrection Miracle?

Perhaps the most important miracle recorded in the Bible is Jesus' resurrection. If your child believes this one event happened, it will set a faith foundation to believe in the others. All of the following facts, taken together, make a great case for Christ's resurrection from the dead.[3]

- God's existence means that miracles are possible.
- Christ predicted that He would be killed and then rise from the dead (Matthew 16:21; 17:23; Mark 10:33–34; Luke 18:31–33).
- The total and near-instantaneous change in the disciples can be explained by Jesus' resurrection.
- Eyewitness testimonies affirm that Jesus rose from the dead (the women, Peter, Paul, James, Thomas).
- Multiple testimonies of those who saw the risen Christ (up to five hundred people) affirm the resurrection.
- Hostile testimonies also affirm that Jesus rose from the dead (Jewish, Greek, Roman).
- Christian teaching about Christ's divinity rapidly emerged following the resurrection.
- Believing Jews changed their worship from Saturday to Sunday.
- The courage of early Christians and their willingness to die for the gospel support the claims of Christ's resurrection.
- The explosion of Christianity throughout the world, in spite of opposition, offers evidence that the resurrection happened.
- The persistence of Christianity over two millennia to this day testifies to the resurrection.
- The power of the gospel to transform lives is one of the most powerful evidences of the resurrection.

Now that's faith! Knowing what God's will is for your life and following it. This wasn't the first time Abraham showed faith. In Genesis, God called Abram (whom he later renamed Abraham) to follow him:

> The Lord had said to Abram, "Leave your country, your people and
> your father's household and go to the land I will show you.
> I will make you into a great nation
>   and I will bless you;
> I will make your name great,
>   and you will be a blessing.
> I will bless those who bless you,
>   and whoever curses you I will curse;
> and all peoples on earth
>   will be blessed through you." (12:1–3)

First, did God make Abram into a great nation? Yes! Do we have proof of that? Yes! The people of the nation of Israel are his descendants. Think of the odds of that alone. How many people were on the face of the earth during Abraham's time? Thousands? Tens of thousands? Hundreds of thousands? More? How many have you heard of? How many have lasting legacies that can be traced back thousands of years? But we know about Abraham, and we know that he was made into a great nation!

Then God said that He would "bless those who bless you." When the nations of the world, including the United States, have stood alongside Israel, have they been blessed? Absolutely! Look at the last part of God's promise to Abraham again: "And all peoples on earth will be blessed through you."

Remember, this was written hundreds of years before Christ came—and Jesus was a direct descendant of Abraham. Did Jesus pay the price for the sins of the world? Perhaps the most frequently quoted verse in the world shows how all peoples on earth were blessed through Abraham: "For God so loved the world that he gave his one and only Son, that whoever believes in him shall not perish but have eternal life. For God did not send his Son into the world to condemn the world, but to save the world through him" (John 3:16–17).

Do we really need any further witnesses? I suppose we do. *We* are to be the witnesses of the resurrection: living proof that we serve a living Savior and that He is working in us "to will and to do for His good pleasure" (Philippians 2:13, NKJV). As we do so, and instruct our children to do so, we won't find any room for doubting. We'll have proven that the Word of God—and every miracle recorded in it—is just as true today as when it was written!

16

How Can I Understand the Bible?

Any fool can know.
The point is to understand.

—Attributed to Albert Einstein

Remember the phrase "Give someone the benefit of the doubt"? If you don't have all the facts about a certain circumstance (especially if the character or motives of someone are called into question), then you are to suspend judgment until you can make a more informed decision. The phrase was originally coined by doctors hundreds of years ago. When a doctor was unsure of a diagnosis, rather than give a patient the *wrong* medicine, which could potentially harm the person, the doctor would let the patient have "the benefit of [my] doubts."[1] Then, as now, it means to wait and gather all the facts before making a judgment.

I think that many children today ought to give the Bible the benefit of the doubt. Our culture teaches us to be skeptical of the Bible, often making assumptions about it. A college student once said to me, "Anything *that* old couldn't possibly still be relevant."

Do you know what one of the best antidotes to such attitudes and bias is? Reading the Bible. Yep, it's that simple. It's amazing how people's perception and perspective on Scripture can change in positive ways when they actually begin to read this much-critiqued book.

Key Concepts

QUESTION RECAP: How can I understand the Bible?

1. The best way to understand the Bible is to dive in and read it. Familiarity will grow into understanding with the Holy Spirit's help. Our faith needs the milk and meat of God's Word to be healthy and whole.

2. Sometimes people avoid reading the Bible because it convicts them. The Bible is a shining light that exposes the deeds of the heart, whether good or evil. If you or your kids don't read the Bible, sin is more likely to creep in and erode your faith.

3. There are six tools for helping you study the Bible: studying the context, considering the manners and customs of the time period, finding out if a word or phrase has been used elsewhere in Scripture, looking up Greek and Hebrew terms and their meanings, examining figures of speech, and paying attention to the details of the passage.

HOPE-FILLED ANSWER: The person who is seeking to truly understand God's Word will be aided by the Holy Spirit. When the words of the Bible impact your life, you'll find that it's a life-changing book filled with wisdom and power.

● ●

If the Bible is boring to you or to a child, it's likely due to these reasons:

You haven't read it.

You don't believe it.

You don't understand it.

Statistics show there's a Bible in nine out of ten American homes.[2] Nevertheless, the Bible seems foreign to many people, and its meaning seems elusive. Your child may be one of them. If so, try this experiment: Read one chapter of Proverbs together every day for a month. It will take only about ten minutes of your time, and in thirty days you'll have taken in the entire book. Then take three weeks and read through all twenty-one chapters of the gospel of John. Your child will be hooked. Chances are your child will *want* to read the Bible for a few moments every day, coming to increasingly deeper levels of appreciation for all it has to say.

If you read three chapters of Scripture each day and five on Sundays, you'll read through the entire Bible each year. I say all these things truly believing that if you and your child begin to read the Bible, keeping an open mind and giving Scripture "the benefit of the doubt," you'll find the content to be amazingly accessible.

What to Do If . . . You Haven't Read It

There's really not anything that a book or anything else can do to cure the first and second reasons why people find the Bible boring. And if you or your children choose not to read the Scriptures, not even the Lord will compel you or them to do so. In fact, if you want to remain unlearned, or ignorant, then so be it: "If anyone thinks himself to be a prophet or spiritual, let him acknowledge that the things which I write to you are the commandments of the Lord. But if anyone is ignorant, let him be ignorant" (1 Corinthians 14:37–38, NKJV).

In today's culture we are so squeezed for time that everything, other than reading and studying God's Word, takes precedence. But in God's eyes, learning His Word isn't optional—it's essential. I'll repeat this verse, because it's key to the Christian life: "Study to [show] thyself approved unto God, a workman that [need] not to be ashamed, rightly dividing the word of truth" (2 Timothy 2:15, KJV).

The word for "study" in Greek is *spoudazo*, which means "to exert one's self."[3] The context of this verse is why the word *study* was chosen in the *King James Version*, but grammatically the emphasis is on exertion of effort, and that effort is to be directed toward "rightly dividing the word of truth." The responsibility for Bible reading falls on each individual to make time in his or her schedule to do so. Parents need to help their kids schedule time for Bible reading.

Just as our physical bodies need healthy food to grow and function properly, our faith needs the milk and meat of God's Word to be healthy and whole (Hebrews 5:12).

What to Do If . . . You Don't Believe It

If you don't believe that the Bible is true, you must ask yourself why you don't believe. Is it because you have legitimate questions about its accuracy

Family Bible Study

Here are some guidelines for successful family Bible study.
- Establish a set time every day for family Bible time. For every family, it will be different. It may be around the breakfast or dinner table, first thing in the morning, or just before bedtime. The time of day isn't important. The key is consistency! Make this a priority. It will happen every day, and everyone will participate, from the youngest to the oldest (even if it's by phone). Read a brief passage, ask questions, and encourage your children to ask questions and share their thoughts. Find a way to apply the lesson to something that happened or will happen that day. Pray together. Family Bible time is nothing fancy, and doesn't require extensive planning. Lots of devotional books and websites are available to choose from, or just choose a book of the Bible to read through.
- Scripture memory is vital for children and adults. The psalmist said, "Your word I have hidden in my heart, / That I might not sin against You" (Psalm 119:11, NKJV).

or integrity? Do you doubt the miracles? Have you honestly examined the evidence that proves it to be true with an open mind? If you have legitimate doubts about the Bible, keep on asking, seeking, and knocking, and God will show you that His Word can be trusted (Matthew 7:7).

On the other hand, do you simply refuse to believe that the Bible is true because you don't like what it tells you about how to live your life? Some people I have spoken with have made a choice not to believe the Bible because it convicts them. The Bible describes such individuals:

> Everyone who does evil hates the light, and will not come into the light for fear that his deeds will be exposed. But whoever lives by the

How else can we defend the gospel, except with the "sword of the Spirit" (Ephesians 6:17)? Choose one verse for the entire family and have everyone learn it. Spend a week or more on each verse to make sure that it's thoroughly learned and not just in short-term memory. Even very young children can learn fragments of a verse. Review the verses from previous weeks in a game format to keep them fresh.

- Get involved with the Bible-teaching programs offered at your church. Bible Drill and Awana are both wonderful discipleship programs that emphasize Scripture memory and Bible-study skills. If your church doesn't have one of these programs, consider starting one or participating in one at a nearby church.
- Look for teachable moments when you can take a real-life situation and apply a Bible verse or story to it. If you catch your child telling a lie, remind him or her of the commandment that says, "You shall not bear false witness against your neighbor" (Deuteronomy 5:20, NKJV).

truth comes into the light, so that it may be seen plainly that what he has done has been done through God. (John 3:20–21)

The Bible is a shining light that exposes the deeds of the heart, whether good or evil. When the light exposes our deeds as evil, we can either run away from the light in fear or confess our sin and receive God's forgiveness. When the light exposes our deeds as good, others will see plainly that what we have done has been "done through God."

Fortunately, as a parent you can strongly influence your child's exposure to Scripture. By making sure your children hear the Bible being read at home, you can help ensure they will grow to love it.

Also, consider this: From the beginning, Satan has a proven track record of causing people to doubt the Word of God. If Satan can cause your children to doubt what God has said, he can keep them from finding that life-giving relationship with Jesus Christ that God intended for them to have. Don't let God's adversary plant seeds of doubt about the Word of God in your children's minds. They could sprout and grow into thorny vines that will choke out their faith and destroy the fruit that God longs to produce in their life.

What to Do If . . . You Don't Understand It

Let's revisit this popular verse that uses a sword as a metaphor for the Word of God: "For the word of God is living and active. Sharper than any double-edged sword, it penetrates even to dividing soul and spirit, joints and marrow; it judges the thoughts and attitudes of the heart" (Hebrews 4:12).

In the Greek, "living" is *zao* and "active" is *energeo*.[4] You'll probably remember from chapter 14 that we get the English words *energy* and *energetic* from the Greek root *energeo*. When we teach our children to set aside time for Bible study, and we model it ourselves, we will truly experience the joy, excitement, and *energeo* that comes from experiencing God through His Word.

Even though the Word of God is living energy, we need to be plugged into it by "rightly dividing" it so that it charges our faith. Unless we take the time to study the Bible and apply honest grammatical skills to it, we risk missing the power of God.

Important Foundational Bible-Study Skills

Please help your children develop the habit of studying the Word of God on their own. They shouldn't leave that habit up to their teacher or pastor or parent. Help them to be responsible for their own walk of faith; every Christian should learn at least a few foundational Bible study skills.

There are six considerations to follow when studying a passage of the Bible. These foundational skills are essential in "rightly dividing the word of truth" (2 Timothy 2:15, NKJV). Let's look at them one by one.

1. Study the context. Context is key when it comes to reading the Bible. The first step in understanding a Bible passage properly is to read it in context. Sometimes it's just the immediate context that will help us understand a verse, but at other times we need to have a broader perspective that spans several chapters or more. Keep in mind that each word in the Bible is part of a sentence, and each sentence is typically part of a larger paragraph or unit of thought that fits into a greater whole. We should set aside a significant amount of time in our lives, for our sake and the sake of our children, to simply read through the Bible on a regular basis, familiarizing ourselves with the people, places, and themes that run throughout the book.

2. Consider the manners and customs of the time period. Some verses don't make sense to us because we're encountering expressions that were unique to the time they were written or words used in the translation that have different meanings. Some recorded events seem odd to us, or we miss the point because we don't understand the culture. For example, Jesus used the following illustration to describe how the angels in heaven rejoice over one sinner who repents:

What woman, having ten silver coins, if she loses one coin, does not light a lamp, sweep the house, and search carefully until she finds it? And when she has found it, she calls her friends and neighbors together, saying, "Rejoice with me, for I have found the piece which I lost!" (Luke 15:8–9, NKJV)

We may think that silver is expensive, but a little research shows that this particular coin was worth only a few cents in Jesus' day—maybe up to a dollar in today's valuation. So why would the woman throw a party over this one missing coin? It turns out that in the Middle Eastern culture of Jesus' day, the ten silver coins were attached to a piece of jewelry that was part of a dowry (think engagement ring). If a modern woman lost a stone out of her engagement ring, we could understand how the stone might have much more sentimental value than intrinsic value. In the same way, Jesus used this illustration to help us understand that sinners who repent have sentimental value to God.

Dozens of books are available on manners and customs of the Bible that can help us understand Scripture from an ancient Middle Eastern mind-set. These books are great to read with your children because they communicate the intent of the passages and explain some verses that might otherwise be perplexing.[5]

3. Find out if a word or phrase has been used elsewhere in Scripture. Sometimes the verse context or the manners and customs of the day don't help us comprehend a particular word, phrase, or sentiment. For example, let's examine the well-known phrase "thorn in [the] flesh." In 2 Corinthians 12, the apostle Paul said that because of the "surpassingly great" revelations that were given to him, he had a "thorn in [the] flesh" to keep him humble. Here's the whole passage:

To keep me from becoming conceited because of these surpassingly great revelations, there was given me a thorn in my flesh, a messenger of Satan, to torment me. Three times I pleaded with the Lord to take it away from me. But he said to me, "My grace is sufficient for you, for my power is made perfect in weakness." Therefore I will boast all the more gladly about my weaknesses, so that Christ's power may rest on me. (Verses 7–9)

Much speculation has been devoted to what the thorn was, but we shouldn't use speculation as a tool to understand the Scriptures. This would be an instance where you would look for a reference to thorns elsewhere in the Bible to help you understand the meaning and context of the phrase in 2 Corinthians.

Another place in Scripture that mentions thorns is Numbers 33:55: "But if you do not drive out the inhabitants of the land, those you allow to remain will become barbs in your eyes and *thorns in your sides*. They will give you trouble in the land where you will live."

> The Bible will keep you from sin, or sin will keep you from the Bible.
>
> —D. L. MOODY

One more reference is in Judges 2: [An angel, speaking for the Lord, said to the Israelites,] "You have disobeyed me. Why have you done this? Now therefore I tell you that I will not drive [the Canaanites] out before you; they will be *thorns in your sides* and their gods will be a snare to you" (verses 2–3).

In the Old Testament, the land of Israel was a gift of God to the sons of Jacob. In each case the phrase "thorns in your sides" is referring to the unbelieving people who were in the land that Israel inhabited. God was warning the Israelites that if they didn't remove the Canaanites from the land, then they would cause problems and be thorns in the sides of God's people.

As you consider the phrase "thorn in [the] flesh" in 2 Corinthians, apply the Old Testament meaning to it. So Paul's thorn may have been a reference to unbelievers who were causing problems for him. In 2 Corinthians 11:23–27, Paul recounted the persecution he suffered at the hands of unbelievers. So we can see why Paul would have prayed for the Lord to remove his thorn. He was asking not to be persecuted. But we can also see why God said His grace would have to be sufficient for Paul. Jesus sent Christians out to the unbelieving people of the world—Jerusalem, Judea,

Samaria, and the "ends of the earth" (Acts 1:8)—therefore, He couldn't answer Paul's prayer to remove the thorn, because unbelievers were part of Paul's mission field!

To locate other places in Scripture where words or phrases have been referenced, you need to use a concordance, which is an alphabetical list of Bible words and corresponding verses, a Bible software program, or online resources.[6] Once you know how and where to check, you can begin a deeper exploration of the Bible with the available tools. Your children can be taught to use a concordance as easily as our generation was taught to use a dictionary or encyclopedia when we were young—and they'll probably figure out the computer programs before you do!

4. *Look up the Greek or Hebrew terms and their meanings.* When I invited Bible teacher Kay Arthur to speak at a conference, she joked to the crowd, "I know a little Greek. He runs a deli in our town." Another funny phrase is "It's all Greek to me," which means that something is so difficult to understand, it seems like a foreign language.

Jokes and hyperbole aside, students of the Bible benefit from knowing how to peel back the English and look at the word meanings of the original Bible languages. This doesn't have to be intimidating, and it isn't as difficult as you may think. Thanks to helpful books and easily accessible online study tools, every interested student can now unpack the rich meanings behind Greek (New Testament) or Hebrew (Old Testament) words. At first this may seem too deep for the average Christian family, but lexicons (basically, dictionaries of foreign languages) are readily available at Christian bookstores or as part of computer-based Bible-study programs. Most of these are easy to use, and like concordances, children can become accustomed to them as well.

The blessing is that most Greek and Hebrew resources include the English word that is being translated, so you don't actually have to learn to read or even pronounce the Greek or Hebrew word. Many lexicons also contain pronunciation guides that tell you how to articulate a particular Greek or Hebrew word.

Many pastors who quote a Greek word during the sermon don't really know how to read the Greek New Testament fluently; they just have the same resources that are available to you and me. Making use of these keys to studying Greek and Hebrew and teaching your children how to use them is important and is within your grasp and theirs.

5. *Examining figures of speech.* There are hundreds of figures of speech in the Bible. God uses figures of speech to illustrate His Word. When you consider that He chose to reveal Himself to us through a book, it makes sense that He would have to be able to impart as much figurative language as possible. Each figure of speech lends itself to emphasizing a different point.

There aren't as many reference books on biblical figures of speech as, say, concordances, lexicons, or books on manners and customs, but there are some, and they would be great resources to add to your personal library. They're fun to use with children because your kids will likely enjoy learning about the different figures of speech as well as recognizing patterns in Scripture that deepen their understanding, which they can share with others.

Because there is so little teaching on biblical figures of speech, many have been omitted from English translations. One example is Isaiah 26:3: "You will keep him in perfect peace / Whose mind is stayed on You / because he trusts in You" (NKJV). In the Hebrew language, the phrase "perfect peace" is actually "shalom, shalom"—it's simply the one word repeated twice for emphasis. However, the translators likely felt it would be confusing for readers if the verse said, "You will keep him in *peace, peace* / Whose mind is stayed on You." Translators probably understood that the Holy Spirit was emphasizing the word *peace* and therefore they "interpreted" it for you as "*perfect* peace," but a more accurate handling of the text would be "You will keep him in peace—*peace!*—whose mind is stayed on You, because he trusts in You!" Hopefully you can see how the repetition of the word *peace* almost sounds as if it's shouting from the pages of Scripture!

This aspect of studying the Word of God takes some effort, but it can be like a treasure hunt: first, learning the different figures of speech, and second, seeing what they're emphasizing.

Sometimes a figure of speech can actually be the omission of a word, where you have to fill in the blank, so to speak. For instance, if you see your son about to do something wrong—take a cookie, push his little brother, climb up a piece of furniture—you might look at him sternly, point your finger at him, and say (in your firm parenting voice), "DON'T!" You don't even have to add the action; your son just understands that "DON'T!" means "Don't do what you're about to do! It's wrong, and there are going to be consequences if you do!" All that information is communicated by one word through the figure-of-speech omission, yet it communicates beautifully.

6. *Pay attention to the details.* Details, details, details! As we learn to pay attention to the details of God's Word (and teach our children to do the same) and recognize that every word in the Bible is important, we also need to be aware of biblical words that affect the flow of thought. Words like *but, however, first of all, therefore, if, when, then, might,* and *may* are examples of words that can indicate preconditions or a change of direction in a Scripture passage. We also need to keep in mind that chapter divisions were added long after the books of the Bible were written, as were the topical section headings some Bibles include.

The writer of Hebrews began chapter 12 with the word *therefore:* "Therefore, since we are surrounded by such a great cloud of witnesses, let us throw off everything that hinders and the sin that so easily entangles, and let us run with perseverance the race marked out for us" (verse 1). Since the word *therefore* is a conjunction that joins two thoughts, we need to find out what the thought connection is.

Hebrews 11 is a passage that some refer to as the Faith Hall of Fame. It recalls the stories of people like Noah, Abraham, Sarah, Joseph, Moses, Rahab, and many others who were known for their great faith. These faithful are the "witnesses" referred to in Hebrews 12:1. We are to look to their example for our inspiration as we run our own race of faith. Without following this flow, we might miss that connection and a deeper appreciation of the intricacies of God's Word.

As an old country preacher once told me, "When you see a *therefore,* find out what it's there for!"

The Holy Spirit's Role

The role of the Holy Spirit is vital to understanding the Word of God. Two Bible passages we've already looked at explain this well. The first is John 16:12–13: "When he, the Spirit of truth, comes, he will guide you into all truth." And the second is like it: "The Counselor, the Holy Spirit, whom the Father will send in my [Jesus'] name, will teach you all things and will remind you of everything I have said to you" (John 14:25–26).

The verses in John 16 show us that the apostles would need the Spirit of truth to help them understand things that they couldn't understand before the Holy Spirit was sent. In John 14, we see that the Holy Spirit will "teach [us] all things," as well as remind us what Jesus said. The Spirit doesn't replace the need for us to study God's Word, but He enlightens us, gives us wisdom, and provides a depth of perspective that is truly out of this world. Many times God will call a verse or passage to our remembrance through His Spirit within us. As we read, we need to apply sound, consistent grammatical skills but also allow for God to lead us, guide us, and inspire us in the journey.

We also need to pray that the Holy Spirit will guide us and our children. First Corinthians 2:14 says, "The man without the Spirit does not accept the things that come from the Spirit of God, for they are foolishness to him, and he cannot understand them, because they are spiritually discerned." Only by God's power can we rightly understand the Scriptures.

Transformed by the Word

There are other skills we can learn to help us study the Bible, but hopefully this chapter has increased your appreciation for the Word of God as an exciting, powerful, life-changing book filled with wisdom and power! As you and your family learn the truths of Scripture and endeavor to live them out during the course of your everyday lives, you'll experience a gradual transformation. Incrementally, God uses His Word to guide us away from being "religious" people toward being sons or daughters of the Most High God! His instruction book for life will begin to read more like a love letter to you, and every day you can wake up excited that God is your Father, that Jesus Christ is your Big Brother, and that the Holy Spirit is ready to guide your every step.

When you read the Bible, pay attention to the details, and make sure you're absorbing what you read. If you find yourself glossing over what you're reading, reread it! Better to read a few verses and deeply understand and contemplate them, comparing them in your mind with other verses and related themes, than to read for half an hour and not really understand what you're reading. Studying God's Word is an acquired but necessary discipline that we should be teaching our children throughout their lifetimes.

This Guy at School Says the Bible Contradicts Itself— Is That True?

As biblical scholarship increases and our knowledge of language, text, and context increases, the problem of (alleged) discrepancy becomes smaller and smaller. There is less reason today to believe that the Bible is full of contradictions than at any time in the history of the church. Prejudice and critical philosophical theories, however, die a very slow and hard death.

—R. C. Sproul, *Reason to Believe*

Guess what? There isn't merely *one* website that tries to get the Bible in "checkmate"; there are *dozens*. There are also hundreds of personal sites run by bloggers who post lengthy articles that criticize the Bible. Such skeptic sites range from the insightful, respectful, and thought provoking to lengthy rants against God and essays peppered with profanity and fallacious arguments.

But your kids rightfully want to know if there are sites that contain a smoking gun, a site that has conclusive proof that disproves the Bible. The answer is no. Have bloggers unearthed a new discovery that exposes

Key Concepts

QUESTION RECAP: This guy at school says the Bible contradicts itself. Is that true? Are there errors in the Bible? How can I know that a really old book can be trusted? And what about websites that list reasons the Bible has flaws?

1. There are hundreds of websites that disparage the Bible. But the sites' arguments and so-called evidence of contradictions are nothing new.
2. Unbelievers who try to persuade Christians that the Bible is untrustworthy are darkened in their understanding.
3. Using study tools, the apparent contradictions in the biblical texts can be reconciled. When interpreting Scripture, scholars consider the intended audience, the context, the purpose of the text, and whether the text is complementary or contradictory.

HOPE-FILLED ANSWER: Your children may be confused if they are presented with a long list of difficult passages in the Bible. However, you can assure them that after careful study, the Bible will prove itself to be reliable.

• •

the Bible as inherently contradictory? Again, no. In fact, many of the sites simply cut and paste lists and recirculate arguments gleaned from other sites. After a decade of reading skeptic literature in an effort to honestly hear the concerns of those with doubts, I have yet to come across a new, truly original issue that hasn't already been clearly answered and resolved. As a matter of fact, most of the challenging questions over verses of Scripture were raised—and substantively responded to—within the first few centuries of Christianity.[1] As Solomon said, "There is nothing new under the sun" (Ecclesiastes 1:9).

Until your kids have studied the Bible for themselves and proven its integrity, they might harbor a silent fear that "maybe the world is right; maybe the Bible *isn't* the Word of God." But if they've become students of the Scriptures, have applied God's Word to their lives, and are seeing the fruit of His work within them, it would likely be difficult for your children to lose confidence in the Bible. That fact, however, doesn't keep many unbelievers from trying to influence Christian kids!

Satan, God's adversary and ours, has been fine-tuning his crafty arguments against the Bible for thousands of years. In the minds of some, he makes a compelling case. I'm often in dialogue with people who, having rejected the authority of the Bible, have become "enlightened" and freed from the "bondage" of religion. At one time, overt attacks on Scripture were largely limited to the more liberal classrooms of some colleges. Increasingly, however, it seems that mainstream university professors are intentionally trying to destroy the faith of our young adults by making arguments against the Bible.

Satan has been seeking to plant seeds of doubt in our children's hearts at earlier and earlier ages. As I mentioned in chapter 15, when fairy tales of Santa, the Easter bunny, the tooth fairy, and other imaginative characters prove to contradict reality, the questioning minds of some children are ready to believe that God's Word is also untrue.

At other times, Satan's tactic is to tear down the Scriptures themselves—the very Word that reveals Jesus to us. If the devil can cause you or your children to doubt the Source of information that reveals Jesus Christ, then he can keep your children from knowing God fully.

The Dark Conspiracy

Is there a conspiracy of evil that is seeking to prevent humanity (i.e., your kids) from learning the truth? I believe there is, because the Bible confirms it (2 Corinthians 4:4).

The antidote is reading more Scripture. The Word of God tells us who we are in Christ and what He accomplished for us on the cross. It shows us that we have access to the same power that raised Jesus from

Exe-what-sis?

Your kids can benefit from knowing the difference between *exegesis* and *eisegesis*. (Oh no! There goes Alex using big words!) Let's break down these terms to see their importance.

Exegesis, or exegetical study, is letting the Bible text speak for itself. It involves careful reading and study of the original language (Hebrew or Greek). The word *exegesis* literally means "to lead out of."[2] Read a passage of Scripture and study what it means in the original language. What truth does it teach? What did the original author intend to say? How does this apply to my Christian walk?

The opposite approach to Scripture is *eisegesis*, which is interpreting the verse based on your own opinion. The word *eisegesis* literally means "to lead into."[3] The danger of this method is when we inject our own ideas and interpretations into the text, making it mean whatever we want.

Topical Bible studies are prone to using *eisegesis*. They tend to propose an idea and then find a Bible verse to support it. The verse offers valid proof for the idea or it may not. Careful *exegesis* of the text will show if it supports your idea, or if it has been pulled out of context to force a particular conclusion.

Concordances, lexicons, and commentaries should be regularly employed by older children. If they can use a dictionary or encyclopedia at school, they can use these resources.

Take advantage of your children's fascination with technology and make the software programs we've already talked about available to them. Your kids are probably computer savvy enough that they'll figure out the programs quickly. If they have a smartphone, e-reader, or other device that has the capability to download applications, put the Bible on it. Reading on your iPod or Kindle is so much cooler than reading a book! The free app available from *YouVersion.com* has multiple translations of the Bible and several versions of reading plans.

the dead—power that can change the way we live. Scripture promises that believers will ultimately spend eternity with Jesus in paradise, and it warns of the dreadful ending that awaits the archenemy of our souls, Satan (and those who believe his lies). Our Enemy wants to erase all nuggets of revelatory truth from our minds, thus keeping us in the dark:

> If our gospel is veiled, it is veiled to those who are perishing. The god of this age has blinded the minds of unbelievers, so that they cannot see the light of the gospel of the glory of Christ, who is the image of God. For we do not preach ourselves, but Jesus Christ as Lord, and ourselves as your servants for Jesus' sake. For God, who said, "Let light shine out of darkness," made his light shine in our hearts to give us the light of the knowledge of the glory of God in the face of Christ. (2 Corinthians 4:3–6)

The attack on the gospel often goes back to Genesis. The first book of the Bible has suffered more abuse and criticism than perhaps any other. Even many Christians (and some Christian colleges) have now embraced a Darwinian view of life's origin. Children are taught that fossils and archaeological finds are (supposedly) millions of years old. Their faith is assaulted, and questions about the Bible arise. But before tossing aside the Word of God, we need to remember several things.

First, there was a time when the Bible was mocked because it spoke of great beasts that didn't fit the description of anything people had ever seen. God spoke of one such beast, the Leviathan, in Job 41. I don't know exactly what type of beast this is talking about, but it sure sounds a lot more like a dinosaur than anything I've ever seen on a nature program.

Before the discovery of fossils, many people were ridiculed for believing the Bible's description of creatures that no one could prove ever existed. Since many fossils of now-extinct species have been discovered, critics say that the Bible doesn't contain *enough* information about these creatures. Do you see how the "scientific" community flip-flopped? First scientists said that the Bible talks about creatures that never existed, and then they said that it doesn't talk enough about them!

The second thing to remember is that the Bible isn't meant to be a textbook on biology. It's a love story about God and His Son rescuing lost humanity, reconciling the world to God. But when it comes to Darwinian evolution, the generally accepted theories fall woefully short. According to "science," the earth was once molten rock that cooled and solidified. The oceans were formed by water that evaporated, condensed, and then fell to the earth. Basically you end up with sterile rock and distilled water. These aren't the conditions from which you can achieve life, and certainly not an abundance of life that covers an entire planet with millions (if not billions) of different animals, plants, insects, mammals, and so forth.

If evolution were true, the fossil record should show an increase in the number of species, right? If there were none to begin with and everything was "evolving," then there would be more and more and more. However, what does the record show? A study of the fossils shows that there was actually more diversity farther back in time. As we move forward in time, we discover that many species have gone extinct. That tells us that everything was created and then gradually started to decay. So what does the Bible say about this? "The creation itself will be liberated from its bondage to decay" (Romans 8:21).

A third thing to remember is that many of the fossil records supposedly proving the theory of evolution, such as so-called missing links, have been intentionally corrupted, misrepresented, or simply made up.[4] Entire "generations" of "prehistoric" man are often based on a tiny fragment of a bone. Other times, scientists have combined bones found hundreds of miles apart and put them together to form a "type" of prehistoric human.

The scientific community is aware of many of these fallacies and fabrications but allows the myths to continue because the alternative would mean admitting that evolution theory has flaws. If evolution is debunked, then the door opens to hypothesizing about a higher power behind creation, and that would lead to belief in God. Ironically, numerous scientists started as atheists or agnostics and have come to believe in God. As they've studied the intricacies of biology, they've recognized the incalculable odds of anything as complex as living creatures coming into existence randomly.

It's not within the scope of this book to compare creation and evolution in depth. But I mention the attacks on the book of Genesis merely to point out that when it comes to the integrity of Scriptures, Genesis is where the attack so often begins. After nearly a century and a half of evolutionary teaching, mistrust of God's Word is ingrained in adults, teens, and even children. If your children can't trust the words in Genesis, then their trust in the entire biblical account is in jeopardy.

The book of Genesis, written by Moses, provides the foundational framework for many important Christian doctrines. We cannot fully understand the gospel unless we understand the fall of humankind and sin entering the world. If we discredit the fall of humankind, we discredit the cross. So in the words of Jesus, "If you believed Moses, you would believe me, for he wrote about me" (John 5:46).

> God has spoken, and He has not stuttered. The God of truth has given us the Word of Truth, and it does not contain any untruth in it.
> —NORMAN L. GEISLER, *When Critics Ask*

Our Lord pointed out that in the Old Testament, Moses recorded how the world got into the mess it's in and prophetically foretold how God planned to rescue humanity and bring us into a lasting relationship with Himself. So if humans didn't fall in the garden of Eden, then why did Jesus really have to die?

Dealing with Apparent Contradictions

A quick search of the Internet will bring up dozens of lists of verses that the writers are convinced contradict each other. A casual reading of them may cause you and your children to wonder as well.

To Whom and When Was It Written?

In the previous chapter we described many of the keys to "rightly dividing the word of truth" (2 Timothy 2:15, NKJV). If these study techniques are applied correctly, most of the hard-to-understand, seemingly contradictory verses can be read so that they fit together.

One of the easiest solutions to many seeming conflicts within Scripture is understanding to whom and when the text was written.

Throughout Scripture we see that there are basically three audiences God addresses: Jews, Greeks or Gentiles[5] (non-Jews), and—after the resurrection of Christ—the Christian church or body of Christ (Jews and Gentiles who have been saved). The apostle Paul referred to all three in 1 Corinthians 10:32: "Do not cause anyone to stumble, whether Jews, Greeks [Gentiles] or the church of God."

On the surface, the following passages would seem to be contradictory statements, and if you were just flipping through the Bible, you might conclude that there's an error:

Passage A: "You are free to eat from any tree in the garden" (Genesis 2:16).

Passage B: "God blessed Noah and his sons, saying to them, "Be fruitful and increase in number and fill the earth. . . . *Everything that lives and moves will be food for you.* Just as I gave you the green plants, I now give you everything" (Genesis 9:1, 3).

Passage C: "*Do not eat any of the fat of cattle, sheep or goats.* The fat of an animal found dead or torn by wild animals may be used for any other purpose, but you must not eat it. Anyone who eats the fat of an animal from which an offering by fire may be made to the LORD must be cut off from his people. And wherever you live, you must not eat the blood of any bird or animal. If anyone eats blood, that person must be cut off from his people" (Leviticus 7:23–27).

Passage D: "I am fully convinced that no food is unclean in itself" (Romans 14:14).

All of these verses, read independently of their context as they are presented here, give the appearance of contradiction. Can we eat meat or not? However, when we dig a little deeper and look at "to whom" these scriptures were written and when, we can unlock the keys to understanding them.

In Passage A, whom was God telling to freely eat of any tree? Adam and Eve. Humans weren't allowed to eat the meat of animals until after Noah and the flood as seen in Passage B.

Later on, God set apart Abraham, Isaac, and Jacob and their descendants (the Jews) to be His chosen people. At this time He gave them new dietary laws. Passage C is a small portion of those laws. Look at the preceding words to better understand to whom it's written: "*The Lord said to Moses, 'Say to the Israelites:* "Do not eat any of the fat of cattle, sheep or goats"'" (Leviticus 7:22–23).

So we see that God, through Moses, was instructing the Israelites regarding these new dietary restrictions that were a part of the law.

After the resurrection of Jesus, Peter was told in a vision that all food was now acceptable for believers to eat (Acts 10:9–33). So in Passage D we hear

> *If we are perplexed by any apparent contradiction in Scripture, it is not allowable to say, the author of this book is mistaken; but either the manuscript is faulty, or the translation is wrong, or you have not understood.*
>
> —SAINT AUGUSTINE, "Reply to Faustus the Manichaean"

Paul's heart affirming that all food is now acceptable to eat. Because Jesus had fulfilled the law (Matthew 5:17), the church was no longer obligated to follow its dietary restrictions.

So these verses are not contradictory after all. They were simply addressing different audiences at different times in the history of the Bible. By using good study techniques, we revealed this truth.

Remember, Context Is King

Another way in which detractors of the Bible find apparent contradictions is to pull passages completely out of their context. Consider these passages: "Not everyone who says to me, 'Lord, Lord,' will enter the kingdom of heaven" (Matthew 7:21), and "Everyone who calls on the name of the Lord will be saved" (Acts 2:21).

So which is it? Jesus said that not everyone who says "Lord, Lord" is going to be saved, but Peter said that everyone who calls on the name of the Lord will be saved. If you read each passage in its context, you'll understand that there is no contradiction.

Peter was preaching to a large crowd in Jerusalem, presenting the gospel and inviting people to put their faith completely in Jesus Christ. This was the New Testament equivalent of an evangelistic crusade. He quoted the prophet Joel to make a point that salvation is possible for everyone who calls on the name of Jesus. He then went on to persuade three thousand people to "repent and be baptized" (Acts 2:38, 41).

In the immediate context of Matthew 7:21, Jesus was preaching on how to recognize false prophets, people who claimed to be saved but weren't. He said these people are like wolves in sheep's clothing, and that we can recognize them by the fruit they produce. This led to the statement "Not everyone who says to me, 'Lord, Lord,' will enter the kingdom of heaven." Notice that Jesus didn't say that everyone *can't* be saved; He said that not everyone *will* be saved.

A careful and honest reading of these and similar passages in their context eliminates the contradiction.

Complementary or Contradictory?

When there is a car wreck, there are usually multiple witnesses. People in other cars behind the wreck, in front of the wreck, or across the road; pedestrians on the street; maybe even traffic cameras all have their unique perspectives on what happened. As police interview each witness, a complete and accurate picture emerges of what actually happened. Likewise, if one story doesn't mesh with all the others, the police know that someone is lying!

The first four books of the New Testament—Matthew, Mark, Luke, and John—are called the Gospels. They record Jesus' earthly life and ministry. Many times two or more of the writers tell the same event from their own unique perspectives. This is true of the story of the demon-possessed man from the Gadarenes in Matthew 8, Mark 5, and Luke 8.

Skeptics will point out the seeming contradictions in these three passages:

> When [Jesus] arrived at the other side in the region of the Gadarenes, *two demon-possessed men* coming from the tombs met him. They were so violent that no one could pass that way. (Matthew 8:28)

> [Jesus and the disciples] went across the lake to the region of the Gerasenes. When Jesus got out of the boat, *a man with an evil spirit* came from the tombs to meet him. (Mark 5:1–2)

> [Jesus and the disciples] sailed to the region of the Gerasenes, which is across the lake from Galilee. When Jesus stepped ashore, he was met by *a demon-possessed man* from the town. For a long time this man had not worn clothes or lived in a house, but had lived in the tombs. (Luke 8:26–27)

The account in Matthew states that there were two men, while the passages in Mark and Luke mention only one man. Some might say that's a contradiction. A contradiction is when one statement makes the other impossible. In this case, Mark's and Luke's references to the one man doesn't mean that there weren't two men present. They just mentioned the one. Could it be that they mentioned only the one man because he was more vocal than the other man? If they had said "only one demon-possessed man," there would be a contradiction. The omission or inclusion of a detail doesn't constitute a contradiction.

The other alleged contradiction in these passages is the name of the region. Matthew called it the region of the *Gadarenes*, while Mark and Luke called it the region of the Gerasenes. This difference could be a simple scribal error. Commentaries mention several other spellings in other manuscripts that are all similar. This isn't a detail that threatens any doctrine, so to make an issue of it is really nitpicking. Recall from an earlier chapter that Christians believe the Word of God is without error in the original manuscripts, but there is a small percentage of errors in *variants*, such as words that are misspelled.

Most commentaries support another possibility: that there was a town called Gerasa, which was part of the city of Gadara. So the people of Gerasa could be called Gerasenes (Mark and Luke) or Gadarenes (Matthew), and both would be correct names for them. It would be the same as the relationship of Manhattan to New York City: Manhattan is a borough within the city of New York. The people of Manhattan may be referred to as Manhattanites or New Yorkers. Both would be correct.

So instead of contradicting each other, these accounts complement each other. When you read all three passages, you get a complete story that you might not see in each individual account.

Contradictions in the Bible? Bring 'Em On!

So which are you going to teach your children to trust: God's Word, which has been shown in these chapters to be trustworthy and without error, or someone with tainted motives who claims that the Bible is full of contradictions? Remember that those who are trying to cast doubt upon the Word of God are seeking to keep your children from coming to know Him.

We've shown you a few of the supposed contradictions in the Bible and how to refute them. It all comes down to accurate and complete study of the Word. Some may say that it takes a lot of work to be students of Scripture and defend the integrity of the Word of God. That's actually true, but it's a worthy endeavor that we're commanded to pursue.

Part 5

Questions about the Church

Why Are Christians Such Hypocrites?

In first century Palestine, Christianity was a community of believers. Then it moved to Greece and became a philosophy. Then it moved to Rome and became an institution. Then it moved to Europe and became a culture. Then it moved to America and became a business.

—Attributed to Sam Pascoe, Anglican priest

Endeavoring to impress upon a class of boys the importance of living the Christian life, a rather pompous-looking church deacon asked, "Why do people call me a Christian?" After a moment's pause, one youngster said, "Maybe it's because they don't know you."

Ever met people like that? They claim to be Christians, but don't act the way Christians should act. Everyone knows that churches are full of such hypocrites. Or are they?

Let's begin this conversation by setting straight the myth that's behind our question for this chapter: Not *all* Christians are hypocrites. Really. But hypocrisy within the church is a problem. It's all the more dangerous because hypocrisy is an excuse that many unbelievers use to reject the church and Jesus Christ.

Key Concepts

QUESTION RECAP: Why are Christians hypocrites? How can I believe in a faith that its own believers don't follow?

1. Not all Christians are hypocrites.
2. Some people go to church and claim to follow Christ, but aren't true believers. Like the Pharisees in Jesus' day, these people like religion for what it can do for them. These people need to repent and truly follow Christ.
3. Believers may appear to be hypocrites because none of us are perfect in our spiritual walk. We need to examine ourselves and seek to rely even more on the Holy Spirit in order to live in a way that honors Jesus.
4. A person should not evaluate Christianity solely on the basis of the bad behavior of a few members. Christianity should be judged on the life of Jesus and the teachings of the Bible.

HOPE-FILLED ANSWER: There are those who attend church and appear religious who are truly hypocrites. These people do not have a true relationship with Christ. For true believers, hypocritical actions can be observed because of our sinful nature that is still within us. We need to encourage one another to walk in the Spirit so that the fruit of the Spirit will be evident in our lives.

• •

There are actually two types of hypocrisy that we're going to look at. First, we'll define each type, and then we'll show how we can help our children avoid using the hypocrisy trap as an excuse to abandon Christianity.

Hypocrisy Defined

The first way the term *hypocrisy* is defined—and the sense that is more frequently used in the Bible—is "to be an actor" or "to wear a mask." It speaks more of outward actions that don't match the beliefs of the heart. This would describe people who claim to follow God, but in their heart of hearts, they don't. It's all a show. In the context of this question, it would be someone who claims to be a Christian and may even be active in the church but isn't truly born again.

A second definition of hypocrisy is "to say one thing and do another" or "to profess to be one thing but to actually be something else." This speaks to a person's words being inconsistent with his or her actions. It would be a Christian who does things that don't honor Christ. If we're honest, we'll admit that we all fall into this category all too often.

The two definitions are similar in that there is a clear and deliberate misrepresentation of the true underlying heart and motives. The only example the world sees of Jesus is His people within His church. We must strive to present a true and accurate representation of what He has called us to be. And when we don't, we must apologize, ask for forgiveness, make amends, and stop sinning.

We're not going to examine all the possible ways someone can be a hypocrite. After all, you can't change the whole church. You can, however, allow God to change you, and this change can influence your children. So we'll look at what Scripture says a Christian is supposed to be and evaluate our lives according to that standard. We can then help our children see that same standard and test their own lives.

The "I'm Just Pretending" Hypocrite

When first launched in 1936, the *Queen Mary* was the largest ship to cross the oceans. Through three decades and a world war, she served until she was retired. In 1967 she was anchored as a floating hotel and museum in Long Beach, California.

During renovations in 1994, the ocean liner's smokestacks were removed for restoration, and all three collapsed. The steel plate from which the stacks had been formed had rusted and the only thing left of them was 110 coats of paint.[1]

It seems like the people in control at church are not necessarily the ones who love the Lord the most, but those who give the most money. I know that God doesn't need our money. Why do Christians have to tithe, when some do it for the wrong motives?

—A. J., age fifteen

In Matthew 23, Jesus addressed the religious leaders of His time, whose "insides" didn't match their outward veneer. The leaders were just pretending to have faith. Seven times He said "Woe" to them (which means "cursed" or "guilty"). He called them *hypocrites* in the temple in front of a large crowd. I doubt He made many friends that day!

The religious leaders (scribes and Pharisees) performed the duties of the temple and interpreted the law for the people. They held powerful positions and were highly respected. But Jesus knew the truth about them. He knew it was all a show. They used their positions of authority to take advantage of people and to make themselves look better. Their religious leadership had become just a duty, a status symbol to them. Just like the smokestacks on the aging *Queen Mary*, the religious leaders of Jesus' time had no substance. The Lord pointed out their lack of a real relationship with God when He said,

> Woe to you, teachers of the law and Pharisees, you hypocrites! You are like whitewashed tombs, which look beautiful on the outside but on the inside are full of dead men's bones and everything unclean. In the same way, on the outside you appear to people as righteous but on the inside you are full of hypocrisy and wickedness. (Matthew 23:27–28)

The Jewish leaders appeared outwardly righteous, but their hearts were filthy. They didn't have an authentic relationship with God.

There are people sitting in the pews of the church every Sunday who are like this. They look good on the outside, but in reality they have no relationship with God. Tragically, and even dangerously, they are outwardly religious but aren't truly saved. Such persons go to church not out of love for the Lord but out of a sense of duty and obligation. They may think, *My family expects me to be here.* Others may attend church services for the status it gives them in the community, or for the business contacts they make.

But they're playing a part, much like an actor in a movie. They go through the motions, trying to look spiritual, but in reality, they're hypocrites, pretending to be something they're not.

Wheat or Tares?

As we saw in chapter 1, Matthew 13:24–30 describes the kingdom of heaven as a field of wheat. The wheat is not pure, however, because tares grow up alongside the wheat. When the tares and wheat are young, there is virtually no way to tell the difference between them. But when the grains are older, they show distinguishing characteristics. Likewise, a church is filled with saved sinners, those who are "works in progress." A church also contains hypocrites, those who aren't truly disciples. On the surface, their behaviors may appear the same. I believe there are three criteria that set apart Christian behavior, even imperfect Christian behavior, from the behavior of a hypocrite. First, true disciples will apologize after making a mistake or after doing something rude or un-Christlike. Second, over time, you'll see the fruit of the Spirit growing in a true believer's life. Third, a well-meaning disciple will develop gifts and begin to give back to the Christian community, not only through works of service, but also through encouragement, love, and true self-sacrifice.

In Basel, Switzerland, each year the townspeople have a festival in which they all don masks. They go throughout the city doing bad things and going to dark places they would never consider doing or going under normal circumstances. The masks, which hide their identities, give them the boldness to do these things. One year, the Salvation Army, concerned about the abandonment of moral standards, put up signs all over the city, which read, "God sees behind the mask."[2] As Proverbs 5:21 puts it, "A man's ways are in full view of the Lord, / and he examines all his paths."

Sadly, some people don't even realize they're acting out a part. They're unwilling to admit to themselves that it's all a show. They think that their religious duty is enough to make them right with God.

Because they have no real relationship with God, they see no reason to apply the teachings of His Word in their lives. They then live their lives in whatever way they choose. When unbelievers see this, they don't know that the person who claims to be a Christian has no real relationship with God. All they see is someone claiming to be a Christian but acting in a way that is anything but Christian. Thus, they see a hypocrite.

Unless the "I'm just pretending" hypocrites genuinely turn from their sin and put their faith completely in Christ, they will one day answer for their hypocrisy.

This is a chilling scenario. Think of it—someone spending years doing the work of the Lord without knowing the Lord of the work. This is heartbreaking.

When kids recognize the duplicity of other people in the church, it can harm their faith.

The "Do as I Say, Not as I Do" Hypocrite

The second type of hypocrite is a Christian who doesn't act like a Christian. These kinds of hypocrites are saved and come to church on Sundays as if they have a vital relationship with Christ. They may overlap a bit with the "I'm just pretending type." They live their lives the rest of the week doing things that are contrary to the Word of God. They talk a good talk, but they don't walk a good walk.

Non-Christians have their own ideas of what Christians should be like and how they should act. Their ideas may or may not be a true biblical reflection of what a follower of Christ should be like. These perceptions—true or false—sometimes lead people to believe that most Christians are hypocrites.

An important fact Christians need to recognize is that there is a standard we're supposed to live up to if we're truly born again. I'm not saying this to condemn anyone. Everyone (including God) knows that we're going to slip up from time to time, but when we accept Christ as

The Gandhi Excuse

Even though Mahatma Gandhi studied the Bible and had many Christian friends over the course of his life, he rejected Christianity. In part this was because he wasn't impressed with materialistic Christians. "I like your Christ," he is reported to have said. "I do not like your Christians. Your Christians are so unlike your Christ."[3]

But is the bad behavior of Christians enough to warrant rejection of Jesus as Savior? More important, does your child have an excuse to write off Christianity because of hypocrites? I would argue no. The person who rejects Christian hypocrisy is aware that there is a missed mark, which is sin. The fact that there are sinners in the world should point to a need for Christ and His redemption—not the opposite. Help your child work through this tough issue with kindness yet firmness. Your child is ultimately responsible for his or her decision about Jesus and salvation. But the basis of that decision should be an examination of the life of Jesus and His teachings and not the sometimes disappointing lives of His followers.

our Savior, there is an understood promise that we're going to allow the Holy Spirit to work in our lives and transform us into Christlikeness (Romans 8:4; Galatians 3:3).

Most Protestant churches agree that the fundamental entry point into Christianity is declared in Romans: "If you confess with your mouth, 'Jesus is Lord,' and believe in your heart that God raised him from the dead, you will be saved" (10:9).

> Nothing is more contagious than a bad example.
>
> —OLD PROVERB

Here, most scholars and theologians agree that Paul was talking about the lordship of Jesus in terms of His authority over us, not necessarily His deity. *Strong's Concordance* defines the Greek word *kurios*, translated in Romans 10 as "Lord," as "supreme in authority."[4] *Thayer's Greek Lexicon* adds "he to whom a person or thing belongs, about which he has the power of deciding; master, lord."[5]

With Christ as our "master," or the One we asked to be "supreme in authority" over us, our lives should be a reflection of His leading, guiding, and inspiring. When we have the Light of the World inside us, He should shine through us to others, as Matthew 5:16 declares: "Let your light so shine before men, that they may see your good works and glorify your Father in heaven" (NKJV).

Some people find this verse confusing when compared to Matthew 6:3–4: "When you give to the needy, do not let your left hand know what your right hand is doing, so that your giving may be in secret. Then your Father, who sees what is done in secret, will reward you."

Understanding these verses in context will help resolve the apparent contradiction. In the earlier verse, Matthew 5:16, Jesus was in the midst of the Sermon on the Mount. He was speaking to His disciples about their mind-set and mission: to be the "salt of the earth" (verse 13).

Salt (as referenced here) was not only a spice to add flavor, but it was also used as a preservative. Salt is *aseptic*, meaning that it prevents bacteria from spreading. As the salt of the earth, we're called to prevent the bacteria of sin from spreading in the world. Our efforts should be focused on presenting an accurate representation of the message of salvation not just in our words but also in our works.

Too often Christians want to leave evangelism to the evangelists. But ask any evangelist what some of the roadblocks are in leading people to Christ, and if they're honest, they'll admit that the body of Christ isn't setting a great example to the world. No one person can correct that, but you and I should work hard to show others what Christ did on the cross on our behalf. Our lives should reflect to the world the life-transforming power of Christ as we walk closely with Him in faith. As the apostle Paul said so well in 2 Corinthians, "We are therefore Christ's ambassadors, as though God were making his appeal through us. We implore you on Christ's behalf: Be reconciled to God" (5:20).

An ambassador for the United States is our authorized representative to another nation. Ambassadors have the authority to speak for the president of the United States, and their responsibility is to faithfully communicate the will of the one they represent. As Christ's ambassadors, we have that authority and responsibility as well.

When people see us, speak with us, and interact with us, they should sense Christ within us. His peace, His patience, His love, His grace, His mercy, and His desire for them to be saved and come into a right relationship with God should be overflowing with fruit of the Spirit from our hearts. For these qualities to overflow, we must first get filled, and to get filled, we must first tap into the Sources: Jesus and the Holy Spirit. The prophet Jeremiah, who spoke for God, recorded this warning:

My people have committed two sins:
They have forsaken me,
    the spring of living water,
and have dug their own cisterns,
    broken cisterns that cannot hold water. (Jeremiah 2:13)

When we forsake God, who describes Himself as "the spring of living water," we find our faith and prayer lives dry and empty. A cistern is either a well or a container used to hold water. If we reject God's living water—His Word and presence in our lives—our natural reaction is to dig our own cisterns, "broken cisterns that cannot hold water." Cisterns represent our religious beliefs, traditions, and habits that don't hold up to the scrutiny of God's Word and don't hold "living water."

Many times we've put our trust in what people say and don't take the time to examine the Scriptures to see whether they're telling us the truth (see, for example, what the Bereans did in Acts 17:11). Too often our lives are without fruit, and we're not shining brightly for the Lord because we've become immersed in our religiosity and not in our relationship with Jesus.

Talk the Talk and Walk the Walk

It's sad when children see people who claim to be Christians, but their lives tell a different story: "Those who are pure in their own eyes and yet are not cleansed of their filth" (Proverbs 30:12). This behavior is a bad example for them.

I'm concerned that young Christians may grow into this category, but there are some things we can do to set a better example for our kids. It's our responsibility as followers of Christ to pursue right living. We need to develop and grow our faith—and by faith I mean our trust in the Lord. To develop our faith, we need to be students of the Scriptures so that we can know what it is that He expects of us and build our faith so that the Holy Spirit can mold us. The book of Romans puts it this way: "Faith comes from hearing the message, and the message is heard through the word of Christ" (10:17).

Parents, one of the best ways to keep your kids from falling into hypocrisy is to avoid it yourself. Consider the following verses in light of pursuing a deep, meaningful relationship with God:

Thus says the LORD:

"Cursed is the man who trusts in man

And makes flesh his strength,

Whose heart departs from the LORD. . . .

"Blessed is the man who trusts in the LORD,

And whose hope is the LORD.

For he shall be like a tree planted by the waters,

Which spreads out its roots by the river,

And will not fear when heat comes;

But its leaf will be green,

And will not be anxious in the year of drought,

Nor will cease from yielding fruit.

(Jeremiah 17:5, 7–8, NKJV)

When we're pursuing a living relationship with the "spring of living water" (Jeremiah 2:13), we'll bear fruit in our relationship with Him (Jeremiah 17:8) and our children will see it. No matter what's going on in society, when our feet are planted on solid rock, our children will see that our lives are different because of the qualities we show in our words and actions. Matthew 7:18–20 says, "A good tree cannot bear bad fruit, and a bad tree cannot bear good fruit. Every tree that does not bear good fruit is cut down and thrown into the fire. Thus, by their fruit you will recognize them."

These are very real evidences of the presence of God in one's life, and the sweet, rich taste and smell of the fruit of the Spirit can be sensed by anyone and everyone—even if they don't choose to acknowledge the Source. Likewise, a lack of spiritual fruit in someone's life is evident to everyone around that person. Harshness, selfishness, rudeness, sarcasm, and self-indulgence are some of the evidences of a lack of relationship with God.

The fruit of the Spirit is listed in Galatians: "The fruit of the Spirit is love, joy, peace, patience, kindness, goodness, faithfulness, gentleness and self-control. Against such things there is no law" (5:22–23). True spiritual fruit is unmistakable when your kids come across it.

Why Do Christians Judge Everybody?

*Students feel safer as doubters
than as believers, and as perpetual
seekers rather than eventual finders.*

—Kelly Monroe, *Finding God at Harvard*

Rick de Gaulle was walking down the infamous Bourbon Street in New Orleans, Louisiana, during Mardi Gras weekend. He wasn't there to participate in the revelries but was a member of a team of men who come to the French Quarter annually to witness and hand out gospel tracts to the partygoers.

As he made his way past the crowded bars, strip clubs, and groups of college coeds who were drinking to excess, he handed out gospel tracts to as many people as would receive them. He prayed that the gospel tracts might spark a spiritual conversation with a few of them. Surprisingly, many people were taking these little bits of good news from him. Some began reading them right away, some stuffed them in their pockets, and others simply threw them on the ground. Most of the people who didn't want them politely refused and went on their way.

As Rick passed by one of the strip clubs, a young woman he knew exited the club and began to cross the street. Rick turned to catch her

Key Concepts

QUESTION RECAP: Why are Christians so judgmental? Is it right for Christians to judge sinfulness? Aren't we called to be loving instead of judging?

1. Everyone makes judgments, not only Christians. Making a judgment isn't necessarily wrong. What is wrong is having an attitude of superiority over others based on our judgments.

2. The Bible tells us not to make hypocritical judgments—pointing out someone else's sin when we are wrong in the same area.

3. Even though we can recognize sin in others' lives, we should always respond with compassion. Jesus had compassion on people, seeing them as sheep without a shepherd, and He began to teach them. We should follow Jesus' example.

HOPE-FILLED ANSWER: Everyone makes judgments. However, Christians should have compassion on others and not be judgmental or have an attitude of superiority over those who are unbelievers. The Holy Spirit does the job of conviction; our job is to share the good news.

• •

attention, and as he offered her the tract, he said, "Sherry, I hope you have a great day!"

Sherry didn't even look him in the face but angrily retorted, "Doesn't the Bible say that Christians shouldn't judge people?" Rick was taken aback. He hadn't said anything judgmental, and yet she seemed to have jumped to the conclusion that just because he was passing out Christian material, he was judging her.

There was a point in time in our culture when almost everyone, believers and nonbelievers alike, could quote John 3:16. Today it would seem that the most widely known and quoted verse is "Do not judge, or you too will be judged" (Matthew 7:1).

A 2007 survey conducted by the Barna Group indicated that among young non-Christians, 87 percent of them perceived Christians as being judgmental.[1]

With a Christians-are-judgmental mind-set in our culture, how are your kids impacted? How can you teach them to hold to Christian standards when the world is telling them that those with standards are annoying prigs? Are Christians, in fact, judgmental?

Do Christians Judge?

Do Christians judge everybody? Yes, we do. But that doesn't mean we have to be spiteful.

The term *judge* refers to making an informed decision and acting upon that decision. All of us, Christian and non-Christian alike, make decisions, or judgments, about the people we encounter every day. We decide whether they are like us or not, whether to befriend them or keep our distance, whether they are worthy of our trust. So in this respect, yes, Christians do judge others—but so do others.

Your children need to learn there's a difference between *making* a judgment and *being* judgmental. Being judgmental implies a feeling of superiority over the one who is being judged. What non-Christians are really asking when they accuse Christians of being judgmental is "Who are you to tell me what I can and can't do? Why do you think that you are better than I am? Only God can judge me."

Today's society has thrown morals out the window. "If it feels good, do it!" became the cry of generations that didn't want anyone, especially the church, telling them how to live their lives. In recent years we've started hearing the word *tolerance* thrown around. Originally it meant "putting up with something you disagree with or don't like." But tolerance has now been redefined to convey the idea that all beliefs should be considered equal, and if it's the belief du jour, it should be not only tolerated but promoted.

We're no longer allowed to say that our beliefs are right and someone else's are wrong. Ravi Zacharias reportedly defined the new tolerance this way:

> These days it's not just that the line between right and wrong has been made unclear, today Christians are being asked by our culture to erase the lines and move the fences, and if that were not bad enough, we are being asked to join in the celebration cry by those who have thrown off the restraints religion had imposed upon them. It is not just that they ask we accept, but they now demand of us to celebrate it too.[2]

So now, in the name of tolerance and everybody getting along, we're supposed to approve of any lifestyle or moral choice. There's a term for this: *moral relativism*. It means that what is right or wrong for you may not be right or wrong for me. The world would like this to be so, but the Bible makes clear distinctions, or judgments, on what is right and wrong. These absolute standards have stood the test of time and still hold true today. In that light, let's see what Jesus actually said about making judgments.

Planks and Specks

When we speak out against sin, Christians are often accused of judging others. But is that what Jesus meant when He said that we shouldn't judge? No. Examining the verse in its context will give us a better picture of what Jesus actually meant:

> Judge not, that you be not judged. For with what judgment you judge, you will be judged; and with the measure you use, it will be measured back to you. And why do you look at the speck in your brother's eye, but do not consider the plank in your own eye? Or how can you say to your brother, "Let me remove the speck from

your eye"; and look, a plank is in your own eye? Hypocrite! First re-move the plank from your own eye, and then you will see clearly to remove the speck from your brother's eye. (Matthew 7:1–5, NKJV)

When we read this verse in its context, it's obvious that Jesus was warning us about the dangers of *hypocritical* judgment: making a judg-ment on someone else's sin when we are doing the same thing, or worse. Confronting your coworker about telling a little white lie when he knows that you called in sick the day before so that you could go fishing would be an example of hypocritical judgment. In the context of parenting, your children would find it hypocritical if you scold them for using profanity when you use the same language.

Paul summed it up well when he wrote,

You, then, who teach others, do you not teach yourself? You who preach against stealing, do you steal? You who say that people should not commit adultery, do you commit adultery? You who abhor idols, do you rob temples? (Romans 2:21–22)

So whenever we talk to other people about sin, we need to exam-ine our own hearts first, recognizing that we, too, are sinners. God will measure us by the same standard we use to measure others. If there's a two-by-four in your eye, remove it before you try to take the splinter out of someone else's eye!

When talking about sin with your children, help them remember that God sees no degrees of sin (Romans 3:23). In His eyes, "little" sins are treated the same as "big" sins. There is only one prescribed remedy for sin, and that is the cross. All who seek forgiveness must find it there.

John Newton's opening words in one of the greatest hymns ever written says it well:

Amazing grace!
How sweet the sound that saved a wretch like me;

I once was lost,
But now am found,
Was blind, but now I see.[3]

There is, however, another type of judgment that Jesus teaches us to carefully apply: a "righteous judgment" (John 7:24, NKJV). This is when we warn others about sin and its consequences with the hope of bringing

---

When Your Kids Think You're Judging Them

Being a parent means setting standards, and oftentimes these standards seem impossibly high to children. To them it seems as if "everybody" has it easier. It can seem as if you're sitting in judgment over them if you don't approve of their music, clothes, or friends.

Obviously the Bible doesn't have a verse we can point to for every issue we face in our modern world. I have yet to find the verse that says, "Thou shalt not have a cell phone until thou art sixteen years old." Sorry, can't help you on that one. But that doesn't mean you permit your children to do everything they want to do if you can't find a verse to back up your position.

Instead of asking how far can you stretch a verse that was written thousands of years ago to apply to your family today, let's ask our children (and ourselves) the question, "What principles in the Bible apply to this situation?"

Let's say Jacob wants to stay up after bedtime playing video games or watching television. You might discuss this scripture with him: "There is a time for everything, / and a season for every activity under heaven" (Ecclesiastes 3:1).

This passage goes on to list many activities that there are times for. Although not specifically stated, we can infer from this passage that there is a time for play, a time for school, a time to eat, a time to do homework, and yes, a time to sleep!

them into a right relationship with God. This kind of judging is actually a biblical responsibility:

> When I [the Lord] say to a wicked man, "You will surely die," and you do not warn him or speak out to dissuade him from his evil ways in order to save his life, that wicked man will die for his sin, and I will hold you accountable for his blood. But if you do warn

The principle from the Bible can be extrapolated and it's easy to see that God would be pleased if Jacob scheduled time for rest.

If your daughter wants to choose the latest fashions that are too revealing, you can point her directly to Paul's teaching:

> I also want women to dress modestly, with decency and propriety, not with braided hair [elaborate hairstyles] or gold or pearls or expensive clothes, but with good deeds, appropriate for women who profess to worship God. (1 Timothy 2:9–10)

Okay, so stretch jeans with a five-inch rise aren't mentioned, but modesty is. "Is this outfit modest? If Jesus were here, what do you think He'd say about the three inches of tummy that is showing?" This is a great opening to discuss modesty and the effects of a girl's clothing on the opposite sex.

There will be situations when the issue isn't a moral dilemma with a clear biblical standard to follow but simply a matter of personal preference and good judgment. God has placed your children in your care, and you need to use your own wisdom and discernment based on your knowledge of the Word and the character of God. As they see you relying on Scripture and the Holy Spirit to lead you, your children will grow to trust your discernment, learn from your example, and realize that you aren't interested in harshly judging them. They'll see you trying to please a higher Authority—God!

the wicked man and he does not turn from his wickedness or from
his evil ways, he will die for his sin; but you will have saved yourself.
(Ezekiel 3:18–19)

In some ways, sin should be treated like rat poison. If I saw that a
child was reaching for a box of rat poison, I would do everything in my
power to stop the child before he or she opened the box, or worse, before
the child began to sample it. If we earnestly believe that "the wages of sin
is death" (Romans 6:23), can we help but present the remedy for sin (the
gospel) in an urgent manner?

Christians Who Really Do Judge

Remember the woman on Bourbon Street, Sherry? Since she was so quick
to jump to the conclusion that Rick de Gaulle was judging her, it seems
obvious that at some point in her life, she had encountered a Christian
who had condemned her lifestyle choices in a judgmental way.

The headlines today feature people who claim to be Christians carrying signs and wearing sandwich boards with messages on them like "God
hates sinners," or "Ask me why you are going to hell," or worse. Their
shock-and-awe tactics present a distorted view of God and the gospel
message, totally lacking in the love and compassion of Christ. Unfortunately, when non-Christians see them, they don't know that the theology
of these so-called Christians is unbiblical. They can only assume that all
Christians believe the same way.

Yes, God hates sin, but He reaches out to sinners!

Unfortunately, the reality is that some Christians are judgmental.
They look down on those who are engaged in sinful behaviors like homosexuality. drunkenness, drug abuse, promiscuous sex, and other behaviors. They speak out against those issues, seeking only to condemn those
who practice them, not to give them the hope of Christ. They condemn
the sinner rather than the sin.

Kindly consider, though, that the greatest man who ever walked the earth, the One in whom "all the fullness of the Deity lives in bodily form" (Colossians 2:9), was the same person of whom it is written: "When Jesus landed and saw a large crowd, he had compassion on them, because they were like sheep without a shepherd. So he began teaching them many things" (Mark 6:34).

Jesus loved sinners and had compassion on them. He wants us to do the same. Do our children see us having Christ's compassion on the lost, or do they see us viewing people as the enemy? Sinful people are not our enemies; Satan is. In fact, the Bible says that the devil "has taken [people] captive to do his will" (2 Timothy 2:26). They are prisoners of war in a great spiritual battle between darkness and light.

Judging Like Jesus

When we encounter people who are in despair and whose lives show obvious signs of trauma, our hearts should beat with our heavenly Father's heart in love and compassion, not in judgment and condemnation. This doesn't mean that we necessarily have to take homeless people into our homes or give money to every alcoholic who has his hand out. (God wants us to have compassion but also discernment.) What's important is that our children see the attitude of our hearts and emulate that attitude in their own lives.

> To love a man enough to help him, you have to forfeit the warm, self-righteous glow that comes from judging.
> —RON HALL, *What Difference Do It Make?*

The religious Sadducees and Pharisees regularly condemned Jesus for spending time with people who were considered unclean or unworthy. Luke describes one such scene:

> Behold, a woman in the city who was a sinner . . . brought an alabaster flask of fragrant oil, and stood at His feet behind Him weeping; and she began to wash His feet with her tears, and wiped them with

the hair of her head; and she kissed His feet and anointed them with the fragrant oil. Now when the Pharisee who had invited [Jesus] saw this, he spoke to himself, saying, "This Man, if He were a prophet, would know who and what manner of woman this is who is touching Him, for she is a sinner." (7:37–39, NKJV)

Woe to us, Christian friends, when we find ourselves on the side of the condemning Pharisees and Sadducees instead of with Jesus. If there was anyone who could rightfully condemn sinful people, it was the perfect Son of God, who never sinned. And yet He never condemned sinners; He came "to seek and to save . . . [the] lost" (Luke 19:10).

One of the hardest facts for some Christians to accept is that lost people act lost. How can we expect them to do otherwise? Without the benefit of the indwelling presence of the Holy Spirit in their lives, they'll continue acting out their sinful nature many times without giving a thought to what God says about the matter.

It's easy to fall into the trap of thinking that if we don't condemn and convict sinners, it will be seen as condoning their wrong behavior. It isn't our job to take the place of the Holy Spirit. He's much better qualified than we are to bring about conviction in the hearts of people. As Jesus said, "When [the Holy Spirit] comes, he will convict the world of guilt in regard to sin and righteousness and judgment" (John 16:7–8).

When nonbelievers start complaining, "You're judging me!" perhaps it's actually the Holy Spirit convicting them of their own sin. Instead of taking responsibility for their own behavior, they try to shift the blame back to the Christian. By the way, if a non-Christian accuses you of being judgmental, hasn't he or she just judged your behavior?

When it comes to judging lifestyles, it's important to remember that we can judge the action while still being loving, kind, and compassionate. Unless we're careful how we confront sin, the church will come off as angry, mean-spirited, and exclusive. As I mentioned in an earlier chapter, Christianity isn't some elite country club that looks down on others and carefully screens its members.

Which is easier, to shun sinners away from our doors or invite them in and help them get their lives cleaned up through the power of the cross? Ministry is messy because people are messy.

Build Bridges; Don't Burn Them

The late Dr. Jerry Falwell founded Liberty University and served as pastor of Thomas Road Baptist Church in Lynchburg, Virginia. Larry Flynt is the publisher of *Hustler* magazine. Both men were known for speaking their minds. Falwell's son, Jonathan, recalls what happened after a debate between his father and Flynt:

> Mr. Flynt asked my dad if we could give him a ride back to Lynchburg in my dad's private jet. Dad said yes, so we traveled to the airport and boarded a beautiful black-and-gold Gulfstream III. As we flew to Virginia, I sat across from Dad and Mr. Flynt as they had a long conversation about sports, food, politics, and other ordinary topics. I was amazed and bewildered because they kept talking like old friends.
>
> After we dropped off Mr. Flynt in Lynchburg, I asked Dad, "How come you could sit on that airplane and carry on a conversation with Larry Flynt as if you guys were lifelong buddies? Dad, he's the exact opposite of everything you believe in; he does all the things you preach against; and yet you were treating him like a member of your own church. Why?"
>
> Dad's response changed my whole outlook on ministry. "Jonathan," he said, "there's going to be a day when Larry is hurting and lonely, and he'll be looking for help and guidance. He is going to pick up the phone and call someone who can help him. I want to earn the right to be that phone call!"[4]

Dr. Falwell employed a significant principle in his dealings with Mr. Flynt: If we're going to reach people with the gospel, we have to build bridges to the lost rather than burn them. By seeing people as God sees them—made in His image and worthy of redemption—and sharing the truth of the gospel in love, we set a strong foundation for a bridge that God can use to rescue them from a Christless eternity.

One convert said to his discipler, "You built a bridge of love between my heart and yours, and Jesus walked over." Jesus was the consummate bridge builder. Through His sacrificial death, He made it possible for humankind to cross the impassable, sin-filled gulf that separated us from God. He has called us to be bridge builders too. If we confront non-Christians in a harsh, judgmental manner, it will only ignite the match that sets the bridge ablaze.

First Timothy states God's ultimate desire for humanity: "God our Savior . . . wants all men to be saved and to come to a knowledge of the truth" (2:3–4). God wants *all* people to be saved and to know the truth. As we seek to walk in fellowship with Him, we need to embrace His goal and endeavor to find a way to help fulfill His mission as members of the body of Christ.

Not everyone is called to be an evangelist, but we are called to be part of God's plan to "make disciples of all nations" (Matthew 28:19). If we follow Jesus' example of compassion toward sinners and endeavor to fulfill our calling to be salt and light on this earth rather than condemning people, we'll help our children understand how to live out their own faith without being offensive.

20

If Church Is Boring, Why Do I Have to Go?

Has it ever occurred to you that one hundred pianos all tuned to the same fork are automatically tuned to each other? . . . So, one hundred worshippers [meeting] together, each one looking away to Christ, are in heart nearer to each other.

—A. W. Tozer, *The Pursuit of God*

Ten-year-old Matthew walked into the room and let out a big sigh. "I'm bo-o-ored."

He just walked past his video-game console, a television with digital cable and more than three hundred channels, his room full of the latest toys, his younger sister, and two neighborhood friends who came by to play.

Next day Matthew sat in church, fidgeting. He picked up a pencil from the little holder on the back of a chair. He wrote a note to his sister on the bulletin: "This is sooooo boring." He underlined sooooo twice.

Kids may get bored at church because the focus isn't on them—nor should it be! Church is not about the worshipper. It's about God and His Son, Jesus. And when kids learn how to effectively engage in a body of believers—a church—then they will want to go.

Key Concepts

QUESTION RECAP: Is going to church really necessary? It's so boring!

1. Church is not about being entertained. Rather, it is about worshipping God, fellowship with other Christians, spiritual education, and evangelism.
2. Parents should make it a priority to help their children engage in church.
3. Get involved with your child's Sunday school class and youth ministry. Meet the teachers and pray for them or become one yourself. Help set your child up for successful learning by making the teacher aware of any special needs your child has.

HOPE-FILLED ANSWER: Yes! Going to church is necessary. Teach your child why we go to church, even if it's not "entertaining." When kids are engaged at church, fruit develops in their life. Try to make it engaging for your child at an appropriate level for their development and understanding.

● ●

The Purpose of Church

Why did God establish the church? (By church, I mean the universal body of Christ, not your individual church family.) God established the church for worship, fellowship, education, and evangelism (Acts 2:42–47). I don't see entertainment in there, and I certainly don't see babysitting. But that doesn't mean church can't become a significant part of your kids' spiritual life. Let's see how the four areas—worship, fellowship, education, and evangelism—can impact the life of your child.

Worship

I believe this is the first and primary task of the church: to praise God and His Son, Jesus, for all they are and all they have done.

The worship model that God expects is that we actively participate in worship (Psalm 29:2; 95:6; John 4:21–24). The leaders of the church, the musicians, and the pastor are the prompters, directing our attention to the star of the show: Jesus! All the focus is on Him.

It doesn't matter if your church uses hymns or praise choruses or Southern gospel or rock 'n' roll. Those are just methods of conveying a message. Tastes may change over time, but the message doesn't. As long as Christ is honored and exalted, as He deserves to be, then it's worship.

Fellowship

Within the fellowship of the church is the caring ministry: meeting each other's needs and ministering to the sick, poor, lonely, homeless, widows, and orphans (Deuteronomy 10:18; 15:11; Matthew 19:21; 1 John 3:17–18). Another word for fellowship is *inreach* (as opposed to "outreach," which certainly has its place too). As members of the body of Christ, we're called to take care of each other, encourage each other, and lift each other up in prayer. Most churches are very good at this.

Education

The educational ministry of the church carries the responsibility of teaching the truths of the Word of God to all ages. These truths must be deeply planted within the hearts of our young people so that they will know *what* they believe. The church must also teach *why* we believe as we do.

The Secret Service is charged with investigating forgeries of money. As the investigators are being trained, they *never* look at a forged bill. They always examine the original. If they are intimately acquainted with that original bill, when they see a forgery, they'll be able to spot it immediately.

The doctrines of the church should be taught over and over so that our children have a firm spiritual foundation. If they have a solid faith in Christ and a sound understanding of God's Word, they'll be able to tell a forgery when they see one. For someone who doesn't have this foundation, when the least trial or doubt comes, they will find their faith on sinking sand (Matthew 7:24–27).

Evangelism

Evangelistic outreach is the means by which the church reproduces itself. *Evangelism* essentially means sharing the good news of Jesus to bring people to a saving faith in Him. Jesus commanded us to "go and make disciples of all nations" (Matthew 28:19). Spreading the gospel message to the unsaved isn't just a task for pastors, evangelists, or missionaries. It's a command for all of us. Jesus wasn't giving His disciples a Great Suggestion; it was the Great Commission. While some people have been specifically called to be evangelists (Ephesians 4:11), all Christians need to be equipped to share the gospel. It's something we all must learn how to do and be ready to do at any time. First Peter 3:15 tells *all* believers, "Always be prepared to give an answer to everyone who asks you to give the reason for the hope that you have." Be obedient to the Word and share Christ, particularly with your children.

Worship, fellowship, education, and evangelism are the roles of the church. It's important that you and your children are a part of a church that is actively practicing these principles. Look around your church. Does it have a worship service that honors the Lord and His Son, Jesus Christ? Do church leaders believe and teach the Word of God? Do they reach in to their members (inreach) and out to the world with the gospel (outreach)? If your church doesn't believe in the power and integrity of the written Word of God, then perhaps you need to consider finding one that does. When the Word of God is being preached and taught accurately and enthusiastically, going to church should be a blessing and a joy! If not, then you have two choices: change the church or change churches.

> *If your children don't want to go to church, there is . . . [an] important question to ask: Why don't your children want to go to church?*
>
> —Natasha Crain, Christian blogger

Leaving a congregation you've been part of for a time can be a stressful and disorienting process and should never be done lightly or flippantly.

Scripture is clear that we're to aspire to keep the "unity of the Spirit through the bond of peace" (Ephesians 4:3), and leaving a church should always be a last resort. The bonds that form in church are important and become an integral part of our lives. Deep ties developed through shared experiences shouldn't be forsaken. But if the health of your child's spiritual life would be enhanced elsewhere, I'd encourage you to consider it.

Ultimately, however, we are to "obey God rather than men" (Acts 5:29), and sometimes finding another congregation that is more conducive to your family's needs is the greater good. New relationships can form, but that doesn't mean the previous ones need to be completely severed. If you leave a church gracefully, without bitterness or complaining, your former church family should be willing to recognize that the body of Christ is greater than one local church.

Should You Make Your Children Go to Church?

Should you make your children go to church? The short answer to this is—absolutely! The easy answer is, "Because I said so!" Even if they are bored sometimes.

The writer of Hebrews wrote this advice to believers: "Let us not give up meeting together, as some are in the habit of doing, but let us encourage one another—and all the more as you see the Day approaching" (10:25).

There are times when we do things simply because we know they must be done. We have to go to work, wash the dishes, take the dog for a walk, and mow the grass. They may be boring, but they have to be done so the family functions smoothly. Are kids bored by homework or chores or eating their vegetables? Yes, but they still have to do these things.

There are also times when we do things because we know that in the end we'll benefit from those activities. I exercise because it's good for my body. I may not see the results today or this week, but I have faith that if I continue to work at it, my health will improve. I also read my Bible every day because it's good for my soul. Are there days I don't feel like doing it? Sure, but I do it anyway, because I have faith that it will benefit me in the end. It's a matter of discipline and commitment.

Going to church and insisting that our children go as well is an exercise in faith too. We trust that someday they'll learn the lessons of prayer, worship, service, evangelism, and more. Most of all we pray that someday they'll choose Christ as their Savior and develop an intimate, authentic relationship with Him.

The book of Proverbs admonishes parents to "train up a child in the way he should go, / And when he is old he will not depart from it"

Keeping Kids Engaged during Worship

When a child says, "Church is boring!" it's usually the worship service and in particular the sermon they're referring to. Let's face it, sitting still for a thirty- to forty-minute sermon isn't easy for us sometimes, much less a child. But that's not to say it isn't important for them to be there.

Following are some tried-and-true techniques other parents have used that can help your child stay focused during a worship service. Remember, our goal is to keep our children engaged in worship, not just quiet.

1. Take your children to the bathroom before worship, and don't allow them to leave during the service. This is an issue of respect for the speaker and fellow worshippers.

2. Insist that your children stand and sing. This seems like a little thing, but if we allow their nonparticipation in the music, it's giving them implicit permission to opt out of anything. If your church uses hymnals, have your children help find the correct page and teach them how to follow the words and music. If your church projects the words on a screen, make sure your children can see the screen.

(22:6, NKJV). Parents are the spiritual leaders of the home, and as such we have the authority and responsibility for the spiritual education of our children. We have the right to say, "Yes, we are going to church. Every Sunday." But that can appear negative. Your attitude on Sunday morning can say a lot. "Let's see who can be ready and in the car first!" you could say with enthusiasm. "First one there gets to pick dessert at lunchtime."

Some parents fear that forcing their children to go to church will cultivate a sense of legalism: If I just show up for church, I've done my duty. This is where the parent's attitude is key. Why do *you* go to church?

3. As your children are starting out in "big church," prepare a bag for them to carry every Sunday. It should contain their very own Bible, crayons, pencils, and some paper. This is intended not as busywork to keep them distracted and quiet but as a tool for them to use during the sermon. Help them find the sermon scriptures in their Bible and read along with the pastor. Start off with a five-minute focus time in which they're expected to just listen to the sermon. This time will grow as they mature. After the listening time, they may draw a picture or write some words on their paper, but those activities *must* have something to do with what they've heard in the music or in the sermon. Eventually this will progress into taking sermon notes, which, incidentally, isn't a bad skill to have as we seek to internalize God's truths.

4. If you know the sermon title or topic before the service, choose one word for your children to listen for. Write it on their papers. Explain what it means and let them know that the pastor will be speaking about that word during the sermon. Ask them to listen for that word and count how many times the pastor says it.

If they see you eager to go to church and wholeheartedly participating in worship and the other ministries of the church, they will be more willing to be involved themselves.

Kids are kids. They're going to get bored sometimes: at home, at school, at church. That doesn't mean it's our responsibility to jump in with the next activity to keep them amused. And it doesn't mean that the church should seek to change its programming to accommodate their every whim either.

However, we can help our church to look at the programs and activities and see if there are ways we can make them more engaging for our children.

Engaging Your Child in Worship

There is a great debate in many churches over sending children to children's church for either all of the service or during the sermon. I can understand both sides of the issue. Sending them to children's church where they have a message and activity that is more on their level has its benefits. One of the disadvantages of that, however, is that worship is meant to be a family event. By separating families by age group, corporate worship is lost. And how will children ever learn from a sermon if they aren't a part of it in their earlier years?

Some say that children won't understand what is being preached. But children understand a lot more than we give them credit for.

Engaging Educational Activities

As a parent you have the primary responsibility for your children's spiritual education. The biblical way places the emphasis squarely on the parents:

> These words which I command you today shall be in your heart. You
> shall teach them diligently to your children, and shall talk of them
> when you sit in your house, when you walk by the way, when you lie

down, and when you rise up. You shall bind them as a sign on your
hand, and they shall be as frontlets between your eyes. You shall write
them on the doorposts of your house and on your gates. (Deuteronomy 6:6–9, NKJV)

These words were written to Israel and were intended as instructions
to individuals. Worship, fellowship, education, and evangelism are to be
regular parts of your family life at home, as well as at church. The teachings in church should reinforce what your children are learning at home.

Do you know the content of the Sunday school lesson your kids
learned last week? Was it biblically correct? Was it taught in such a way
that kept your children engaged and eager to learn more? Here are several suggestions on how you can be diligent in protecting your children's
education at church:

1. First of all, pray for your children's teachers and leaders. En-
    courage them. Often they feel abandoned and forgotten in
    their posts, especially if they've served for many years.

2. Be involved! Go visit your children's classrooms. Get to know
    their teachers. Volunteer to help with an outing or activity.
    Offer to substitute teach as needed. You may even feel God's
    sense of calling to teach in that area yourself. Offer to serve on
    committees that oversee these areas.

3. Encourage your church to offer training for your teachers or to
    send them to training conferences. There's nothing like some
    fresh ideas to give a teacher a shot in the arm!

4. If one of your children has special needs, such as ADHD,
    ADD, a learning disability, or a behavioral disorder, be sure
    the teachers are aware of them. A good teacher can work with
    these issues if they know about them ahead of time. If they
    don't, it will serve only to frustrate the teacher and the student.

5. Make sure that your children understand that they are ex-
    pected to follow the rules and expectations of the teachers
    in their classes. They follow rules at school and at home, but

some children come into church and think that all bets are off, since they're not at church for a grade and Mom's not around.

6. If you serve in a position that is responsible for recruiting teachers, be diligent in placing the right teachers in the right positions. Some teachers may not have been called by God. Instead, they were called by the nominating committee and guilted into filling a position for which they don't have a passion. One of the worst things a committee can do is put someone into a position who says, "Well, if you can't find anyone else, I'll do it." Be very careful here. We cannot see what God is doing in someone's life and heart. The last thing you want to do is to cause pain or dissension in the church. Tact, love, and prayer should go before anything in this area.

7. If you have concerns, don't talk about it with other parents until first you have talked about it with God and then with the pastor, youth leader, or children's director. Avoid gossip; it accomplishes nothing but hard feelings and distrust.

8. Work with the committee that chooses the curriculum to examine what you're using now as well as compare it to what else may be available. Many churches chose a particular denominational curriculum years ago and haven't looked at anything since that time. There are multiple publishers available now that offer excellent products. A thorough, informed survey of what you are using now versus what is available may be something that you can help evaluate.

A word on curriculum: I'm concerned about a trend I see in some educational curricula to water down the message of Scripture. Bible stories teach character lessons instead of the power and greatness of God. Biblical characters are commended for their wisdom rather than their reliance on God. Pictures of Jesus often portray Him with a cartoony look on His face.

Our children (particularly the boys) need to see Jesus as a rugged man. He got angry and overturned the tables of the money changers in the temple. He was a carpenter who worked with His hands and had muscles. His suffering on the cross involved tremendous physical endurance and stamina. Jesus was a hero, not a wimp!

Attracting children can be helpful to grow the church in general, but to that end some churches offer a type of spiritual fast food that's more about fun and making it easy for the teachers than about the truth of Jesus. It's vital that our children are being fed true spiritual food and not just a stimulating experience that leaves them happy but undernourished.

Teenagers

If I could sum up the problems with teenagers and church attendance, it would be this: relationships. With teenagers, relationships are essential to everything. When asked to attend a particular function at church, a teenager will never reply, "What doctrinal truths will you be teaching?" Instead, they want to know, "Who's going to be there?" (And will there be food?)

Many teenagers wonder, *Does anyone like me? Am I her friend? Will I be rejected? Am I cool? Am I popular?*

Nowhere is it more important for them to feel loved and accepted than at church. If they feel rejected by their peers within their youth group, they'll also feel rejected by God. Work with your youth leadership to try to minimize cliques within the youth group. To some extent they will always be there, but try to help the youth see how their actions are a direct reflection of the love of Christ.

Church is not an option; it's a biblical requirement. When the church functions as God intended, it can be a wonderful place for parents and children to concentrate on inreach, outreach, and the great spiritual truths that emphasize Christ's love and sacrifice for us and the world.

21

Why Don't Most Churches Care about Pollution and Global Warming?

If you are to be a Christian, you should, as I like to say, have the Bible "running out of your ears." Most people only read a certain number of verses for some devotional thoughts, not to know what the book is actually saying.

—J. I. Packer, *Scholar's Corner* interview, November, 1994

Pollution and global warming are considered by some to be among the most controversial issues in our day. Before we dive into the subject, let's establish what is typically meant by the term *global warming.* Global warming specifically refers to *man-caused* global warming and not any naturally occurring observable phenomenon in our environment. Your opinions on the topic are relatively irrelevant. But know that your kids probably think global warming and environmental issues are important and they look to the church to do something about it.

The arguments for or against this issue are typically driven by emotion and politics rather than reason. The very words *pollution* and *global warming* usually evoke a sense of anger or outrage, dread or fatigue.

QUESTION RECAP: Why doesn't the church do anything about pollution or global warming? Don't Christians care about the earth?

1. One reason many pastors may avoid discussing these issues is that they are highly political and controversial topics. Pastors may not want to get involved in what is often perceived as a political fight.
2. As Christians we are stewards of the earth. Everything in the earth belongs to God, and He has given it into our care. We should use the best practices to take care of the earth and keep it clean for future generations. However, this must be a balanced approach.

HOPE-FILLED ANSWER: Environmentalism is a political hot topic. Regardless of our political view on the issue, Christians should strive to take care of the resources God has given us in the best way possible.

• •

Many conservatives are angry because they believe that global warming is a complete hoax and that any climate change we see is part of a natural environmental cycle, not caused by humans.

Some believe that the government is using these false assumptions to take control of things that are not commonly within its scope of constitutional authority. Conservatives believe that the government should have minimal involvement in the lives of its citizens. For example, there are rumors that the federal government wants to regulate the thermostat within your house. You may think the government wouldn't possibly go that far, but consider that many local governments have already banned cigarette smoking in public places and have attempted to ban smoking in private homes. It seems that the US government has taken certain liberties in taking away certain liberties (pun intended).

On the flip side, many progressives and liberals see only the mark that each human makes on the environment throughout the course of his or her life in terms of consumption (food, clothing, packaging, excrement, carbon-dioxide emissions from operating vehicles, energy consumption, and so forth). The ultimate goal of environmental activists is to get everyone to "offset" their carbon footprint[1] by reducing consumption, eliminating nonbiodegradable packaging, driving fuel efficient cars (preferably electric), planting trees and greenery wherever possible in the

---

Pollution Points

Perhaps you've heard the phrase *cap and trade* bandied about during political conversations but don't know what it means. In a very simplified explanation, cap and trade basically means that a country agrees not to produce any additional pollutants year after year.

Every industry that creates pollution—and virtually all do in differing degrees—gets assessed based on the amount of pollution it generates and a "credit" is issued if they are clean enough. Credits become assets that can be sold or traded. If a business wants to expand or a new business wants to start, it must either find ways to avoid producing new polluting emissions or trade (read, "buy") credits from a company that has reduced its emissions or gone out of business.

The government could raise or lower the annual cap to allow for expansion of business or to decrease the number of pollutants, thus giving the government a backdoor method of imposing restrictions on free enterprise. This is a very real proposal that has been circulating in the halls of Congress for many years, but as of this writing it hasn't yet become the law of the land. (Bet you didn't think an innocent parenting book would talk about this issue, eh?)

hopes of reducing or reversing humanity's negative effect on nature, and other "green" practices.[2] Many times these activists accomplish their goals by lobbying the government to craft and impose new legislation, thus forcing everyone into compliance.

Then there are the ultraextremists who don't really fit into any political category and aren't embraced by any mainstream political party. These people believe that humans are a blight on the planet—a genetic anomaly who don't belong on earth. They point out that humans are the only species that creates toxins that endure; bombs that kill masses; and plastics, Styrofoam, and other materials that Mother Nature herself can't break down. Some who lean that way almost worship animals (and the earth) and believe that any and all use of animals, even for medical research, is inhumane. Even if experimentation on a rat were to produce a cure for cancer, they argue, the rat ought never to be exposed to the pains of trials and testing.

Yet another group is corporate industry. Since the beginning of the Industrial Revolution, unscrupulous corporations have dumped known toxins into water supplies and landfills without regard for the environmental impact, let alone the human lives that might be lost because of their action. Their attitude? It's cheaper to dump rather than treat—human life can be forfeited. Their irresponsible acts, motivated by greed and callousness, have impacted many lives, resulting in terminal cancers, birth defects, and other debilitating ailments.

These dramatic representations of the extremes illustrate why many people don't even want to discuss the issues of pollution and global warming. Bless you if you're still reading along. Be encouraged; help is on the way! There is a godly balance on this issue, even if it's precariously perched between these wildly divergent views.

Global Warming and the Church

Children are bombarded with "Save the Planet" messages at school and in the media, and even in their cartoons. If you were to believe the hype they see (and kids do believe it!), the planet is destined for annihilation next Tuesday, and we have to *do something now!* No wonder they think that Christians don't care, when they hear this message everywhere except church. Parents also find themselves without clear scriptural guidance and feel compelled to form a personal opinion that they may or may not be comfortable taking a stand on.

Many Christians do care about pollution and global warming, but the church has been conspicuously silent on these matters. Perhaps just by reading this far, you can see why many pastors choose to steer clear of the subject. Perceptions of political infighting, disputed research and conclusions, forced compliance, and extremist viewpoints are only a few of the reasons why pastors may decide not to speak on the issue. Furthermore, pastors may choose to distance themselves from the modern-day environmental movement because of its frequent ties to anti-Christian teachings, such as evolution and New Age pantheism. Unfortunately, this allows our enemy (Satan) to seize an important issue that rightfully belongs to the Creator.

In general, it's perceived that the majority of Christian churches are "conservative" and thus more aligned with Republicans, and that the minority of "liberal" churches are aligned with Democrats. In reality, the Scriptures are the Scriptures, and we need to put the honor of being part of the kingdom of God above any and all other groups or affiliations. When and where a political party embraces your sense of values, then it deserves your support. However, we shouldn't fall into the trap of hating those who are different from us or support a different party.

It All Belongs to God

One of the major doctrines taught in Scripture is stewardship. When Christians hear the word *stewardship*, the first thing they typically think of is the proper handling of money. When non-Christians hear the word *stewardship*, they often think, *The church only wants my money.* But biblical stewardship goes beyond money; it also includes our time, our talents, and yes, even proper management of the environment.

Our understanding of stewardship begins with the truth that God not only created everything we see—and continues to sustain it all through His power—but He also owns everything:

> To the LORD your God belong the heavens, even the highest heavens,
>   the earth and everything in it. (Deuteronomy 10:14)
> The earth is the LORD's, and everything in it,
>   the world, and all who live in it. (Psalm 24:1)
> Every animal of the forest is mine,
>   and the cattle on a thousand hills. (Psalm 50:10)

God, the Owner and Creator of all, has allowed us to manage (be stewards of) the things that belong to Him and use them for our benefit and the benefit of others. God cannot be pleased when we squander our financial resources on excessive material possessions or sinful lifestyles rather than using them to provide for the basic needs of our families. It would then seem logical that God expects us not to destroy the earth He created but to steward it well so that our children and our children's children will have an earth worth living on. The book of Genesis reminds us that God assigned the responsibility for stewardship of the earth to humans:

> God said, "Let us make man in our image, after our likeness. And let them have dominion over the fish of the sea and over the birds of the heavens and over the livestock and over all the earth and over every creeping thing that creeps on the earth."
>
> So God created man in his own image,
>   in the image of God he created him;
>   male and female he created them.
>
> And God blessed them. And God said to them, *"Be fruitful and multiply and fill the earth and subdue it, and have dominion over the fish of*

the sea and over the birds of the heavens and over every living thing that
moves on the earth." (Genesis 1:26–28, ESV)

Having "dominion" over and being told to "subdue" the earth doesn't
mean that we have free license to wreck God's world. Rather, in the
broader context of Christian teachings, our responsibility, as I've stressed,
is to care for creation as God's good stewards.

God, the Sovereign of the universe, made humankind the crown of
His creation. Since humans are made in the image of God, we have the
ability to reason, to make moral choices, and to understand the consequences of our actions. No other creature is made in God's image,
and therefore, humans are uniquely qualified to rule (be sovereign) over
creation just as God is sovereign over us. Therefore, God gave Adam
dominion over the earth and its creatures. Adam's job was to bring everything that God had created under his control, to govern it, and to take
responsibility for it: "The LORD God took the man and put him in the
garden of Eden to tend and keep it" (Genesis 2:15, NKJV).

The very first task God gave to Adam was to tend the garden of Eden.
That task didn't end after Adam and Eve were ejected from the garden
because of their disobedience. At that time God told Adam, "Cursed is
the ground because of you; through painful toil you will eat of it all the
days of your life" (Genesis 3:17). It's clear that Adam's responsibility to
be a steward of creation was to carry beyond Eden.

Also, we read in Genesis 4:2 that Adam's first son, Cain, was a "tiller
of the ground" and Abel, his second son, was a "keeper of sheep" (NKJV).
Both of these jobs required proper stewardship of God's created resources,
not reckless abuse.

So Adam was put in the garden to tend and keep it. Even though God
didn't specifically say, "Tell all your children for all generations to do the
same," without any recorded change in God's sentiment, we would expect
that His desires have remained the same from generation to generation.

Before the fall, humanity was perfect, and therefore Adam's stewardship of the world was arguably perfect. After sin entered the world

and corrupted humankind's sense of judgment, the possibility arose that Adam and his descendants would abuse, misuse, and even deplete the resources God entrusted to their care. Since that time, some have taken the idea of "dominion" to the extreme, believing that they have a right to take whatever they want without repercussions. History is replete with examples of this, from the overfishing of the whale population during the nineteenth century to the modern-day destruction of the rain forests.

Evolutionists often assert that Christians and their belief in the doctrine of dominion are solely responsible for the environmental problems we face today. However, this charge is false because evolutionists misunderstand dominion. Their understanding of dominion is that human beings are reckless consumers who take without regard to the earth or their fellow humans. A biblical understanding of dominion, however, should lead us to greater environmental responsibility and stewardship. Incidentally, given the Darwinian position, there are no real foundations for morally right or wrong behavior at all. So charging Christians with environmental wrongdoing is inconsistent with the evolutionists' worldview.

If we're looking for someone to blame for the woes of the environment, I would point the finger at a more obvious and likely culprit: fallen human beings.

Stewardship and the Law

Our obligation to properly steward God's creation can further be seen in some of the laws God gave to the nation of Israel in Leviticus:

> The LORD said to Moses on Mount Sinai, "Speak to the Israelites and say to them: 'When you enter the land I am going to give you, the land itself must observe a sabbath to the LORD. For six years sow your fields, and for six years prune your vineyards and gather their crops. But in the seventh year the land is to have a sabbath of rest, a sabbath to the LORD. Do not sow your fields or prune your vineyards.' " (25:1–4)

Conservationists and farmers have long known the value of allowing land to lie fallow—to remain unplanted for a short period of time. This period of rest for the land allows it to replenish nutrients, restore moisture to dry areas, and regain fertility without the application of fertilizer. The plants that grow during this time of rest help to further maintain the land by preventing erosion. Many believe this is the reason why God commanded the nation of Israel to observe a sabbath rest for the land every seven years.

In addition to giving instructions regarding the proper care of farmland, God also gave numerous instructions in the law on the proper treatment of animals. He commanded the Israelites to ensure that any livestock they used to tend their land was also given a day of rest on the Sabbath. In Deuteronomy 25:4, God instructed His people not to muzzle an ox while it was "treading out the grain," which meant the animal was allowed to eat while working. Here are two other references that point to the need to properly care for the creatures God created:

> *Each year, Americans throw out enough plastic film to shrink-wrap the entire state of Texas.*
> —The Utterly, Completely, and Totally Useless Fact-O-Pedia

A righteous man cares about his animal's health,
but even the merciful acts of the wicked are cruel.
   (Proverbs 12:10, HCSB)

Be diligent to know the state of your flocks,
And attend to your herds. (Proverbs 27:23, NKJV)

Throughout the Old Testament, God provided many instructions on the handling of food, human waste (excrement), blood, corpses, and other hygienic issues.

A recurring theme of Scripture from Genesis through Revelation is cleanness versus uncleanness. God even used gardening analogies about unkempt vineyards and overgrown plantations to chastise laziness or slothfulness (Mark 12:1–9 and John 15:1–15 are but two examples). While the comparison is mostly applied to the spiritual realm, it wouldn't make sense unless it was true in the physical realm first. In fact, the terms *washing, regeneration, renewal,* and *sanctification* all have their roots in a physical context that was then translated and elevated into the spiritual realm.

There's a natural sense that any logical person would agree that the Bible promotes cleanliness, order, and respect for the earth. When Scripture was being written, there weren't any harmful man-made materials littering the highways and byways. Virtually everything people utilized was biodegradable, and the things that weren't, such as metal, were considered valuable. Those items would be recycled or melted down and put to another use. Trash was normally burned in a public place, and building materials were either combustible or recyclable.

With the knowledge that we have today about population growth, the length of time it takes for man-made materials to decompose/biodegrade, and the very real smog that lingers over our cities, it should be common sense, if not a biblical mandate, to take care of our surroundings.

All life is a gift. When we're careless or shortsighted and don't steward the resources God has given us, we're being less than grateful toward Him.

So as Christians, we should be quick to acknowledge that God has made us stewards over the whole of His creation. The privilege of having dominion over the land means that we are to govern its use with great care and respect, seeking not to take too much or to neglect or abuse it. Neither should we allow Satan the freedom to co-opt this issue through the false teaching of naturalistic evolution and New Age rhetoric.

Working together in the church body to find common-sense practical alternatives will help us pass on the cleanest, greenest planet to our children, grandchildren, and all generations that follow until the Lord returns.

Part 6

Questions Parents Ask and My Question to You

22

Questions Parents Ask

*The greatest question of our time is not
communism vs. individualism, not Europe vs.
America, not even the East vs. the West; it is
whether men can bear to live without God.*

—Will Durant, *On the Meaning of Life*

"How can a book written more than nineteen hundred years ago answer the questions kids ask today? After all, Moses didn't have an iPad or a cell phone, did he?"

Parents across the country ask me questions like this on a regular basis. I want to assure you that even though the Bible was written long ago, its relevance for our lives today—and particularly for parenting—is evident because it addresses what truly matters.

Does the Bible include instructions on how to fix a cell phone that dropped into the toilet? No. But it does teach you how to handle that situation with grace and patience. Will you find a driver's manual on how to navigate bumper-to-bumper traffic? No again. But you will find scriptures on patience and time management.

Have situations changed? Yes, but people haven't—and neither has God. As parents, your role in your children's lives is to teach them the character of God and how to live out that character in their own lives with the power of the Holy Spirit. Then when they encounter a challenge or temptation, they won't have to wonder what to do; they'll know because they have the Bible and the Holy Spirit as their guide: "Whether you turn to the right or to the left, your ears will hear a voice behind you, saying, 'This is the way; walk in it'" (Isaiah 30:21).

Is It in There?

So does the Bible address any of the issues that parents in the twenty-first century face on a day-to-day basis? Let's see . . .

Children rebelling against their parents? We don't have to read very far in Genesis to see the first two people, Adam and Eve, rebel against their Father—God!

Sibling rivalry? One chapter later in the same book, Cain kills Abel!

Family disputes? Later in the Old Testament, the sons of Jacob (Israel) sell their brother Joseph into captivity!

Marriage? Absolutely. The Bible includes some very vivid case studies of couples that did it right and those that did it very wrong.

Drunkenness? It's in there. *Prostitution?* Check. *Anger management?* Yup. *Dealing with life's stresses and anxieties?* A recurring theme. *Handling finances wisely?* Just happens to be one of the most talked about subjects in Scripture. *Homosexuality?* It's addressed. *Love? Hate? Fear? Integrity?* Yes, yes, yes.

What about Sexual Immorality?

Exodus 20:14 and 1 Corinthians 6:12–20 speak directly to this issue. The Bible's prohibition against adultery includes any act of sex outside of the bonds of marriage, as well as sensual images and behaviors that are designed to entice. Pornography, erotica (romance books with explicit adult material, sometimes called "bodice rippers," and are on the best-seller list for ebooks), lewd jokes, and even the manner of dress are all things that lead to sexual temptation and should be avoided. As kids would say today, "Don't even go there." Teach and expect sexual purity from your children. Abstinence is possible and should be the accepted norm for a Christian family.

What Can I Teach about Homosexuality?

The Bible specifically states that homosexuality is a sin as far back as Genesis 19. Other clear verses are Romans 1:24–28 and 1 Corinthians 6:9. Homosexual sex is still sex outside of marriage and is therefore considered premarital sex or adultery. God has established a natural order for the family in which a husband and wife join together in marriage. Our culture doesn't see it this way, however. Your kids are being bombarded with the message that homosexuality is normal and healthy and that homosexual marriage is the same as a union between one man and one woman. To find current information on how to stand up for the Bible's authority with sensitivity, visit *citizenlink.com/understanding homosexuality* and *refugefm.com/online-messages/?series=52*. These two books are also great resources: *The Complete Christian Guide to Understanding Homosexuality* and *When Homosexuality Hits Home.*

Is Abortion Wrong?

At the heart of the abortion issue is the question, When does life begin? Does it begin at conception, during the twentieth week of pregnancy, at birth? According to God's Word, He knows us from the time we are formed in our mothers' wombs (Psalm 139:13–16; Jeremiah 1:5). If He knows us before we're born, then we must be alive in the womb. Life begins at conception; the moment the sperm joins with the egg. From that moment life is to be revered and protected. Taking any life, even an unborn child's life, is murder according to God's Word (Exodus 20:13). Our culture puts little value on life today. Murder and violence on television and video games are just a matter of sport. So why should we expect someone to respect a life that isn't even here yet and will be such an inconvenience? Women's rights groups insist, "It's a woman's body! It's her choice." But the Bible reminds us that "you are not your own; you were bought at a price. Therefore honor God with your body" (1 Corinthians 6:19–20). The choice is made when two people choose to have sex.

Be aware, though, that many Christian women end their pregnancies and experience overwhelming emotional and spiritual pain as a result. If

Tuning in to Jesus

Pretend you have a room with one hundred pianos in it. They're all out of tune, so the piano tuner is called and tunes piano number one to perfect pitch. He then tunes piano number two using piano number one as his standard. Piano number three is tuned to piano number two, and piano number four to piano number three, and so on, until every piano has been tuned to its predecessor. Enter one hundred pianists. Are you ready for this, or are you already cringing with fear and dread? What will it sound like? Even if the hundred pianists are all playing the same piece of music, it will sound horrible because the pianos will be out of tune with each other.

No matter how good the piano tuner might be, without using the same standard on every piano, each time the tuner moved from one piano to the next, the pitch changed ever so slightly. One standard pitch must be used as the basis for the tuning. If that tuner had used a single tuning fork as his standard for each piano, all the pianos would be tuned the same and would sound wonderful when played together.

God has set a standard for us to "tune" our lives to His Holy Word: His Son, Jesus. The melody never changes. To help us know how to live up to that standard, He has given us His commandments and laws. These aren't merely suggestions but rules that He set up for our benefit, and if we follow them through the power of the Holy Spirit, He promises that we will have "life, and . . . have it more abundantly" (John 10:10, NKJV).

someone you know is grieving an abortion and needs counseling, contact Focus on the Family at 1-800-A-Family (232-6459) weekdays 6:00 AM to 8:00 PM (Mountain Time). Please be prepared to leave your contact information for a counselor or chaplain to return your call as soon as possible. The consultation is available at no cost to you.

What Do I Tell My Kids about Money, Materialism, and Greed?

God's concern isn't about material things themselves but about how we *relate* to them. The love of money and the handling of money are actually something that Jesus talked about many times (see Matthew 6:19–21, 24; 23:25; Luke 12:13–21). Money isn't the issue; the love of money is the bigger issue: "The love of money is a root of all kinds of evil. Some people, eager for money, have wandered from the faith and pierced themselves with many griefs" (1 Timothy 6:10). But God's Word tells us to "keep your lives free from the love of money and be content with what you have, because God has said, 'Never will I leave you; never will I forsake you'" (Hebrews 13:5).

Which Verses Talk about Drugs, Smoking, and Drinking Alcohol?

As Christians, we're commanded to obey those God has placed in authority over us (Romans 13:1–7). This includes obeying the laws of the land. If something is illegal, we shouldn't do it, because it would damage our witness for Christ. We've already seen in 1 Corinthians 6:20 that we should honor God with our bodies. The evidence is clear that drugs and smoking do great harm to the body. Many scriptures talk about being of sober mind and judgment—1 Corinthians 15:34, 1 Thessalonians 5:4–8, 2 Timothy 4:5, and 1 Peter 1:13, 4:7, and 5:8 are just a few.

There's also a strong link between witchcraft (sorcery) and drug use. The Greek word for "sorcery" is *pharmakeia*, which literally means "the use or administering of drugs."[1] It's the root word for our English words *pharmacy* and *pharmaceutical*. Witchcraft often involved using herbs and poisons while administering spells. Galatians 5:19–21, Revelation 9:20–21, 21:8, and 22:15 all give stern warnings about participating in these activities. Some people try to use Genesis 2:9 as justification for using plant-based drugs like marijuana. But this verse clearly states that plants were to be used for food, not to alter the mind and conscience.

Many people use the fact that Jesus turned water into wine and actually drank wine as a justification to drink alcohol. The Bible doesn't forbid drinking alcohol, but it does say not to drink to excess (Proverbs 23:29–35; Ephesians 5:18). The apostle Paul also warned that believers shouldn't allow their bodies to be enslaved by anything (1 Corinthians 6:12).

What Happens to People Who Commit Suicide?

The Bible tells of six people who committed suicide: Abimelech (Judges 9:54), Saul (1 Samuel 31:4), Saul's armor-bearer (1 Samuel 31:5), Ahithophel (2 Samuel 17:23), Zimri (1 Kings 16:18), and Judas Iscariot (Matthew 27:5). God prohibits murder, and it logically follows that He would not condone self-murder (Exodus 20:13). Only God has the authority to choose the time of our death. Many faiths teach that suicide is an unforgivable sin, since the one who commits suicide cannot ask forgiveness for the act after he or she dies. This isn't what the Bible teaches. The only unpardonable sin is rejecting Jesus Christ as our Savior, because He is the only way to be reconciled to God.

If a Christian commits suicide, he or she is still assured of eternal life (John 10:27–29; Romans 8:38–39; Ephesians 1:13–14), but God will surely not be pleased that a child of His made this choice. If He is grieved when we don't trust Him in life, how much more grieved would He be if we choose not to entrust to Him the day and manner of our death? Although not specifically discussing suicide, 1 Corinthians 3:15 certainly could apply to someone who is saved but commits suicide: "He himself will be saved, but only as one escaping through the flames."

> *Remember—children are precious, and no product replaces adult supervision.*
> —Notice accompanying a pair of Gerber-brand baby nail clippers

Unfortunately, your children may have friends who commit suicide. Your role as a parent in this case is to help your children work through their feelings of guilt for not seeing the signs in time and doing something to prevent the suicide. You must give them hope that if their friend knew Christ, he or she is in heaven. Open and honest discussions about the issues your child's friend felt so desperate about can help your child work through grief and prevent him or her from falling into despair as well (John 10:27–29; 1 Thessalonians 4:13–14).

Should I Warn My Kids about Witchcraft and the Occult?

Young people today are fascinated by witchcraft, Wicca, and the occult. This subject is addressed in several places in the Old Testament, including Leviticus 19:26, 31, and 20:6. Those who practiced witchcraft, séances, sorcery, and similar practices were said to have the face of God against them and were to be stoned (Leviticus 20:27). These practices were actually borrowed from the pagan religions of other nations and had no place in the nation of Israel, God's people. Galatians 5:20 lists sorcery as one of the "acts of the sinful nature." This list appears just before and in contrast to the fruit of the Spirit.

Watch Your Mouth!

Ever want to snatch a word back after it's been said? Oh, how I wish we could do that. God's Word speaks often about guarding our words, especially in the books of Psalms and Proverbs. In the New Testament, Ephesians 4:29, 5:4, and Colossians 3:8 are the primary passages about watching what we say. The tongue is so small, and yet it causes so much trouble (James 3:2–10)! We use words to express our hearts and minds. We interact with other people using words. And we worship and praise God with words. It used to be that we never heard curse words on television until after a certain time of night. Now the censors have loosened the standards, and foul language is being heard in commercials and even kids' cartoons. In our changing society, words that once were considered offensive aren't viewed that way anymore. Children will repeat everything we say, usually at the most inopportune times! They pick up words easily and use them in the same way they hear them, without knowing they're improper. So, watch your mouth! Like the psalmist, ask God daily to "set a guard over my mouth, O Lord; keep watch over the door of my lips" (Psalm 141:3).

•••

These are a few of the issues your children may ask you about. Hopefully, you've seen in this chapter that the Bible is relevant and does speak to modern issues in parenting. God's Word never changes! Even though the grass may wither and the flowers may fall, "the word of the LORD endures forever" (1 Peter 1:25, NKJV).

Now that you have a better understanding of how to incorporate Scripture when discussing difficult topics with your kids, see if you can find additional scriptures that will help you address other topics of interest to your children.

23

What Will Your Family Legacy Be?

Do not fear death so much,
but rather the inadequate life.

—Bertolt Brecht, *The Mother*

A man named John Fleming lived a quiet, unassuming life in a small town. He had only a tenth-grade education, but he worked hard as a farmer and lived frugally. Known for his gentleness and compassion, John always had a kind word for his grandchildren, his older family members, and anyone else who came into contact with him. His involvement in the local church was always low-key; he did many things behind the scenes and never sought recognition for his service.

His daughter told me that the family was surprised, perhaps even a bit overwhelmed, that at John's death more than five hundred people came to pay their respects to this unassuming farmer. Before his funeral service began, many of the people came to comfort his daughter with stories of how John had discreetly helped them over the years.

One woman said, "Once my family had no heat in our home and no money to purchase firewood. John cut a load of firewood on a Sunday afternoon and brought it to us free of charge." Another said, "John used his four-wheel-drive truck to take my daughter to the hospital during the big ice storm two years ago. He may have saved her life!"

John's daughter heard story after story about her father, the quiet farmer with a big heart. She had no idea of the extent of his generosity or that he had helped so many people in their times of need. The stories filled her grieving heart with joy as she settled into a pew at the front of the church.

As the service began, the pastor held up an obviously well-used Bible; it was held together with strips of inglorious gray duct tape. "Our dear brother John was a believer in Jesus Christ," he said. "Not only did he read and believe this book, but he also put it into practice in his day-to-day life. The impact the Bible made on John Fleming's life is evident by your presence here today."

Everyone Will Leave a Legacy

Have you given much thought to the legacy you'll leave to your family when you depart from this life? Not to be melancholy, but death is a reality all of us must face. The book of James says, "You are a mist that appears for a little while and then vanishes" (4:14).

Every day you write another page of your legacy. The words and paragraphs you pen aren't based on how successful you are or the amount of money you'll leave to your children. The brand of clothing you wore, the size of your house, or the value of your stock portfolio won't even be mentioned. But the influence you had on your family and the people around you through your words and actions will be written all over the pages you compose.

Eventually, your legacy, good or bad, will be passed on to another generation. Are you troubled by the legacy you will pass on to your children, or are you at peace with it?

Society is crying out for role models, and your children desperately need you to be a person of integrity who lives according to the Scriptures. Consider this exhortation from King Solomon:

My son, do not forget my teaching,
    but keep my commands in your heart,

for they will prolong your life many years
>   and bring you prosperity.
Let love and faithfulness never leave you;
>   bind them around your neck,
>   write them on the tablet of your heart.
Then you will win favor and a good name
>   in the sight of God and man. (Proverbs 3:1–4)

The concept of having a "good name" isn't as popular as it used to be in small-town America. Here in Proverbs it says, "Let love and faithfulness never leave you," and that means living an authentic Christian lifestyle with integrity. Proverbs has more to say about the value of a good name, or the lack thereof: "The memory of the righteous will be a blessing, / but the name of the wicked will rot" (10:7), and "A good name is more desirable than great riches; to be esteemed is better than silver or gold" (22:1).

Does your family have a reputation for honor, integrity, and being a *true* Christian family? Are the words *kind, sweet, generous,* and *wholesome* affiliated with your reputation?

From God's perspective, "a good name is more desirable than great riches"—is it to you?

A Fresh Start

Even if you have some regrets from the past—a divorce, an addiction, parenting failures—a healthy legacy is within your reach. It's time to start writing a new chapter in your legacy. There are numerous examples of people in the Bible who made course corrections in their walk with God. Most went on to be notable heroes of the faith.

Moses, seeking to bring about deliverance for his people, took a wrong turn when he killed an Egyptian who had beaten a Hebrew slave. After Moses spent forty years in the wilderness, God sent him back to Egypt and used him to lead His people out of captivity.

It's Never Too Late to Change

"If it wasn't for Christ—coming into my life when He did—our marriage and home would have simply fallen apart."

With those words, a man named Jay began to share his testimony of God's power to change the direction of an entire family. I had met Jay while on the road, speaking for several days at a church conference.

"It was my second marriage, her first," Jay continued. "My wife had been raised in a churchgoing family, and once we were married, she went pretty much every Sunday. From day one, my response to her invitations was 'No thanks.' "

For Jay, growing his heavy equipment business was the main priority. He poured himself into his work, and success came—but with a price. "I was drinking heavily, running around on my wife, and by now we had a daughter," Jay reflected.

Over the course of a dozen years, Judy stayed with her husband, patiently living out her Christian faith before him. Jay remembers, "My wife never raised her voice to me, not once. She had every right to leave me, but she didn't. I sometimes thought, 'What is wrong with this woman?' "

Jay's eyes became moist with emotion as he shared details of his story. During these years Jay's wife had been praying for him. And their daughter, Jennifer—by this time in middle school—was going to church and praying for him, too.

What Jay didn't know was that during these years his wife was leaning on the strength of God's Word to endure an unhealthy marriage. First Peter 3:1 says, "If any of them do not believe the word, they may be won over without words by the behavior of their wives."

The unconditional love that Judy extended to Jay on a daily basis began to make an impact. "I could see my young daughter becoming strong in her walk with God. When Judy would share a Bible story with Jennifer before bed, I would listen to them pray. I began to want what they seemed to have. My wife and daughter had developed a certain joy about them, while chasing success and illicit relationships had left me empty."

One Easter, Jay decided to go with the family to church. "I told myself that the reason I was going was to hopefully make some business connections. Deep down, I didn't want to admit that I needed God or was finally seeking Him." That first Sunday made a strong impression, but opening up to a personal relationship with Jesus didn't come immediately. But Jay was, for the first time in his life, thinking about spiritual issues. When the Reverend Billy Graham was on television two weeks later, he decided to watch.

"It all seemed to come together," Jay remembers. "I clearly understood that Jesus died for my sins, and that by placing my faith in Him I could be forgiven."

At home, things began to change immediately. At night as a family, there would be a devotional reading and prayer before bed. Much to the surprise of many in the community, Jay became a model husband, father, and servant within his church. "People who knew me around town and longtime friends—they could see that I had changed. My mother-in-law and father-in-law, who knew how badly I had treated their daughter, could tell that things were different!"

Now, more than twenty-five years later, Jennifer serves in full-time ministry. She leads the children's program at the church where she and her mom faithfully attended, so many years ago.

"Our family's goal is that people see Jesus Christ through our lives," Jay says. "The best advice I could give a young couple? Seek the Lord together, pray together, worship together. Model godliness and consistency before your kids. And be honest with your mate."

King David committed adultery with Bathsheba, the wife of one of his band of mighty men, Uriah the Hittite. After discovering that Bathsheba was pregnant, David sought to cover his indiscretion by arranging for Uriah to be killed during a fierce battle. David then took Bathsheba into his house as his wife. Despite this dark blotch on his legacy, David is still known as a "man after [God's] own heart" (1 Samuel 13:14).

Peter, one of the members of Christ's inner circle, vowed to fight to his last breath after the Lord spoke of His betrayal at the hands of Judas Iscariot and His impending crucifixion. But when the pressure was on and Jesus was enduring hours of suffering prior to His death, Peter denied even knowing Him. However, after the resurrection, Jesus restored Peter, and Peter became the key leader in the church at Jerusalem.

> *The secret of good family life is disarmingly simple: Cultivate the family's relationship with Jesus.*
> —LARRY CHRISTENSON,
> *The Christian Family*

Saul, later known as Paul, actively took part in the persecution of believers in the early church. He not only consented to their deaths, but he also went from house to house arresting men and women in order to imprison them for their faith. After being blinded by a vision on the road to Damascus, Saul was converted, began preaching the gospel, and ended up writing a majority of the New Testament books.

For the Lord's sake, for our children's sake, and for the world's sake, we need to search our hearts and ask Jesus to strengthen us where we need to be strengthened so that we can be people of integrity.

It's important, however, that we don't make ourselves out to be perfect—it will be obvious to all that we're not. Rest assured, your children will spot your character flaws—usually they find them before the age of fifteen.

If you have a big blunder or skeleton in the closet that your kids don't know about, tell them about it when they're mature enough to understand the moral issues involved in your decisions. Don't dwell on the "exciting" details of the transgression; the emphasis of your story should always be on God's forgiveness, your repentance, and the lessons you learned as a result of those choices. We can be honest and tell our kids about our failures and shortcomings, but we should also emphasize how the Holy Spirit is changing us daily.

God can take your broken legacy and restore it if you'll turn back to Him with your whole heart. God can give you "beauty for ashes, the oil of joy for mourning," and "the garment of praise for the spirit of heaviness" (Isaiah 61:3, NKJV).

Creating a New Family Legacy

Nathan Stuben's father was not a nice man. Mr. Stuben wasn't a Christian, and he had a history of mental illness and alcoholism. In his drunken rages he would abuse his wife and children physically and emotionally.

Nathan grew up, got married, and went to college, and to his dismay, he began making the same evil choices his father had made. Nathan's wife finally persuaded him to go to church with her. Through her godly influence and the witness of the men at church, Nathan gave his heart to Christ. Nathan gave up the drinking and drugs, but he still had anger and mistrust issues that stemmed from his father's abuse. Once Nathan had little Stubens of his own, he realized that if he didn't allow God to change his heart, those strongholds would affect his children and be passed down to them. The dark Stuben legacy would continue.

As Nathan discovered, our personalities and habits are deeply influenced by our parents and grandparents. Bad habits are passed down from one generation to the next with comments like, "Well, she came by it honest," or "He can't help it. Look how he was raised." Too often we use these attitudes as excuses for our own sin.

We all have traits we've picked up from our ancestors, but it's our choice whether we'll pass on that legacy to our children. Take an honest look at the legacy of your parents, grandparents, aunts, and uncles. Has a sinful family legacy been passed down to you? Do you want to pass it on to your children?

Identify where sinful habits came from and attempt to understand the motivation behind them. Analyze your own life to see how your family legacy is manifesting in you. Then seek God's forgiveness and healing in any areas you identify. Ask God to reveal to you when you're exhibiting sinful attitudes and patterns of behavior to your children.

No one says that you have to live under the shadow of your past for the rest of your life. Choose a new godly heritage for your children.

Your Spiritual Legacy

What about the spiritual legacy you'll leave behind? As a follower of Christ, it isn't enough to simply keep your nose clean; God wants you to make an impact on your world and to bring glory and honor to His name. Modeling a Christian walk and taking an active part in the spiritual formation of your children are the greatest ways you can make an impact on the world around you.

Many of the great spiritual leaders in Christian history can trace their heritage back to a godly father or mother. Charles Wesley was one of history's most prolific hymn writers. He wrote at least 6,500 hymns in his lifetime. His brother John Wesley, an itinerant minister, is said to have preached more than forty thousand sermons. John is considered to be the principle founder of the Methodist Church. Both men owed much to their parents, Samuel and Susanna Wesley. Their father was an Anglican rector, and their mother actively taught them the Scriptures and Bible stories from their earliest years. The influence of their parents can't be overstated; it is still being felt three centuries later.[1]

Reverend Billy Graham has preached the gospel to more people than any other person in Christian history. He was one of four children born to William and Morrow Graham, dairy farmers from Charlotte, North Carolina.[2] Graham said of his parents in his autobiography *Just As I Am*:

When [my parents] read the family Bible in our home, they were not simply going through a pious ritual. Mother told us that they had established a family altar with daily Bible reading the very first day they were married. They accepted that book as the very Word of God, seeking and getting heavenly help to keep the family together.[3]

Not only did Billy Graham's parents have a huge influence on him during his formative years, but Billy and his wife, Ruth, also influenced their children and grandchildren to continue his legacy of evangelism. His son Franklin now serves as president of the Billy Graham Evangelistic Association and Samaritan's Purse, a worldwide relief agency. His daughter Anne Graham Lotz leads AnGeL Ministries and speaks to thousands of women worldwide. Several of Reverend Graham's grandchildren are also active in full-time ministry.

It's hard to say whether you're raising the next Charles or John Wesley or Billy Graham. One thing is sure: Godly parents set a firm foundation that God can use to change the world. Dr. Albert Mohler says,

> Parenthood is not a hobby, but represents one of the most crucial opportunities for the making of saints found in this life. . . . This reminds us of our responsibility to raise boys to be husbands and fathers and girls to be wives and mothers. God's glory is seen in this, for the family is a critical arena where the glory of God is either displayed or denied. It is just as simple as that.[4]

When the apostle Paul wrote to his son in the faith, Timothy, he reminded him of the influence that his mother and grandmother had on him: "I have been reminded of your sincere faith, which first lived in your grandmother Lois and in your mother Eunice and, I am persuaded, now lives in you also" (2 Timothy 1:5).

If you have been negligent in imparting a spiritual legacy to your children, don't wring your hands in regret and anguish. Get busy! Teach them. Let them see the light of Christ in you. And by all means, pray for your children. First, pray that they will come to know Jesus. Second, pray that they will follow Him faithfully throughout their lives.

I came across this beautiful puritan prayer titled "The Family," which I believe sums up how we ought to pray for our families:

> O God, I cannot endure to see the destruction of my kindred.
> Let those that are united to me in tender ties
>   be precious in thy sight and devoted to thy glory.
> Sanctify and prosper my domestic devotion, instruction, discipline,
>   example,
>   that my house may be a nursery for heaven,
>   my church, the garden of the Lord,
>   enriched with trees of righteousness of thy planting, for thy glory.[5]

Your Greatest Command

Perhaps when you began this book, you were skeptical about whether the Bible was trustworthy or even relevant for today. Maybe you're a strong believer who was simply looking for help for questions that children ask their parents about Christianity. Regardless of where you were coming from, please be assured in your heart that I am overjoyed you took this journey with me, and I pray that this book will help you fulfill what our Lord Jesus Christ called the "most important" commandments. Follow these by allowing the Holy Spirit to work through you, and your legacy will be assured:

> "The most important [commandment]," answered Jesus, "is this:
> 'Hear, O Israel, the Lord our God, the Lord is one. Love the Lord
> your God with all your heart and with all your soul and with all
> your mind and with all your strength.' The second is this: 'Love your
> neighbor as yourself.' There is no commandment greater than these."
> (Mark 12:29–31)

Introduction

1. Hebrews 8:12 (NASB).

Chapter 1

1. Famous line from *The New England Primer*, which used biblical imagery to teach children the alphabet and reading. Originally published in 1687, the better-known 1777 edition was reprinted in 2003 by WallBuilders Press, Aledo, Texas.

Chapter 2

1. Alex McFarland and Elmer Towns, *10 Questions Every Christian Must Answer* (Nashville: Broadman and Holman Academic, 2011), 33.
2. Rudolf Clausius, "The Second Law of Thermodynamics," in *The World of Physics: A Small Library of the Literature of Physics from Antiquity to the Present* (New York: Simon and Schuster, 1987), 1:734.
3. *Encyclopedia Britannica*, s.v. "entropy," accessed February 21, 2013, http://www.britannica.com/EBchecked/topic/189035/entropy.
4. See the article "Science: The Benefits of Hurricanes," *Time*, September 24, 1973, www.time.com/time/magazine/article/0,9171,90 7967,00.html. I also recommend an informative DVD titled *A God of Suffering?* (Petersburg, KY: Answers in Genesis, 2005). It's available at www.answersingenesis.org.

Chapter 4

1. Charles Wesley, "And Can It Be?" public domain, in Robert K. Brown and Mark R. Norton, eds., *The One Year Book of Hymns* (Wheaton, IL: Tyndale, 1995), 29.

Chapter 5

1. C. S. Lewis, *Mere Christianity* (New York: HarperCollins, 2001), 137.
2. *Strong's Concordance*, s.v. "Greek 5281, *hypomonē*," accessed February 8, 2013, http:// biblesuite.com/greek/5281.htm.

3. *Strong's Concordance*, s.v. "Greek 1382, *dokimé*," accessed February 8, 2013, http://biblesuite.com/greek/1382.htm.

4. *Thayer's Greek Lexicon*, s.v. "Greek 1680, *elpis*," accessed February 8, 2013, http://biblesuite.com/greek/1680.htm.

Chapter 6

1. Ellen Tumposky, "Rare 'Double Eagle' Gold Coins Ruled Property of U.S. Not Collector's Family," *ABC News*, July 21, 2011, http://abcnews.go.com/US/ten-rare-gold-coins-property-us-treasury-jury/story?id=14124595; and Susan Headly, "The 1933 Saint Gaudens Gold Double Eagle—World's Most Valuable Coin," About.com, http://coins.about.com/od/famousrarecoinprofiles/p/1933_Gold_Eagle.htm.

Chapter 7

1. Linda Falter, "A Beautiful Anger," *Christianity Today*, April 27, 2011, 36–37, http://www.christianitytoday.com/ct/2011/april/beautifulanger.html?start=2.

Chapter 9

1. An online version of *An Enquiry into the Obligations of Christians to Use Means for the Conversion of the Heathens* can be found at the William Carey University website: http://www.wmcarey.edu/carey/enquiry/enquiry.html. Excellent coverage of William Carey's story and the development of modern missions is found in Ruth A. Tucker, *From Jerusalem to Irian Jaya: A Biographical History of Christian Missions* (Grand Rapids: Zondervan, 2004), 121ff.

2. For a fascinating look at what many unreached people groups admitted knowing about God before Christian missionaries arrived with the explicit news of Jesus, I highly recommend Don Richardson's book *Eternity in Their Hearts* (Ventura, CA: Regal, 2005).

3. C. S. Lewis, *Mere Christianity*, rev. ed. (New York: HarperCollins, 1980), 136–37.

Chapter 10

1. Sylvester Bliss, *Memoirs of William Miller* (Boston: Joshua V. Himes, 1853), xiv, http://books.google.com/books?id=hfU_dOu9p6YC&p rintsec=frontcover&source=gbs_ge_summary_r&cad=0#v=onepage &q&f=false.
2. "Preacher Harold Camping Gets Doomsday Prediction Wrong Again," FoxNews.com, May 21, 2011, http://www.foxnews.com /us/2011/05/21/preacher-harold-camping-gets-doomsday-prediction -wrong/.
3. Lester R. Brown, "The New Geopolitics of Food," *Foreign Policy*, November 7, 2012, http://www.foreignpolicy.com/articles/2011 /04/25/the_new_geopolitics_of_food; and Mindy Belz, "Feed My People," *World Magazine*, May 3, 2008, http://www.worldmag.com /2008/05/feed_my_people.
4. *Today in the Word*, Moody Bible Institute, vol. II (April 1989), no. 4:27.

Chapter 11

1. St. Augustine anecdote, adapted from Stephen Seamands, *Ministry in the Image of God* (Downers Grove, IL: InterVarsity, 2005), 101.
2. Jeremy Begbie, "Can We See God? Jeremy Begbie Explores the Question at the Veritas Forum," YouTube, uploaded June 24, 2010, http://www.youtube.com/watch?v=t2u20RxqPvo.
3. Information on modalism, Arianism, tritheism, and other heresies can be found on the Christian Apologetics and Research Ministry website, http://carm.org/heresies.
4. Matt Slick, "Modalism," Christian Apologetics and Research Ministry, accessed February 13, 2013, http://carm.org/modalism.
5. Ryan Turner, "Arianism and Its Influence Today," accessed February 13, 2013, http://carm.org/arianism-and-its-influence-today.

Chapter 13

1. The Doors, "When the Music's Over," *Strange Days*, copyright 1967, Elektra Records.

2. Dr. Barry Leventhal, discussion with the author, January 2013.

3. *Strong's Concordance*, s.v. "Hebrew 2459, *cheleb*," http://biblesuite
.com/hebrew/2459.htm.

Chapter 14

1. Francis J. Beckwith and Gregory Koukl, *Relativism: Feet Firmly
Planted in Mid-air* (Grand Rapids, MI: Baker, 1998), 20, quoting
from *The Presbyterian Layman*, July-August 1996, 8.

2. Michael Vitcavitch, *Deciduous Belief: Letting Go of the Old You So the
New You Can Embrace a Healthy and Meaningful Relationship with
God and Others* (Bloomington, IN: Cross Books, 2011), 162.

3. Marcia. Manna, "A Historical Heavyweight: The San Diego Natural History Museum Hosts the Biggest Exhibition of the Dead Sea
Scrolls Ever Assembled," *San Diego Magazine,* June 2007, http://
www.sandiegomagazine.com/San-Diego-Magazine/June-2007
/A-Historical-Heavyweight/.

4. Bruce M. Metzger, *Chapters in the History of New Testament Textual Criticism* (Grand Rapids, MI: Eerdman's, 1963), 144. Further
verification can be found in Lee Strobel, *The Case for Christ* (Grand
Rapids, MI: Zondervan, 1998), 70, quoting Princeton scholar and
Metzger colleague Benjamin Warfield: "The New Testament [is]
unrivaled among ancient writings in the purity of its text as actually transmitted and kept in use." Reflecting on more recent textual
discoveries and scholarship, Metzger published an updated work
affirming the accurate preservation of the Testament manuscripts.
Published by Oxford University Press in 2005, *The Text of the New
Testament: It's Transmission, Corruption, and Restoration*—which, in
academic terms, documents that the content of the New Testament
has been preserved—was written in collaboration with skeptic and
scholar Bart Ehrmann.

5. *The NAS New Testament Greek Lexicon*, s.v. "*dokimazo*," accessed
February 4, 2013, http://www.biblestudytools.com/lexicons/greek
/nas/dokimazo.html.

6. David M. McCasland, "A Clear View," *Our Daily Bread*, March 12,
2011, http://odb.org/2011/03/12/a-clear-view/.

7. *The NAS New Testament Greek Lexicon*, s.v. "*energeo*," accessed February 14, 2013, http://www.biblestudytools.com/lexicons/greek/nas /energeo.html.

Chapter 15

1. C. S. Lewis, *Miracles* (New York: Macmillan, 1960), 106.
2. For more information about the historical validity of biblical miracle claims, see, on a popular level, my book *Ten Answers for Skeptics* (Ventura, CA: Regal, 2011), 193–96. For a much more in-depth treatment, see Michael R. Licona, *The Resurrection of Jesus: A New Historiographical Approach* (Downers Grove, IL: InterVarsity, 2010), chapter 2; and William L. Craig, *Reasonable Faith: Christian Truth and Apologetics*, 3rd ed. (Wheaton, IL: Crossway, 2008), chapter 6.
3. For a more thorough defense of the resurrection, I recommend Gary R. Habermas and Michael R. Licona, *The Case for the Resurrection of Jesus* (Grand Rapids: Kregel, 2004).

Chapter 16

1. Cited in *The Foster Letter, Religious Market Update* (Van Wert, OH: Gary D. Foster Consulting, 2011), 4.
2. American Bible Society, 2011 "State of the Bible" survey, cited in "Bible Statistics: America's Bible IQ and Beliefs about the Bible," DeMossNews.com, accessed February 15, 2013, http://www .demossnewspond.com/americanbible/press_kit/bible_statistics.
3. *The KJV New Testament Greek Lexicon*, s.v. "*spoudazo*," accessed February 15, 2013, http://www.biblestudytools.com/lexicons/greek/kjv /spoudazo.html.
4. *The NAS New Testament Greek Lexicon*, s.v. "*zao*," accessed February 15, 2013, http://www.biblestudytools.com/lexicons/greek/nas/zao .html; *The NAS New Testament Greek Lexicon*, s.v. "*energeo*," accessed February 14, 2013, http://www.biblestudytools.com/lexicons/greek /nas/energeo.html.
5. Two excellent resources on biblical culture are John Walton, Victor H. Matthews, and Mark W. Chavalas, *The IVP Bible Background Commentary: Old Testament* (Downers Grove, IL: InterVarsity,

2000); and Craig S. Keener, *The IVP Bible Background Commentary: New Testament* (Downers Grove, IL: InterVarsity, 2000).

6. One free, helpful online resource is BibleGateway.com, http://www .biblegateway.com/. Another is BibleStudyTools.com (www.Bible StudyTools.com). Both of these websites feature a variety of online Bible versions, commentaries, concordances, and other Bible-study tools.

Chapter 17

1. For an interesting look at the robust apologetics work of the earliest Christian leaders and how little the basic questions and objections have changed, I recommend L. Russ Bush, ed., *Classical Readings in Christian Apologetics AD 100–1800* (Grand Rapids, IL: Zondervan, 1983).

2. *Random House Dictionary*, s.v. "exegesis" (New York: Random House, 2013) http://dictionary.reference.com/browse/exegesis?s=t.

3. *Random House Dictionary*, s.v. "eisegesis" (New York: Random House, 2013), http://dictionary.reference.com/browse/eisegesis?s=t.

4. For analysis of this topic, the following books are recommended as starting points: Jonathan Wells, *Icons of Evolution* (Washington, DC: Regnery Publishers, 2002); Jonathan Sarfati, *The Greatest Hoax On Earth?* (Powder Springs, GA: Creation Book Publishers, 2010); Gary Parker, *The Fossil Book* (Green Forest, AZ: Master Books, 2005). Also, note the following admission from an evolutionist, regarding how evolutionary presuppositions shaped the conclusions of scientists rather than tangible fossil evidences: "Gradualism was never 'proved from the rocks' by Lyell and Darwin, but was rather imposed as a bias upon nature. (This) has had a profoundly negative impact by stifling hypotheses and by closing the minds of a profession toward reasonable empirical alternatives to the dogma of gradualism. Lyell won with rhetoric what he could not carry with data." Source: S. J. Gould, "Toward the vindication of punctuational change," in W. A. Berggren and J. A. Van Couvering, eds., *Catastrophes and Earth History: The New Uniformitarianism* (Princeton, NJ: University Press, 1984), 14–16.

5. Note that Paul often referred to the Gentiles as "Greeks" and this word is used in lieu of *Gentiles* in many versions, but the intended sense is clearly the non-Jewish community, which by definition would be the Gentiles.

Chapter 18

1. Carol Bidwell, "Long Beach's Opulent Queen," *Daily News (Los Angeles)*, May 31, 1996, L.A. Life section.
2. Adapted from sermon illustration by Dr. Kenneth Gangel, Scofield Memorial Church, May 22, 1983, in "The Salvation Army," Bible .org, http://bible.org/node/11398.
3. Mahatma Gandhi quoted in *Famous Quotes from 100 Great People* (Mobile Reference, Google eBook, 2011).
4. *Strong's Concordance*, s.v. "Greek 2962, *kurios*," accessed February 16, 2013, http://www.bibletools.org/index.cfm/fuseaction/Lexicon .show/ID/G2962/kurios.htm.
5. *Thayer's Greek Lexicon*, s.v. "*kurios*," accessed February 16, 2013, http://www.bibletools.org/index.cfm/fuseaction/Lexicon.show/ID /G2962/kurios.htm.

Chapter 19

1. Barna Group, "A New Generation Expresses Its Skepticism and Frustration with Christianity," Barna.org, September 24, 2007, http://www.barna.org/barna-update/article/16-teensnext-gen/94 -a-new-generation-expresses-its-skepticism-and-frustration-with -christianity.
2. Ravi Zacharias as quoted on Goodreads, "Ravi Zacharias Quotes," http://www.goodreads.com/author/quotes/3577. Ravi_Zacharias.
3. John Newton, "Amazing Grace," public domain.
4. Reverend Jonathan Falwell, quoted in Macel Falwell, *Falwell: His Life and Legacy* (New York: Howard and Simon and Schuster, 2008), 178.

Chapter 21

1. Sarah Dowdy, "How Carbon Offsets Work," HowStuffWorks.com, accessed February 16, 2013, http://science.howstuffworks.com /environmental/green-science/carbon-offset.htm.
2. Ibid.

Chapter 22

1. *The NAS New Testament Greek Lexicon*, s.v. *"pharmakeia,"* accessed February 18, 2013, http://www.biblestudytools.com/lexicons/greek /nas/pharmakeia.html.

Chapter 23

1. Although Wesley composed a huge corpus of hymns—more than 400 are still sung today—there is no consensus as to the exact number, since several important issues complicate the ascription of authorship. "The numerical calculation of Charles's hymns runs from a high of 9,000 down to a low of 3,000—if one excludes the lyric poems." Source: John R. Tyson, ed., *Charles Wesley: A Reader* (Oxford: Oxford University Press, 1989), 20–21.
2. "Billy Graham Biography," Bio.com, accessed February 19, 2013, http://www.biography.com/people/billy-graham-9317669?page=1.
3. Billy Graham, *Just As I Am: The Autobiography of Billy Graham* (New York: HarperCollins, 1997), 19.
4. Albert Mohler, "Deliberate Childlessness: Moral Rebellion with a New Face," AlbertMohler.com, June 7, 2005, http://www.albert mohler.com/2005/06/07/deliberate-childlessness-moral-rebellion -with-a-new-face-2/.
5. "The Family," quoted in Arthur G. Bennett, *The Valley of Vision: A Collection of Puritan Prayers and Devotions* (Edinburgh: Banner of Truth Trust, 1975), 113.